The Impact of COVID-19 on Corporations and Corporate Law in Malaysia

Loganathan Krishnan · Wai Meng Chan
Editors

The Impact of COVID-19 on Corporations and Corporate Law in Malaysia

Springer

Editors
Loganathan Krishnan
Department of Business Law and Taxation
Monash University Malaysia
Bandar Sunway, Selangor, Malaysia

Wai Meng Chan
Faculty of Business and Economics
University of Malaya
Kuala Lumpur, Malaysia

ISBN 978-981-19-5518-1 ISBN 978-981-19-5519-8 (eBook)
https://doi.org/10.1007/978-981-19-5519-8

This Springer imprint is published by the registered company Springer Nature Singapore Pte Ltd.
The registered company address is: 152 Beach Road, #21-01/04 Gateway East, Singapore 189721, Singapore

I dedicate this book to my mother, Sarojinee Rajoo, who always believed in my capabilities, my dearest late father, Krishnan Govindan, who instilled confidence and self-esteem in me, my wife, Hema Malini Tharman, who is a constant pillar of strength for me, my twin children, Mahilavan and Maadhavi, who are my inspirations, my teachers, particularly Prof. Dr. Choong Yeow Choy, who was my PhD supervisor, for giving me all the guidance I need in this journey of life.

–Dr. Loganathan Krishnan

I dedicate this book to my late parents, Chen Yee Kow @ Chan Yee Khow and Cheah Kwai Mei @ Cheah Kwai May, who showered me with their unconditional, unfettering and unfailing love, as well as gave me invaluable lessons on life; to my mentor, the late Prof. Dato' P. Balan, who took me under his wings and showed me the ropes in research and writing; and to my friends and students, who supported, encouraged and cheered me on, especially during the COVID-19 pandemic.

–Assoc. Prof. Dr. Wai Meng Chan

Foreword

The pandemic of COVID-19 came without a warning and hit us like a tsunami. Many succumbed to the consequences brought forth by COVID-19, be it individuals or businesses. Some lost their lives, some saw their finances in tatters. The government initiated various incentives and moratoriums to ease the financial burdens borne by businesses and people. Many pondered then if there would be light at the end of the tunnel. Thankfully, after two years, many countries including Malaysia have learnt to live with the virus and transited to the endemic stage. Businesses are beginning to get back on their feet. This is much welcomed as the calm after a rough storm and it is timely to reflect on the lessons learnt.

In light of all that, this book is timely for it captures the impact of the pandemic on corporations in Malaysia and the application of the Companies Act 2016 to deal with the situation. Thus, I am delighted that Dr. Loganathan Krishnan of Monash University Malaysia and Assoc. Prof. Dr. Wai Meng Chan of University of Malaya together with academicians and practitioners of diverse backgrounds and experience, brought about this book entitled "The Impact of the COVID-19 on Corporations and the Companies Act 2016."

This book provides a thorough discussion of the impact of the pandemic on businesses in Malaysia from various perspectives. It explored how the pandemic affected or would affect directors' duties, auditors' roles, board meetings, general meetings, shareholder activism, compliance with laws, companies' duties, capital market and corporate rescue mechanisms. Each of these perspectives must be reassessed to ensure businesses withstand future challenges and where necessary reforms must be made to the current legal framework so that Malaysia is able to withstand another like situation. This book will be useful to policymakers, legislators, practitioners and researchers to assist them in their work in exploring and ensuring a sustainable and comprehensive legal framework.

I heartily commend and congratulate the authors/contributors of all book chapters on the publication of this book and I wish them the best for future research endeavours.

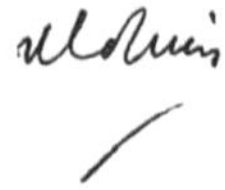

YAA Tun Tengku Maimun Tuan Mat
Chief Justice of Malaysia
Palace of Justice
Putrajaya, Malaysia

Preface

This book is timely since Malaysia has now moved to an endemic phase and thus it is pertinent to reflect on the impact of the pandemic on corporations and Companies Act 2016. Essentially, many lessons can be gleaned from this unfortunate episode. As each country has different sets of issues and tackles them in different ways depending on the country's culture, environment and resources, Malaysia is no exception. In the beginning, the focus of most nations was on health and ways to curb the spread of COVID-19. Not many realized that the pandemic may also have an impact on the legal framework governing businesses. On this note, businesses are affected the most, as there were total lockdowns in some cases and subsequently partial lockdowns.

The aim of this book is to carry on a discourse on the impact of COVID-19 on corporations in Malaysia. Challenges faced by corporations and their responses to them will be discussed. The relevant provisions in the Companies Act 2016 will be examined, and where necessary reforms will be proposed. Thus, it is anticipated that this book will be helpful for practitioners who are in need of a guide to manage the impact of COVID-19 on corporations and the Companies Act 2016. The book will also be a reference point for regulators and policymakers on the issues raised by the authors on the initiatives and measures taken by regulators and policymakers in combating the impact of COVID-19. Judges may also refer to this book for solutions offered by the authors in addressing the challenges caused by COVID-19. Other researchers may develop research gaps pointed out by the authors and elevate the research to greater heights and seek greater attention from regulators and policy-makers. Researchers from other jurisdictions involved in comparative studies may refer to this book to obtain a clear picture of the circumstances faced by the corporations in Malaysia. Last but not least, the industry players themselves may take a leaf from this book in managing the impact of COVID-19 on their businesses.

Chapter 1 gives an overview of the issues that arise as a result of the impact of the pandemic on businesses. As companies are managed by the Board of Directors, Chaps. 2 and 3 focus on how directors had to carry out their duties in light of the pandemic. Chapter 4 proceeds to explore the challenging role of the auditors in auditing a company due to the lockdowns. Chapter 5 then examines the interplay of the challenging roles played by board meetings, general meetings and shareholder activism. As all companies in Malaysia are regulated by the Companies Commission of Malaysia, a company that sources funds from the public is also regulated by the Securities Commission of Malaysia and if the company's shares are listed on the stock exchange, by Bursa Malaysia too, Chaps. 6 to 9 explore the roles played by the regulators to facilitate companies in the fulfilment of their statutory obligations, as well as providing lifelines to tide them over the crisis brought by the pandemic. We observe the relaxation of rules, the easing of financing and the increase in the threshold of insolvency.

Nevertheless, the pandemic has also revealed some weaknesses. Some of the laws are rigid. Some laws place importance on the company's responsibilities towards its shareholders. The pandemic exposed the need to acknowledge the impact of a company towards its other stakeholders such as its employees, suppliers and creditors, both secured and unsecured, as well as its surrounding community. Thus, one of the positive outcomes of the pandemic is the relevance of corporate social responsibility has been brought to the fore. Another positive outcome is the forced adoption of information and communication technology (ICT). People who resisted ICT prior to the pandemic had to adopt ICT or be left behind. This also applies to companies and all matters related to them. Due to the movement control orders and the strict standard operating procedures, virtual meetings became the new norm. Digitalized documents are preferred. All these will reduce carbon footprint and prayerfully heal the world.

Though COVID-19 has ravaged the world, it has given us valuable lessons which should not be forsaken nor forgotten. Actions should be taken to overcome weaknesses exposed by the pandemic. It is hoped that the discourses put forth in this book by the various contributors of diverse backgrounds, training and experience will provide fodder for law reforms.

We would like to thank the contributors Assoc. Prof. Dr. Usharani Balasingam, Ms. Wei Fong Wong, Ms. Li Chen Mah, Assoc. Prof. Dr. Yusramizza Md Isa, Dr. Anis Shuhaiza Md Salleh, Ms. Shanti Geoffrey and Prof. Dr. Hasani Mohd Ali for their contribution towards this book. We also wish to record our sincere appreciation to Springer, particularly to Ms. Anushangi Weerakoon, Mr. Rajasekar Ganesan and Mr. Vishnu Muthuswamy, for giving us this opportunity and their tremendous support.

Bandar Sunway, Malaysia Loganathan Krishnan
Kuala Lumpur, Malaysia Wai Meng Chan

Contents

About the Editors

Loganathan Krishnan obtained an LL.B (Hons) from the University of London, England. He then pursued an LL.M at the University of Malaya, Malaysia. He obtained his postgraduate qualification in Tertiary Education from the Curtin University of Technology, Perth, Australia. He then obtained his PhD at the University of Malaya in Company Law. Dr. Loganathan Krishnan was in legal practice for over two years in London and in academia for over 20 years in Malaysia. He has taught at several institutions namely, SEGI, Curtin University of Technology (Sarawak Campus), Universiti Tunku Abdul Rahman and he is currently attached to Monash University Malaysia. He lectures Business and Company law to undergraduate and postgraduate students. He supervises research projects for undergraduate students and dissertation/thesis for postgraduate students. He is also an Examiner and Moderator for the above-mentioned subjects at several institutions and professional examinations. Dr. Loganathan Krishnan has presented research papers at national and international conferences held in Malaysia, Bangladesh, China, Indonesia, Italy, Japan, New Zealand, Philippines, South Korea, Taiwan, Thailand, Turkey and the United Arab Emirates. He has also published papers in scholarly refereed journals, namely: Asian Law Journal, Consumer Review, Current Law Journal, INSAF The Journal of the Malaysian Bar, International Islamic University Malaysia Law Journal, Journal of Governance and Development, Journal of Legal Studies, Journal of Malaysian and Comparative Law, Journal of Syariah and Law, Malayan Law Journal, Malaysian Journal of Law and Society, Malaysian Labour Review, Quarterly Law Review, Rekayasa Journal of Ethics, Legal and Governance, Syariah Journal and The Law Review. Dr. Loganathan Krishnan is also a paper reviewer for several journals. His research expertise is in Business Law, Company Law and Constitutional Law. He has also received several research grants to conduct research in Company Law and Constitutional Law. Dr. Loganathan Krishnan is a member of ASEAN Law Association of Malaysia, a Committee Member of Constitutional Law and Human Rights Committee, LAWASIA.

Wai Meng Chan is an Associate Professor at the Faculty of Business and Economics, University of Malaya, Kuala Lumpur, Malaysia. She lectures on Company Law and Commercial Law since she joined the Faculty in 1998. Wai Meng has published extensively. Among her publications are Third Party Rights in Insurance Law in Malaysia, Essential Company Law in Malaysia: Navigating the Companies Act 2016, and Navigating the Companies Act 2016 for SMEs. She contributed to The Annotated Malaysian Companies Act 2016 published by Sweet & Maxwell Asia. Wai Meng is an Examiner and Assessor for Company Law in a number of professional examinations. She is also an Associate Trainer for the Companies Commission of Malaysia. Prior to joining academia, Wai Meng was in legal practice and in the banking industry for ten years.

Chapter 1
The Pandemic, Businesses and the Companies

Loganathan Krishnan

The Companies Act

The Companies Act 1965 ("CA 1965") has been in existence until it was replaced in January 2017 by the Companies Act 2016 ("CA 2016"). Although before the CA 2016 was enacted, the CA 1965 was amended over 35 times, the amendments were not holistic.[1] Additionally, the amendments were not in tandem with the various developments that have taken place in developed countries[2] such as the United Kingdom, Australia and Singapore.[3] Nevertheless, the CA 2016 has taken into account the developments that have taken place in those countries as they have been tested and tried.[4] As remarked by the Companies Commission of Malaysia's Chief Executive Officer, Datuk Zahrah Abd Wahab, the CA 2016 had to replace the CA 1965 as it is vital for companies to remain relevant and competitive.[5] Furthermore it is crucial for the CA 2016 to reflect the developments taking place elsewhere if Malaysia wishes to

[1] MAICSA Annual Conference 2006, Corporate Updates, Malaysian Association of Institute of Chartered Secretaries and Administrators, Kuala Lumpur, July 10–11, 2006.

[2] Adeline Paul Raj, "Companies Bill 2015 to Bring Major Reform," *The Edge Malaysia*, April 18, 2016, 24.

[3] MAICSA Annual Conference 2007, Challenges in Leading Governance, Malaysian Association of Institute of Chartered Secretaries and Administrators, Kuala Lumpur, July 16–17, 2007.

[4] Kenneth Foo Poh Khean & Lee Shih, *Companies Act 2016: The New Dynamics of Company Law in Malaysia*, Ampang: CLJ, 2017, 35.

[5] MAICSA Annual Conference, Challenges of the Changing Corporate and Regulatory Landscape Malaysian Association of Institute of Chartered Secretaries and Administrators, Kuala Lumpur, September 9–10, 2014.

L. Krishnan (✉)
Monash University, Selangor, Malaysia
e-mail: loganathan.krishnan@monash.edu

L. Krishnan and W. M. Chan (eds.), *The Impact of COVID-19 on Corporations and Corporate Law in Malaysia*, https://doi.org/10.1007/978-981-19-5519-8_1

be an attractive business hub locally, regionally and globally.[6] The enactment of the CA 2016 is a result of the proposals made by the Corporate Law Reform Committee set up by the Companies Commission of Malaysia.[7] However, it took 13 years before the proposals came into effect in the form of the CA 2016.[8] Be that as it may, the concern at hand is whether the CA 2016 was able to withstand the impact COVID19 pandemic has on businesses and companies.

Background

The pandemic of COVID-19 hit the Malaysian shores in early 2020. Consequently, this severely affected businesses and companies and there were various movement control orders ("MCO"). The MCOs restricted the movement of people and operation of businesses.[9] The Malaysian government enacted the Prevention and Control of Infectious Diseases (Measures within the Infected Local Areas) Regulations 2020 in order to issue the MCOs. The Regulations were enacted under the Prevention and Control of Infectious Diseases Act 1988 and the Police Act 1967. The MCO was from March 18, 2020 till April 1, 2020, phase 2 was from April 1, 2020 till April 14, 2020, phase 3 was from April 14, 2020 till April 28, 2020 and phase 4 was from April 29, 2020 till May 12, 2020. The Conditional MCO which was announced on May 1, 2020 ended on June 9, 2020. The Recovery Movement Control Order was announced by the Government of Malaysia on June 5, 2020 and was effective from June 10 until August 31, 2020. On 28 August, Prime Minister Muhyiddin Yassin announced the extension of the RMCO by a further 4 months until December 3, 2020. The second MCO was implemented across a number of federal territories and states in January 2021. The restrictions on movements have since been lifted and companies are gradually getting back on their feet. Malaysia has now transitioned to an endemic phase. Nevertheless, companies are still experiencing the post-pandemic effect.

---

[6] Malaysian Legal and Corporate Conference–Shifting Sands: Is the Law Reshaping Our Legal and Corporate Sectors? Current Law Journal Sdn Bhd and Malaysian Bar Council, Kuala Lumpur, July 3–4, 2013.

[7] Companies Commission of Malaysia National Insolvency Conference: Companies Bill 2015—Modernising Corporate Insolvency Framework in Malaysia, Companies Commission of Malaysia, Kuala Lumpur, October 11, 2016.

[8] Workshop on the New Companies Act, Corporate Securities and Financial Law and Regulation, Civil Law Department, Ahmad Ibrahim Kulliyah of Law, International Islamic University Malaysia, August 2–3, 2016.

[9] It was enforced under the Control and Prevention of Infectious Diseases Act 1988 and the Police Act 1967, and encompasses, among others, the closure of all government and private premises except those involved in essential services (water, electricity, energy, telecommunications, post, transportation, irrigation, oil, gas fuel, lubricants, broadcasting, finance, banking, health, pharmacy, fire prevention, prisons, ports, airports, security, defense, cleaning, food supply and retail).

COVID Act 2020

At the time when the COVID-19 pandemic started, various calls were made to enact a specific law on COVID-19 similar to the approach taken by Singapore.[10] On October 23, 2020, the Temporary Measures for Reducing the Impact of Coronavirus Disease 2019 Act 2020 was gazetted ("COVID Act 2020"). The aim of the legislation is to reduce the impact of COVID-19 on businesses and people. Hence, it modified certain provisions in the Limitation Act 1953, the Sabah Limitation Ordinance, the Sarawak Limitation Ordinance, the Public Authorities Protection Act 1948, the Insolvency Act 1967, the Hire-Purchase Act 1967, the Consumer Protection Act 1999, the Distress Act 1951, the Housing Development (Control and Licensing) Act 1966, the Industrial Relations Act 1967, the Private Employment Agencies Act 1981, the Land Public Transport Act 2010, the Commercial Vehicles Licensing Board Act 1987, the Courts of Judicature Act 1964, the Subordinate Courts Act 1948 and the Subordinate Courts Rules Act 1955.

Section 1(2) of the COVID Act 2020 provides that except where the date of commencement and period of operation have been provided in respect of the respective Parts in the Act, the Act shall come into operation on the date of publication of the Act and shall continue to remain in operation for a period of two years from such date of publication. It will end in October 2022. Nevertheless, the COVID Act 2020 makes no reference to CA 2016. Hence, reference should be made to guidelines issued by the Companies Commission of Malaysia ("CCM"), Securities Commission of Malaysia ("SC"), Bursa Malaysia and the Central Bank of Malaysia ("BNM") on the requirements and compliance by companies in light of the pandemic.

In view of this, various aspects of company law must be re-examined as the pandemic has major impacts on those aspects. The ensuing discussion will explore the extent the pandemic impacted areas concerning directors' fiduciary duties, directors' duty of care and skill, auditors' dutics and obligations, board meetings, company meetings, shareholder activism, compliance with statutory requirements, criminal liability risks for corporations, effect on capital markets, corporate restructuring and insolvency. Subsequent chapters will discuss in detail the impact COVID-19 had on companies and CA 2016 on the respective topics as aforementioned.

Directors' Duties to Act in Good Faith

It is a trite fact that every director of a company is under a fiduciary duty. This duty is owed to the company since it is a legal entity.[11] This is a common law duty which is incorporated in the CA 2016. Lord Greene MR in *Re Smith and Fawcett Ltd*[12] stated that:

---

[10] "Companies Need More Relief", *The Star*, May 11, 2020.

[11] Siew Cheang Loh, *Corporate Powers Accountability* (Petaling Jaya: LexisNexis, 2018), 347.

[12] [1942] Ch 304.

> The principles to be applied in cases where the articles of a company confer a discretion on directors are, for present purposes, free from doubt. They must exercise their discretion bona fide in what they consider – not what a court may consider – is in the interests of the company, and not for any collateral purpose. The question, therefore, simply is whether on the true construction of the particular article the directors are limited by anything except their bona fide view as to the interests of the company.

Hence, in the context of the topic at hand, directors must consider whether the decisions made by reason of the impact of COVID-19 are in the best interests of the company. Certainly the difficulty arises as to what company's interests constitute. In any case directors must ensure that they act in the interests of the company,[13] collective shareholders,[14] employees,[15] creditors[16] environment and society.[17] Nevertheless, the term 'interest' is usually taken by the courts to mean financial interests.[18] Furthermore, it was rightly pointed out in *Board of Trustees of Sabah Foundation & Ors v Datuk Syed Kechik bin Syed Mohamed & Anor*[19] by Ian Chin J that 'the distinguishing obligation of a fiduciary is the obligation of loyalty." Therefore, where there is conflict of interests of the various parties, directors should have in mind the interests of the company. During the COVID-19, many businesses were affected and socio-economic status of individuals were affected. A director should not breach his duty in order to save his socio-economic status. This is because his position is one of those where trust is placed on him by the company, shareholders, employees and creditors as clearly enunciated by the court in *Dato' Abul Hasan bin Mohamed Rashid v Multi-Code Electronics Industries & Anor.*[20] Therefore, a director is under a duty to report to the company if there is any conduct which is detrimental to the company. This was well explained by the court in *Sundai (M) Sdn Bhd v Masato Saito & Ors.*[21]

Every aspect of the law on fiduciary duty namely the duty to act for a proper purpose,[22] retain discretion,[23] avoid conflict of interest,[24] not to make a secret profit,[25] not to accept bribes,[26] not to misuse the company's funds,[27] not to take up corporate

---

[13] *Swinfen Eady J in Percival v Wright* [1902] 2 Ch 401.

[14] *Lum Sow Kuen v Chuah Choong Heing & Ors.* (1998) MLJU 39 where the court stated that duty is not owed to individual shareholders.

[15] In view of the director's duty to prepare a report under S. 252 of the CA 2016.

[16] *West Mercia Safetywear Ltd v Dodd* [1988] BCLC 250.

[17] S. 252 of the CA 2016.

[18] Paul Desmond Finn, *Fiduciary Obligations* (Sydney: Law Book Co, 1977), 203.

[19] [1999] 6 MLJ 497.

[20] [2012] 5 MLJ 176.

[21] [2013] 9 MLJ 729.

[22] Lord Wilberforce in *Howard Smith Ltd v Ampol Petroleum Ltd* [1974] UKPC 3.

[23] *Thorby v. Goldberg* [1964] 112 C.L.R. 597.

[24] Lord Selbourne in *Great Eastern Railway v Turner* (1872) LR 8 Ch App 149.

[25] Lord Russell of Killowen in *Regal (Hastings) Ltd v Gulliver* [1942] UKHL 1.

[26] *Boston Deep Sea Fishing & Ice Co. v Ansell* (1888) 39 ChD 339.

[27] *Totex-Adon Pty Ltd v Marco* (1982) 1 ACLC 228.

opportunity,[28] not to misuse confidential information,[29] and not to compete with the company[30] must be carefully examined in relation to the directors' conduct especially in light of the pandemic. This is because although the powers of the management of a company must not be stifled, neither can unfettered, unsupervised, absolute discretion be permitted.[31] The requirement of good faith is that it must not only be done but must manifestly be seen to be done.[32]

In addition to the duty imposed under common law, various provisions of the CA 2016 impose a duty on directors too namely S. 213—act in good faith, S. 218—not to misuse property, information, position and opportunity, S. 219—general duty to make disclosure, S. 221—duty of disclosure of interests in contracts, S. 222—interested director not to participate or vote at board meetings, S. 223—obtain approval from company for acquisition or disposal of property of substantial value, S. 75—obtain approval from company before allotment of shares, S. 224—not to accept loans from the company, S. 226—not to accept tax free payments from the company and S. 227—not to accept compensation for loss of office. A point to be noted is that although the aforementioned provisions use the term "director", S. 210 of the CA 2016 states that the term includes chief executive officer, chief operating officer and chief financial officer for the purposes of S. 213, 214, 215, 216, 217, 218, 223 and S. 228.

Hence, it can be observed that ample duties are imposed on directors by common law and the CA 2016. This is to ensure that directors do not misuse their powers and position. This is because the success and failure of a company rests on directors. A detailed discussion on the impact of COVID-19 on companies in the context of directors' fiduciary duty under common law and the CA 2016 can be seen in Chap. 2. The author takes us back to the development of these duties and how directors will have to cope as a result of the impact of COVID-19.

Additionally, what is also important is the directors' duty to act with reasonable care, skill and diligence. This is extremely important considering directors are the ones who make decisions on behalf of the company. The COVID-19 has certainly made many directors of companies to be cautious in their decision making. This is simply because the impact of COVID-19 is severe and the future remains uncertain. Hence, the ensuing section will explore this to give a hindsight on the topic.

---

[28] Lord Buckmaster LC in *Cook v Deeks* [1916] UKPC 10 i.

[29] Megarry V-C in *Thomas Marshall (Exports). Ltd. v. Guinle* [1978] I.C.R. 905.

[30] Lord Atkin in *Bell v Lever Brothers Ltd* [1931] UKHL 2.

[31] John H Farrar, Nigel E Furey, and Brenda M Hannigan, *Farrar's Company Law* (London: Butterworths, 1991), 379.

[32] Lawrence Cecil Bartlett Gower, *Gower's Principles of Modern Company Law*, 4th ed (London: Stevenson 1979), 583.

Directors' Duty to Exercise Due Care, Skill and Diligence

This aspect of duty has undergone drastic changes since the time the common law set the standards. In fact, the case of *Re City Equitable Fire Insurance Co*[33] had set a very low standard. Romer J at the High Court stated that:

> (1) A director need not exhibit, in the performance of his duties, a greater skill than may be reasonably expected from a person of his knowledge or experience. A director is not bound to exercise any skill he does not have. A director is not expected to be an expert unless appointed as such.
>
> (2) A director is not bound to give continuous attention to the affairs of the company and his duties arise intermittently while performing his functions at Board meetings. He is not bound to attend all such meetings but should attend whenever he is reasonably able to do so.
>
> (3) In the absence of suspicious circumstances, a director may trust another company official to carry out those duties which may properly be delegated.

If the duty is based on the above standard, it is very unlikely that a director can be made responsible and liable for his actions as it is based on a subjective standard. Every director has different knowledge and skills. There will not be uniformity of standard expected of directors. In fact, decisions are made by the Board of Directors ("the Board"). A director should not be permitted to hide behind his personal knowledge and skill to declare that a lower standard should be expected of him especially where decisions are made by the Board. Moreover, a lower standard was expected of directors as the standard was set during Victorian times.

Today, directors live in a trying and challenging environment. This is more so due to the pandemic which requires directors to make very careful decisions otherwise they could be liable and could cause the company to make major mistakes and collapse financially. Directors have to ensure that their decisions are reasonable. They must exercise due care, skill and diligence. In *Dorchester Finance Co v Stebbing*[34] Foster J held that directors had to display such skill and care as should be reasonably expected from people with their knowledge and experience. Hence, it can be observed that an objective test is imposed. Furthermore, there is no longer a distinction between an executive and non-executive director. In *Daniels v Anderson*,[35] the Australian Court of Appeal held that a director's duty of care is not merely subjective, limited by the director's knowledge and experience or ignorance or inaction. In another Australian case of *AWA Ltd v Daniels (t/as Deloitte Haskins & Sells)*[36] Rogers CJ remarked that directors must take reasonable steps and understand the effect the economy has on the business of the company to always monitor the management of the company. In fact in the New Zealand decision of *National Mutual Life Nominees Ltd v Worn*,[37] Henry J in *obiter* remarked that the standard set by Romer J in *Re*

---

[33] [1925] Ch 407.

[34] [1989] BCLC 498.

[35] (1995) 37 NSWLR 438.

[36] (1992) 7 ACSR 759.

[37] [1990] 3 NZLR 641.

City Equitable Fire Insurance Co cannot be used as yardstick in today's world of business. In the context of the discussion at hand this is extremely apt as the pandemic has completely overturned companies in the way they do business. Hence, it can be observed that the common law standard has been reexamined in Australia and New Zealand in light of the way business is being run today.

As for the domestic front, the director's duty of care, skill and diligence is governed by S. 213(2) of the CA 2016. The provision incorporated an objective and subjective test in determining whether a director has exercised his duty of care, skill and diligence reasonably. The provision reads as follows:

A director of a company shall exercise reasonable care, skill and diligence with —

(a) the knowledge, skill and experience which may reasonably be expected of a director having the same responsibilities; and

(b) any additional knowledge, skill and experience which the director in fact has.

Hence, in view of the pandemic, directors have to ensure that the decisions they make are reasonable and in tandem with the decisions of other directors of the same responsibilities. Be that as it may, directors may rely on the defence of the business judgment rule as provided by S. 214 of the CA 2016. The provision reads as follows:

It is a defence to a director where he:

(a) makes the business judgment for a proper purpose and in good faith;

(b) does not have a material personal interest in the subject matter of the business judgment;

(c) is informed about subject matter of the business judgment and reasonably believes the decision made is appropriate under the circumstances; and

(d) reasonably believes that the business judgment is in the best interests of the company.

The likelihood of this defence being relied upon is very high given the uncertainties the pandemic has caused. Moreover, the courts may adopt a lighter approach in establishing liability in cases where directors acted reasonably and in the best interests of the company.

As regards to reliance, S. 215 of the CA 2016 imposes a duty on a director to ensure only a reliable and competent person is relied upon. As for delegation, S. 216 of the CA 2016 requires a director to ensure work is only delegated to a reliable and competent person. Hence, a director must exercise due care, skill and diligence before relying on another person or delegating to another person. Hence, Chap. 3 explores in detail the impact of the pandemic on the director's duty of care, skill and diligence.

The impact of the pandemic was not only felt by directors but auditors too as they audit the company's accounts and prepare the auditors' report. In doing so, various documents will be accessed and various personnel will be interviewed to source information in ensuring that the report is reliable and correct. The succeeding section will explain the extent the pandemic has impacted auditors.

Auditors' Duties and Obligations

The term auditor is not defined in the CA 1965 nor CA 2016. Nonetheless, S. 2 of the Capital Markets and Services Act 2007 states that an auditor is an approved company auditor within the meaning of the Companies Act. The term approved company auditor is interpreted in S. 2(1) of the CA 2016 which reads that "a person who has been approved under S. 263 as an auditor and whose approval has not been revoked." Hence, there is no precise definition provided in the statutes as to who an auditor is.

In Latin, the term auditor means listening as it came from the word *audire*.[38] The origins of audit can be traced to the medieval times whereby the accounts of the Exchequer, boroughs, public bodies, merchants, commercial ventures, manors and landed estates must be verified.[39] They are required to examine the financial information of a company.[40] They verify the companies' accounts in detail and thus audit is a monitoring device.[41] The aim is to prevent fraudulent actions.[42] Thus, audit is defined as "a skilled examination of such books, accounts and vouchers which will enable auditors to verify the balance sheet of a company".[43] Although there is reliance and dependence on the information provided by the company, auditors are required to use their own professional judgment and skill. They are required to ask the right questions.[44] They are trained professionally to audit the companies' accounts independently since independence is the foundation of the audit profession.[45] This is what audit means, in most countries.[46] Furthermore, they perform important advisory, reporting, investigatory, regulatory and administrative functions.[47]

Therefore, there are various duties and obligations imposed on auditors under common law and CA 2016. There are also other laws which are applicable namely Capital Markets and Services Act 2007, Financial Services Act 2013, Central Bank

---

[38] Aishah Bidin, *Undang-Undang Syarikat Di Malaysia* (Kuala Lumpur: DBP, 2001), 230.

[39] Mae Baker, and Michael Collins, "Audit and Control in the Not-For-Profit Sector: An Endowed Charity Case 1739–1853", *Accounting and Business Research* 35 (2005): 2–7.

[40] Sin Boon Ann, "The Duty of Care of Auditors: To Whom Should the Duty be Owed," *Malayan Law Journal* 3 [1990]: iii.

[41] Wanda A Wallace, "The Economic Role of the Audit in Free and Regulated Markets: A Look Back and A Look Forward," *Research in Accounting Regulation* 17 (2004): 267–298.

[42] Waheed Abdel-Qader, "An Evaluation of the International Auditing Standards and Their Application to the Audit of Listed Corporations in Jordan," (PhD diss., University of Western Sydney, Australia, 2002), 53.

[43] Geoffrey R Masel, *Professional Negligence of Lawyers, Accountants, Bankers and Brokers*, 2nd ed., (North Ryde, N.S.W: CCH Australia Ltd, 1989), 23

[44] Eddie Lee, "Sniffing Out Fraud," *Accountants Today,* 25 no 2 (March/April 2012): 26.

[45] John L Carey, The Rise of the Accounting Profession: To Responsibility and Authority, 1937–1960 182 quoted in Panel on Audit Effectiveness.

[46] Elizabeth L Normanton, *The Accountability and Audit of Governments* (New York: Manchester University Press, 1966), 22–23, 57–58.

[47] Rupert M Jackson, and John L Powell, *Professional Negligence*, 4th ed. (London: Sweet & Maxwell, 1997), 804.

of Malaysia Guidelines, Bursa Malaysia Listing Rules and the Malaysian Code of Corporate Governance 2021. However, those laws are not within the ambit of the discussion here.

The English laws have taken the position that auditors were required to be familiar with the company's constitution,[48] report on any matter which is illegal or improper,[49] make a qualified report if unable to obtain the full information on a company's accounts,[50] check on the management of the company,[51] employ own tests to determine whether the company's internal system is reliable,[52] duty to take further steps if that is so[53] and maintain confidentiality.[54]

As for the position under Malaysian case law, auditors were required to detect any material errors and omissions[55] and maintain confidentiality.[56] Additionally, the CA 2016 imposed various duties on auditors namely, the duty to report to members of the company,[57] to state whether the financial statements of the company are in their opinion properly drawn up so as to give a true and fair view of the matters required by S. 248, to state the particulars of any defect or irregularity in respect of any of those matters,[58] whether the accounts of the company have been properly drawn up in accordance with the CA 2016[59] and the applicable approved accounting standards,[60] to report to the CCM of any breach or non-observance of the CA 2016[61] and to report fraud to the CCM if it is a public company or a company which is controlled by a public company.[62]

These duties pose a challenge during the pandemic since there was a lockdown. Auditors had to engage in remote auditing. To what extent this is effective is questionable. Consequently, auditors will have to rely on digital transformative processes. As the pandemic caught many by surprise, the question is certainly whether companies were prepared for a digital transformative process to enable auditors to carry out

---

48 *Re Republic of Bolivia Exploration Syndicate Ltd* [1914] 1 Ch 139 and *Leeds Estate Building & Investment Co v Shephard* (1887) 36 Ch D 787.

49 *Thomas v The Corporation of Devonport* (1900) 1 QB 16.

50 *Berg Sons & Co Ltd v Adams* [1993] BCLC 1045.

51 *Re City Equitable Fire Insurance Co* [1925] Ch 407, 481 [1924] All ER Rep 485: 133 LT 520.

52 *Roberts v Hopwood* [1925] AC 578, 605.

53 *Re Kingston Cotton Mill Co (No 2)* [1896] 2 Ch 279.

54 *Prince Jefri Bolkiah v KPMG (a firm)* [1999] 1 All ER 517, 518.

55 *RHB Capital Bhd v Tan Sri Dato' Abdul Rashid bin Haji Mohamed Hussain* [2006] 4 MLJ 80.

56 *Tat Sang Sdn Bhd v Saw & Co* [2002] 3 MLJ 457 and *Onestop Software Solutions (M) Sdn Bhd v Masteritec Sdn Bhd & Ors* [2009] 8 MLJ 528 though the court took a different approach in *Teoh Peng Phe v Wan & Co Kuala Lumpur High Court (Commercial Division) Suit No D5-24-339-1999 (unreported)*.

57 S. 266(1) of the CA 2016.

58 S. 266(2)(d) of the CA 2016.

59 S. 266(2)(a)(ii) of the CA 2016.

60 S. 266(2)(a)(iii) of the CA 2016.

61 S. 266(8)(a) of the CA 2016.

62 S. 266(9) of the CA 2016.

remote auditing. In some cases, companies were reluctant to rely on digital transformative processes on the grounds of security. One of the main concerns is the challenge faced by auditors in obtaining evidence. Furthermore, since many businesses were facing financial difficulties, a heavier responsibility is placed on the shoulders of auditors to make a statement whether a company is a going concern company. The pandemic has made things so uncertain and hence it will be extremely difficult for auditors to gauge the financial situation and the future. Additionally, since companies were given leeway to comply with regulatory requirements, auditors will also have to follow suit. More can be observed as the author of Chap. 4 has examined auditors' duties and obligations in the context of the pandemic from various perspectives in detail.

Board Meetings, Company Meetings and Shareholder Activism

Due to the pandemic and the lockdown, the holding of board meetings and company meetings were severely affected. Since there was no physical platform for shareholders to voice their concerns, shareholder activism was impacted. Although a company is a legal entity as enumerated by Lord Macnaghten in *Salomon v A Salomon & Co Ltd*[63] and explicitly provided in S. 20 of the CA 2016, decisions are made by the Board and shareholders at meetings. Nevertheless, directors usually have the power to manage the business of the company, with the members being entitled to vote only on matters expressly reserved for them by the constitution or under CA 2016.[64] Having said that, decisions must be made by the majority directors at the Board meetings as the board is the primary organ of the company as succinctly put by V C George J (as he then was) in *Chan Choon Ming v Low Poh Choon & 4 Ors.*[65] This is because it clearly provided that the business and affairs of a company shall be managed by or under the direction of the Board.[66] The Board has all the powers necessary for managing, directing and supervising the management of the business and affairs subject to any modification or exception or limitation in the CA 2016, or the constitution.[67] Therefore, members do not have an overriding or residual power over the directors' management powers. In *John Shaw & Sons (Salford) Ltd v Shaw*,[68] Greer LJ stated that.

---

[63] [1896] UKHL 1, [1897] AC 22.

[64] Aiman Nariman, Aishah Bidin, Pamela Hanrahan, Ian Ramsay and Geof Stapledon, *Commercial Applications of Company Law in Malaysia*, 3rd ed (Malaysia: CCH Asia Pte Limited, 2008), 135.

[65] [1995] 1 CLJ 812.

[66] S. 211(1) of the CA 2016.

[67] S. 211(2) of the CA 2016.

[68] [1935] 2 KB 113.

> They cannot themselves usurp the powers which by the articles are vested in the directors any more than the directors can usurp the powers vested by the articles in the general body of shareholders.

Similarly in *Automatic Self-Cleansing Filter Syndicate Co Ltd v Cuninghame*,[69] Lord Collins MR stated that the simple majority of shareholders was not enough to override the requirement in the constitution that the directors may only be given instructions through a three quarter majority.

In light of the pandemic, there is high likelihood that directors may have differing opinions among themselves before arriving at a decision. Be that as it may, the directors owe their duty to the company individually.[70] Furthermore, there is a likelihood that the Board may have a different opinion than the shareholders. As stated earlier, it is the Board which will make decisions in determining the direction of the company unless the company's constitution requires shareholders' approval in certain matters. Nevertheless, in the event there is a deadlock in the Board, the members at the general meeting do have the power to manage the company as stated by Sundaresh Menon CJ at the Singapore Court of Appeal in *Chan Siew Lee v TYC Investment Pte Ltd and Ors and anor appeal*.[71]

Regard should also be made to S. 195 of the CA 2016 as this is a new provision which is not found in the CA 1965. Despite the aforementioned cases on the powers of the Board to determine the direction of the company, S. 195 sheds an interesting light on the matter. The provision provides that the chairperson of a meeting of members of a company shall allow members a reasonable opportunity at that meeting to question, discuss, comment or make recommendations on the management of a company. Since the provision uses the term "shall", it is obligatory for the chairperson to allow this opportunity for the members. Subsection (2) proceeds to state that members may pass a resolution to make recommendations to the Board on matters affecting the management of the company. The recommendations are only binding if it is in the best interest of the company and the rights to do so are provided in the constitution or it is passed by way of special resolution as provided by S. 195(3) of the CA 2016.

This provision shows that shareholder activism is alive though there are criteria to be satisfied. In light of the pandemic, this provision will be very useful for shareholders to question, discuss, comment or make binding recommendations. Hence, the aforementioned cases must be re-examined in light of S. 195(3) of the CA 2016.

Be that as it may, due to the pandemic and the lockdown, physical meetings were not possible. Thanks to technology, there were various platforms which enabled companies to hold virtual meetings. This is further facilitated by guidelines and directives issued by the regulators which allowed such meetings. Additionally, the CA 2016 contained provisions which enabled virtual meetings. Nevertheless, the pandemic was the testing ground whether the provisions were effective or needed further reforms. Furthermore, companies had to be prepared to use such technologies.

---

69 [1906] 2 Ch 34.

70 *Re Westmaid Packaging Services Ltd; Secretary of Trade and Industry v Griffiths* [1998] 2 BCLC 646.

71 [2015] 5 SLR 409.

Their employees need to have the knowledge and skill and the companies must have the technological infrastructure. On the other hand, shareholders face the same dilemma as to whether they have the knowledge and skill to use such technology and whether their homes are equipped with adequate technological infrastructure. Hence, it is certainly a challenge for the company, chairman, directors and shareholders. For example, the AGM of Maybank was disrupted by a technical glitch and this certainly affected the meeting. Chapter 5 will scrutinise in detail the impact of the pandemic on this area and provide the readers a new perspective on this issue. Related to this topic is the succeeding section which focuses on compliance with statutory requirements and as the responsibility is to be shouldered by the management of the company.

Compliance with Statutory Requirements

One of the biggest challenges for any businesses during the pandemic is to comply with the statutory requirements. Compliance with the statutory requirements is imperative as otherwise it would attract a criminal penalty causing the company and/or its officers liable to a fine or imprisonment in certain circumstances. The CA 2016 has further enhanced the criminal penalties to ensure compliance with statutory requirements is strictly adhered to. Moreover, the compliance will benefit various stakeholders who have an interest in the way the company does its business.

The regulators are fully aware of the difficulties for businesses to comply with statutory requirements due to the lockdown. Hence, various interim measures were provided to assist companies to effectively comply with the statutory requirements. Additionally, the regulators provided moratoriums and extension of time in order to ensure that companies will not be in breach of the CA 2016. The regulators provided practice directions and guidelines for companies in order to make it easier for the companies to comply with the statutory requirements. In many circumstances, compliance with the CA 2016 would first require the company to hold board meetings and/or company meetings. As discussed in the preceding section that due to the lockdown, a physical meeting was not permissible. Hence, the only option left was a virtual meeting. It was also discussed earlier the challenges in holding a virtual meeting. This would mean that a company is faced with double challenges namely holding a virtual meeting effectively and complying with statutory requirements. In the common law case of *Re Bonelli's Telegraph Co. Collie's Claim,*[72] the court held that as long as the directors decided unanimously, a board meeting can be held informally. However, in light of the Third Schedule of the CA 2016, it is unlikely that this will still be the case. Hence, although a virtual meeting is permissible, it must still be formal. In fact, a hybrid meeting was held as far back as 1990, in the case of *Byng v London Life Association Ltd*[73] though it was not a fully virtual meeting.

[72] (1871) LR 12 Eq 246. For newer cases, see *Charterhouse Investment Trust Ltd v Tempest Diesels Ltd* (1985) 1 BCC 99, *Runciman v Walter Runciman plc* [1993] BCC 223.

[73] [1990] Ch 170.

A point to be noted is that the replacement of the CA 1965 with the CA 2016 which contained many new provisions is much to be appreciated as the provisions were found to be very useful for companies to comply with during the pandemic. Nevertheless, the pandemic has also revealed the necessary reforms that should be made to the CA 2016 in order to address problems that may recur in the future. Hence, taking a leaf from other countries such as the United Kingdom, Australia and Singapore will prove to be useful.

Compliance with the statutory requirements were seen as a challenge since not all documents can be submitted electronically. Hence, the only option was to submit over the counter. However, the regulator's office itself was closed during the lockdown. Furthermore, not in all cases that the regulators have provided an extension of time and due date. The authors of Chap. 6 have certainly ingeniously unearthed many perplexing issues concerning compliance with the CA 2016 during the pandemic. It is hoped that the regulators will take a cue from the concerns raised and make the necessary reforms to the CA 2016.

It should be noted that the impact of the pandemic is not only experienced by businesses but also employees of an organization. This will be discussed in the succeeding section and the author of Chap. 7 will discuss the impact on employees and the organisation from various perspectives.

The COVID-19 Diffusion and Criminal Liability Risks for Corporations

As stated earlier, the impact of the pandemic was severely felt by the employees. This is because employees have to ensure that they comply with the standard operating procedures ("SOP") as set by the Ministry of Health ("MOH"). Additionally, organisations may have further rules to ensure that the pandemic is diffused at the workplace. This is for the safety of all employees at the organisation.

In fact, S. 213(1) of the CA 2016 is under the heading of "Duties and responsibilities of directors". This connotes that the provision places a responsibility on directors. Furthermore, the provision states that a director of a company shall at all times exercise his powers in accordance with the Act, for a proper purpose and in good faith in the best interest of the company. The term best interest is not defined in the CA 2016. Nevertheless, one of the categories of persons the directors should have in mind is the employees since they are the assets of the organisation. Hence, the directors must ensure that the company complies with its obligations relating to the health, safety and welfare at work of its workers, under health and safety legislation.

Furthermore, reference should be made to S. 252 of the CA 2016 which requires directors of a company to prepare for each financial year a report and such report shall be attached to the financial statements prepared under S. 248. Section 253(1)(c) of the CA 2016 proceeds to state that the directors' report for a financial year in relation to a company shall contain the matters set out in the Fifth Schedule. Part

II of the Fifth Schedule then states that a director's report may include a business review. Paragraph 2(d)(ii) states that the business review may, to the extent necessary for an understanding of the development, performance or position of the company's business, contain information about the company's employees. Although the requirement is not obligatory, it can be observed that the policymakers have in mind the interest of employees in the organisation. Hence, in this context, directors may state the measures taken by the organisation to diffuse the pandemic in order to ensure a safe and proper place of work is provided.

Hence, companies must ensure that hand sanitisers, face masks and face shields are provided to all employees. The management must also ensure that employees are wearing their masks at all times and that the employees sanitise their hands regularly. Additionally, only those employees who have been vaccinated as per the rules set out by the MOH be allowed entry to the workplace. On that note, an employee must co-operate and be obedient to the employer's instructions unless they require him to do an unlawful act or to expose himself to unreasonable danger as remarked by Karminsk J in *Pepper v Webb.*[74] Moreover, S. 15 of the Occupational Safety and Health Act 1994 ("OSHA"), imposes duties on employers to secure workplace health and safety for all employees and others who may be affected by the activities at the workplace.

Moreover, it is an implied duty under common law for employers to ensure a safe place of work is created for its employees. The employer is also under a duty to provide safe plant and equipment. This includes providing appropriate tools, machinery and materials maintained to an adequate standard as emphasised by the *Scottish Industrial Tribunal in Pagano v HGS.*[75] This is particularly important as during the pandemic, there is a likelihood that different types of tools, machinery and materials are required.

In the event an organisation does not comply with the SOP as set out by the government, the organisation will be open to liability. Although there is no direct provision which penalises the directors and the company for failure to comply with the SOP, S. 213(1) of the CA 2016 require directors to act in the best interests of the company. Non-compliance of SOPs would bring disrepute to the company. Section 213(3) of the CA 2016 provides that a director who contravenes this section commits an offence and shall, on conviction, be liable to imprisonment for a term not exceeding five years or to a fine not exceeding three million ringgit or to both. Besides the CA 2016, S. 52(1) of the OSHA 1994 imposes liabilities on directors, managers, secretaries, or other like officers, if the organisation fails to provide a safe place and system of work.

A more detailed analysis is made by the author of Chap. 7 on the company's duty to ensure a safe place and system of work is provided to diffuse the pandemic for the welfare of all employees at the workplace. The succeeding section will then explore the effect of the pandemic on capital markets.

---

[74] (1969) 1 WLR 514 CA.

[75] [1976] IRLR 9.

Effect on Capital Markets

The effect of the pandemic is certainly felt by many by public listed companies. This is because public listed companies usually have large shareholding. In fact, the danger of the impact of pandemic on companies is the likelihood of the companies engaging in fraudulent activities in order to survive in the economic downturn. This will certainly not reflect well on the reputation of the company.

Since the impact of the pandemic was so severe, various measures were taken to ensure that businesses survive, namely changes to the Overnight Policy Rate and introduction of moratoriums. Investors had difficulties in investing in companies due to financial constraints. Consequently, shareholders were not able to sell their shares at desired price. This resulted in losses in margin trading. The regulators introduced measures to address this. Moreover, one of the ways for companies to avoid being in financial turmoil during the pandemic is to raise capital by issuing shares. Doing so during the pandemic could be a big challenge and the regulators had eased certain rules to make this possible. Furthermore, the government introduced some measures to assist in fundraising by the company. Additionally, the regulators issued directives which redefined the meaning of inability to pay debts in the context of S. 466(1)(a) of the CA 2016. This is to ensure that companies will not be easily categorised as unable to pay debts and consequently a petition against the company for insolvency could be avoided. Furthermore, Bursa Malaysia has also provided temporary relief for financially distressed companies in order to avoid being categorised as PN17. Flexibilities were also offered in relation to takeovers and mergers as the regulators were fully aware that submission of hard copy documents is a challenge due to the lockdown. What is obvious is that it is a major challenge for the regulators to provide interim measures across all types of companies i.e. public, public listed companies, and micro, small and medium sized enterprises.

On the other hand, it should not be construed that the impact of the pandemic has made the regulators loosen its reins completely. There are circumstances whereby the regulators have tightened the rules to ensure there is no manipulation of the circumstances for instance in the area of short selling. Furthermore, although it has been repeatedly echoed that the pandemic has severely affected businesses, certain sectors were doing very well such as producers of masks, sanitisers, face shields, personal protective equipment, gloves, etc. Be that as it may, the regulators must be wary of financial fraud that may be committed by companies. The author of Chap. 8 has remarkably assessed the situation and explored various perspectives on the impact of the pandemic on capital markets.

The succeeding section will focus on corporate restructuring and insolvency as this is the most important aspect as it concerns the survival of the company. If corporate restructuring is not possible it will end the life of the company due to insolvency.

Corporate Restructuring and Insolvency

When a company is severely financially hit by the pandemic, there are only two options left i.e. corporate restructuring or liquidation. Hence, the concern is the extent the current laws will help the company restructure itself in order to avoid liquidation. At the same time, the duties of the directors are of utmost importance as fingers will begin to point towards them for poor management skills. Hence, the concern is also the extent the current laws address this matter. The discussion will also centre on the manner the regulators redefined the concept of insolvency to ensure not many companies will fall within that category and result in the company to be liquidated.

During the pandemic, corporate rescue mechanisms ("CRM") have certainly gained popularity since companies faced financial difficulties. Corporate voluntary arrangement[76] and judicial management[77] were introduced in the CA 2016 though they only came into force on March 1, 2018 whereas the scheme of arrangement was already in CA 1965.[78] It provides an avenue for a company to manage its financial affairs by first having discussions with its creditors. The provisions of the CA 2016 which govern CRM are supported by the Companies (Corporate Rescue Mechanism) Rules 2018 and the Practice Directive No. 4/2018 (PD No. 4/2018). The Rules sets out the process and procedure of the Court under the CA 2016 whilst the Practice Directive states the general requirements for the documents to be lodged with the Registrar of Companies.

It is imperative to take note of the effectiveness of CRM in rescuing a company from being liquidated and therefore regard should be made as to whether they are applicable to all types of companies. There have been cases where applications were rejected on the ground they were not eligible for example Scomi Group Berhad and *CIMB Islamic Bank Berhad v Wellcom Communications (NS) Sdn Bhd*.[79] The procedure to be complied with may be tedious but it is for the benefit of all parties involved i.e. the company, shareholders, creditors and the courts. Much developments have taken place in this area as can be seen in several cases. In *Spacious Glory Sdn Bhd v Coconut Three Sdn Bhd*,[80] the issue before the High Court was that the applicant was a judgment creditor and whether he has a right to apply for judicial management. The court held that the creditor had a pecuniary claim against the company and therefore has a right and the same reasoning was applied in *Loh Teck Wah v Fintree Capital Sdn Bhd*.[81] Most importantly, the court must be satisfied that the company is or will be unable to pay its debts and hence, there is a duty to make a full and frank disclosure as remarked by the Honourable Judicial Commissioner Wong Chee Lin in *Leadmont*

---

[76] See S. 394 to 402 of the CA 2016.

[77] See S. 403 to 430 of the CA 2016.

[78] Now see S. 365 to 371 of the CA 2016.

[79] Civil Appeal No. W-02(IM)-1888-09/2018.

[80] [2020] MLJU 1827.

[81] [2021] MLJU 995.

Development Sdn Bhd v Infra Segi Sdn Bhd.[82] That was the reason an application for judicial management was rejected by the High Court in *Twin Unitrade Sdn Bhd v TSK Hardware Sdn Bhd.*[83]

The CRM are certainly offering a better protection to creditors than if a company is being wound up and this is echoed by the courts in *Loh Teck Wah v Fintree Capital Sdn Bhd*[84] and *Spacious Glory Sdn Bhd v Coconut Three Sdn Bhd.*[85] The decision of the Court of Appeal which overturned the High Court's decision in *Million Westlink Sdn Bhd v Maybank Investment Bank Berhad & Ors*[86] on the issue of whether secured and unsecured creditors may oppose an application for judicial management is now seen to have been reconciled with the decision of *Goldpage Assets Sdn Bhd v Unique Mix Sdn Bhd (unreported).*[87] As regards to the scheme of arrangement, the landmark case is *Airasia X Berhad v BOC Aviation Ltd & Ors.*[88]

In relation to insolvency, developments have taken place on S. 465(1)(e) of the CA 2016 which provides the ground a company can be compulsorily wound up i.e. the company is unable to pay its debts. Section 466(1) of the CA 2016 explains what is meant by the term unable to pay its debts. Due to the pandemic, the amount of indebtedness and the duration provided to the company to pay the debts have been revised. This is to provide some form of relief to ailing companies. The author of Chap. 9 will dwell on this matter in depth. Nevertheless, what is unfortunate is the extent of director's liability in preventing the company from being insolvent even in cases where the directors have taken reasonable steps. Developments in other countries have shown that directors have a defence in such cases. Perhaps, policymakers should look into this matter.

Concluding Remarks

The pandemic of COVID-19 has certainly affected many businesses not only in Malaysia but in other regions of the world too. Many governments have taken immediate steps to provide assistance to ailing businesses so that they will not be liquidated. Otherwise, it will affect the economy of the country. The ones who were drastically affected were micro and small medium enterprises and private companies. The way businesses could be affected can be observed in snippets' view in the aforementioned discussion. Authors of succeeding chapters have dwelled in their respective field of

---

[82] [2019] 8 MLJ 473.

[83] [2020] MLJU 2326. For other cases see *Vision Development Concept Sdn Bhd v Low Sheh Ling* [2020] MLJU 2387 and *Re Biaxis (M) Sdn Bhd* [2020] MLJU 1188 on the application of S. 405(5)(a) of the CA 2016.

[84] [2021] MLJU 995.

[85] [2020] MLJU 1827.

[86] Civil Appeal No. B-02(IM)-1590-08/2019).

[87] Decided on June 10, 2020.

[88] [2021] 1 LNS 188.

expertise to give the readers a thorough understanding of the impact of the pandemic on companies and the Companies Act 2016.

References

1. Abdel-Qader, Waheed, "An Evaluation of the International Auditing Standards and Their Application to the Audit of Listed Corporations in Jordan." PhD Diss., University of Western Sydney, Australia, 2002.
2. Bidin, Aishah. *Undang-Undang Syarikat Di Malaysia.* Kuala Lumpur: DBP, 2001.
3. Baker, Mae and Michael Collins. "Audit and Control in the Not-For-Profit Sector: An Endowed Charity Case 1739–1853," *Accounting and Business Research* 35, (2005): 2–7.
4. Carey, John L. (1970). The Rise of the Accounting Profession: To Responsibility and Authority, 1937–1960 182 quoted in Panel on Audit Effectiveness.
5. Companies Commission of Malaysia National Insolvency Conference: Companies Bill 2015 – Modernising Corporate Insolvency Framework in Malaysia, Companies Commission of Malaysia, Kuala Lumpur, October 11, 2016.
6. "Companies Need More Relief". *The Star*, May 11, 2020.
7. Farrar H. John, Nigel E. Furey and Brenda M. Hannigan. *Farrar's Company Law.* London: Butterworths 1991.
8. Finn, Paul Desmond. *Fiduciary Obligations.* Sydney: Law Book Co, 1977.
9. Foo, Kenneth Poh Khean and Shih, Lee. *Companies Act 2016: The New Dynamics of Company Law in Malaysia.* Ampang: CLJ, 2017.
10. Gower, Lawrence Cecil Bartlett. *Gower's Principles of Modern Company Law.* 4th edn. London: Stevens, 1979.
11. Jackson, Rupert M, and John L. Powell. *Professional Negligence.* 4th ed. London: Sweet & Maxwell, 1997.
12. Lee, Eddie. "Sniffing Out Fraud." (March/April 2012) 25(2) *Accountants Today* 26.
13. Loh, Siew Cheang. *Corporate Powers Accountability.* Petaling Jaya: LexisNexis, 2018.
14. MAICSA Annual Conference 2006, Corporate Updates, Malaysian Association of Institute of Chartered Secretaries and Administrators, Kuala Lumpur, July 10 - 11, 2006.
15. MAICSA Annual Conference 2007, Challenges in Leading Governance, Malaysian Association of Institute of Chartered Secretaries and Administrators, Kuala Lumpur, July 16 - 17, 2007.
16. MAICSA Annual Conference 2014, Challenges of the Changing Corporate and Regulatory Landscape Malaysian Association of Institute of Chartered Secretaries and Administrators, Kuala Lumpur, September 9 - 10, 2014.
17. Malaysian Legal and Corporate Conference – Shifting Sands: Is the Law Reshaping Our Legal and Corporate Sectors? Current Law Journal Sdn Bhd and Malaysian Bar Council, Kuala Lumpur, July 3 - 4, 2013.
18. Masel, Geoffrey R. *Professional Negligence of Lawyers, Accountants, Bankers and Brokers.* 2nd ed. North Ryde, N.S.W: CCH Australia Ltd, 1989.
19. Nariman, Aiman., Aishah Bidin., Pamela Hanrahan., Ian Ramsay., and Geof Stapledon. *Commercial Applications of Company Law in Malaysia.* 3rd ed. Malaysia: CCH Asia Pte Limited, 2008.
20. Normanton, Elizabeth L. *The Accountability and Audit of Governments.* New York: Manchester University Press, 1966.
21. Raj, Adeline Paul. "Companies Bill 2015 to Bring Major Reform" *The Edge Malaysia*, April 18 2016.
22. Sin Boon Ann. "The Duty of Care of Auditors: To Whom Should the Duty be Owed." *Malayan Law Journal* 3, [1990]: iii.

23. Wallace, Wanda A. "The Economic Role of the Audit in Free and Regulated Markets: A Look Back and A Look Forward." *Research in Accounting Regulation,* 17 (2004): 267–298.
24. Workshop on the New Companies Act, Corporate Securities and Financial Law and Regulation, Civil Law Department, Ahmad Ibrahim Kulliyah of Law, International Islamic University Malaysia, August 2 -3, 2016.

Chapter 2
Directors' Fiduciary Duties

Wai Meng Chan

Abstract Section 211 of the Companies Act 2016 ("CA 2016") provides that the general powers to manage the company is given to the board of directors ("the Board"). The members of the Board are the appointed directors. When exercising his powers, the director owes a fiduciary duty to the company and thus, has to act for the best interest of the company. A company is a body corporate, and has members. Usually, the interests of the company as an entity overlap with that of its members, and thus members would not protest if an act is for the good of the company. However, where an act benefits the company as an entity but not some of the members, the directors cannot sacrifice the interest of the company in favour of that group of members. This chapter will discuss whether the duty of the directors was limited to that owed to the company and the members as a whole even during the COVID-19 pandemic. It will also discuss whether a company which was in doldrums could terminate its employees' services and hibernate to preserve its resources, and whether a company should maximise its profits instead of acting for the benefit of humanity and nation during this testing period. This will bring to the next issue of the directors' liabilities if they were to also act in the best interest of humanity and the nation, instead of solely in the best interest of the company and its members as a whole.

Introduction

When the COVID-19 pandemic hit Malaysia in early 2020, the government promulgated the movement control order under the Prevention and Control of Infectious Diseases Act 1988 and the Police Act 1967 to curb the spread of the virus. There were restrictions on movement, assembly and travel. All businesses and government departments, other than those involved in essential economic and social services, were mandated to close. The restrictions were gradually relaxed in May 2020, but re-imposed when the number of cases skyrocketed in January 2021, and again in June 2021. It hit the peak in August 2021. On August 26, 2021, there was a record of

W. M. Chan (✉)
University of Malaya, Kuala Lumpur, Malaysia
e-mail: chanwm@um.edu.my

L. Krishnan and W. M. Chan (eds.), *The Impact of COVID-19 on Corporations and Corporate Law in Malaysia*, https://doi.org/10.1007/978-981-19-5519-8_2

24,599 new cases. The cumulative number of COVID-19 positive cases in Malaysia hit the one million, two million and 2.5 million marks on July 25, 2021, September 13, 2021 and November 6, 2021 respectively.[1] The number of cases started to decline in September 2021 when more adults were vaccinated. The economy re-opened.

How did businesses fare during these periods of lockdown? Businesses which were engaged in essential economic and social services could continue to trade and thus might not have felt the brunt of the lockdown. In fact, some companies recorded unparalleled profits. But businesses in many industries suffered. Some businesses were closed, resulting in no income being generated. Yet, employees still have to be salaried, utility bills settled, rentals paid, and loans serviced. The crisis facing most companies was unprecedented. The board of directors which was tasked with the management and supervision of the company's business and affairs was put to test.

In Malaysia, the general powers to manage the company is given to the board of directors ("Board"). This is codified in S. 211 of the Companies Act 2016 ("CA 2016") which reads as follows:

> (1) The business and affairs of a company shall be managed by, or under the direction of, the Board.
>
> (2) The Board has all the powers necessary for managing and for directing and supervising the management of the business and affairs of the company subject to any modification, exception or limitation contained in this Act or in the constitution of the company.

The term "Board" is defined in S. 2(1) to mean:

> (a) directors of the company who number not less than the required quorum acting as a board of directors; or
>
> (b) if the company has only one director, that director.

The Board is to manage the company's business and affairs subject to the CA 2016 and the company's constitution. The members of the Board are the appointed directors of the company. The company's constitution may lay down the proceedings of the Board. If not, S. 212 states that the Board proceedings are governed by the Third Schedule to the Act. The Board makes decisions by passing resolutions. According to paragraph 11, each director has one vote and a board resolution is passed if it is agreed to by all directors present without dissent or if a majority of the votes are casted in its favour. Paragraph 12 further provides that a director present at the Board meeting is presumed to have agreed to, and to have voted in favour of, a resolution unless he expressly dissents from or votes to object against the resolution at the meeting.

[1] "Malaysia: What is the Cumulative Number of Confirmed Cases?" Our World in Data, accessed November 28, 2021. https://ourworldindata.org/coronavirus/country/malaysia#what-is-the-cumulative-number-of-confirmed-cases.

Director as a Fiduciary

A fiduciary is a person who has undertaken to act for and on behalf of another person in a particular manner in circumstances which give rise to a relationship of trust and confidence. According to Millet LJ in *Bristol and West Building Society v Mothew (t/a Sapley & Co)*[2]:

> The principal is entitled to the single-minded loyalty of his fiduciary... A fiduciary.. may not act for his own benefit or the benefit of a third person without the informed consent of his principal.

In sum, a fiduciary has to act bona fide in the interest of his principal, and that of no one else. It is settled at common law, that a director is a fiduciary. When exercising his powers, the director owes a fiduciary duty to the company and thus, has to act for the best interest of the company. He is not to abuse his power or position. He should avoid any conflict of interest.

Further, in *Great Eastern Ry v Turner* (1872), Lord Selbourne aptly said this about directors:

> Directors are the mere trustees or agents of the company, trustees of the company's money and property; agents in the transactions which they enter into on behalf of the company.

Therefore, a director is an agent of the company. The law of agency requires an agent to exercise reasonable care, skill and diligence with the knowledge, skill and experience which may reasonably be expected of a person having the same responsibilities; and any additional knowledge, skill and experience which the agent actually has.

The CA 2016 has also enacted the directors' fiduciary and non-fiduciary duties in S. 213(1) and (2) respectively. They read as follows:

> (1) A director of a company shall at all times exercise his powers in accordance with this Act, for a proper purpose and in good faith in the best interest of the company.
>
> (2) A director of a company shall exercise reasonable care, skill and diligence with—
>
> (a) the knowledge, skill and experience which may reasonably be expected of a director having the same responsibilities; and
>
> (b) any additional knowledge, skill and experience which the director in fact has.

This chapter will focus on the directors' fiduciary duties, whereas the directors' non-fiduciary duties will be spotlighted in the next chapter.

Who are Directors?

Before we dive into the discussion of directors' fiduciary duties, we must first clarify the scope of the term "director" in S. 213(1). Section 2(1) defines the word "director"

---

[2] [1998] 1 Ch 1, at p.18. This view was endorsed by the Malaysian Federal Court in the case of *The Board of Trustees of the Sabah Foundation & Co v Datuk Syed Kechik bin Syed Mohamed & Anor* [2008] 5 MLJ 461.

to include any person occupying the position of director of a company by whatever name called ("*de facto* director") and includes a person in accordance with whose directions or instructions the majority of directors of a company are accustomed to act ("shadow director") and an alternate or substitute director. The term is defined in an inclusive manner and thus, should include a person who is appointed as a director of the company following the procedure laid down in the CA 2016 or the constitution ("*de jure* director"). He is certainly a director of the company.

Only a person who has been appointed as a director of the company and whose term is still continuing is a member of the board of directors. The others in the list such as the de facto director and shadow director are not members of the Board. However, they are imputed with the statutory duties and obligations imposed on a director under the CA 2016. They cannot claim they are not directors of the company and thus say that they are not liable if they breach the duties of a director.

In addition, S. 210 provides that for the purpose of certain provisions in the Act, including S. 213, the term "director" includes not only that defined in S. 2(1) but also "includes chief executive officer ("CEO"), chief financial officer ("CFO"), chief operating officer ("COO") or any other person primarily responsible for the management of the company". Hence, the S. 213 duties are imposed on the following persons:

- *de jure* director;
- *de facto* director;
- shadow director;
- alternate or substitute director;
- CEO;
- CFO;
- COO; and
- any person primarily responsible for the management of the company.

It is noteworthy that the duty imposed by S. 213(1) on directors is strict. To illustrate its strict application, there are persons who are appointed as directors by virtue of their positions as employees of the majority members or holders of debentures to represent a member of the company, his employer or a debenture holder. He is known as a nominee director. Section 217 provides that a nominee director:

> shall act in the best interest of the company and in the event of any conflict between his duty to act in the best interest of the company and his duty to his nominator, he shall not subordinate his duty to act in the best interest of the company to his duty to his nominator.

Thus, even a nominee director has to act in the best interest of the company. In the event of any conflict, his duty towards the company prevails over that to the person who nominated him. Though the appointment of a nominee director is initiated by his employer, majority member or debenture holder, it is the members at the meeting who cast their votes for his appointment. Therefore, as he is appointed by the members as a director of the company, he owes a fiduciary duty to the company.

Directors Owe Their Fiduciary Duties

This brings us to the next issue i.e., who comprises the company and to whom the director owes his fiduciary duty? Reference is made to S. 2 which defines "company" to mean a company incorporated under the CA 2016 or under any corresponding previous written law. As a company is an artificial legal person, having its own legal entity, the director owes his duty to the company as an entity.[3]

Nevertheless, piecing together S. 9, 18 and 20 also reveals that a company is a body corporate,[4] and has members.[5] The members together are the body corporate by the name in its notice of registration.[6] Usually, the interests of the company as an entity overlap with that of its members, and thus members would not protest if an act is for the good of the company. However, where an act benefits the company as an entity but not some of the members, the directors cannot sacrifice the interest of the company in favour of that group of members. Further, where the act impacts classes of members differently, the directors must act fairly as among them, and needless to say, the directors must always act within their limits.[7] Failing which, the unhappy member may take action on the ground that he is unfairly discriminated against and thus seeks remedies under S. 346 of the CA 2016.

During the COVID-19 pandemic, many companies suffered as they could not carry on their businesses as usual. Some businesses had to stop operation; some were allowed to continue but had to scale down. The worst would be a company with no income but with mounting expenses to be paid. At the other end of the spectrum were companies in businesses which were very much in demand or critical in managing the war against COVID-19, such as those manufacturing personal protection equipment and providing health care services. As S. 213(1) of the CA 2016 requires the directors of a company at all times, to exercise their powers in accordance with the Act, for a proper purpose and in good faith in the best interest of the company, the issue is whether the duty of the directors is limited to that owed to the company and the members as a whole? Should the companies which were in doldrums terminate their employees' services and hibernate to preserve their resources? Should companies be dealing in much demanded products, maximising its profits during this crisis? Would the directors be in breach of their fiduciary duties if they were to also act in the best interest of humanity and the nation, instead of solely in the best interest of the company and its members as a whole?

In the UK Companies Act 2006, the provision on the fiduciary duties of directors is found in S. 172.[8] It provides that a director has a duty to promote the success of the company for the benefits of members as a whole, and in doing so have regard to inter

[3] See Siew Cheang Loh, *Corporate Powers Accountability* (Petaling Jaya: LexisNexis, 2018), 347.

[4] S. 20 of the CA 2016.

[5] S. 9(b) of the CA 2016 provides that a company must have at least one member.

[6] S. 18 of the CA 2016.

[7] *Re BSB Holdings Ltd (No 2)* [1996] 1 BCLC 155, at 222.

[8] S. 172 of the UK Companies Act 2006 reads as follows:

alia, the company's stakeholders such as employees, suppliers, customers, community and others. The provision recognises the paramount interest of the members as a whole, yet the interests of the other stakeholders cannot be ignored.

Malaysia does not have similar provisions in its CA 2016. The Act does not expressly recognise the interests of stakeholders, other than the members. Indeed, when the CA 2016 was being drafted, the guiding principle was the shareholder theory. This was gleaned from paragraph 6 of the Scope of the Corporate Law Reform Committee ("CLRC") which was established on December 17, 2003 to review the then Companies Act 1965[9]:

> two main approaches in the corporate governance debate on the issue of directors' accountability are the shareholder theory and the stakeholder theory. The shareholder theory considers that directors have a duty to consider shareholders' interests in company's management whilst the stakeholder theory allows, or requires directors to consider the interests of other persons who are involved in a company's management for example creditors and employees. We take note of these theories in our review but will be guided by the shareholder theory whilst taking account of the interests of other stakeholders.

This is reaffirmed in the Consultative Document No 5 issued by the CLRC on "*Clarifying and Reformulating the Directors' Role and Duties*" ("CLRC CD No 5").[10] Though it admitted that the rigid application of the rule "which requires company directors to only act in the interest of the company can at times result in decisions that do not conform with public expectations and the company's social obligations",[11] the CLRC took the stand that social obligations of the company should not be incorporated in the Act. Similarly, it did not recommend the regulation of the relationship between a company and its creditors and employees to be included in the Act.[12]

"(1) A director of a company must act in the way he considers, in good faith, would be most likely to promote the success of the company for the benefit of its members as a whole, and in doing so have regard (amongst other matters) to—

(a) the likely consequences of any decision in the long term,

(b) the interests of the company's employees,

(c) the need to foster the company's business relationships with suppliers, customers and others,

(d) the impact of the company's operations on the community and the environment,

(e) the desirability of the company maintaining a reputation for high standards of business conduct, and.

(f) the need to act fairly as between members of the company.

(2) Where or to the extent that the purposes of the company consist of or include purposes other than the benefit of its members, subsection (1) has effect as if the reference to promoting the success of the company for the benefit of its members were to achieving those purposes.

(3) The duty imposed by this section has effect subject to any enactment or rule of law requiring directors, in certain circumstances, to consider or act in the interests of creditors of the company.".

[9] See Companies Commission of Malaysia, "Scope of the Corporate Law Reform Committee ("the CLRC")," accessed on September 21, 2021. https://www.ssm.com.my/Pages/Publication/CLRC/Scope.aspx.

[10] Paragraph 4.4 of the CLRC CD No 5.

[11] Paragraph 4.6 of the CLRC CD No 5.

[12] This is gleaned from para 4.7 to 4.10 of the CLRC CD No 5:

The shareholder theory imposes on companies the obligation to maximize profits for its shareholders. Though the CLRC had softened its impact by stating that the directors are to take into account the interests of other stakeholders as well, the effect remains that the CA 2016 requires directors to put the interests of the shareholders above that of other stakeholders. Indeed, the stand taken by the CLRC is aligned with that of the High Level Finance Committee Report on Corporate Governance (1999, p.10), which defines corporate governance as, "… the process and structure used to direct and manage the business and affairs of the company towards enhancing business prosperity and corporate accountability with the ultimate objective of realizing long-term shareholder value, while taking into account the interest of other stakeholders."

Nevertheless, the acknowledgment of the company's other stakeholders is gaining momentum. While Malaysia was in the midst of battling COVID-19, with stories abound about the sufferings of her people and businesses, the Securities Commission of Malaysia issued the Malaysian Code of Corporate Governance 2021 ("MCCG 2021") on April 28, 2021. Paragraph 1.2 says, "corporate governance is not only concerned with shareholder interests but requires balancing the needs of other stakeholders such as employees, customers, suppliers, society and the communities in which the companies conduct their business."[13] This is affirmed in its Principle A1 that the board of directors "is collectively responsible for the long-term success of a company and the delivery of sustainable value to its stakeholders." Principle A1

"4.7 Whilst the CLRC supports the proposition that a company must be a good corporate citizen and for the long-term, sustainability of a company must foster a relationship with its stakeholders, the CLRC is of the view that social obligations of the company should not be incorporated in the Companies Act 1965. The CLRC noted that there are jurisdictions which have expressly provided that company directors are empowered to make provisions for company employees on the cessation of the company's business, are allowed to consider employees' interest when exercising their powers, or are required to consider, amongst other things, the impact of its operations on the community and the environment, these statutory provisions do not replace the fundamental rule that requires company directors to act in the interest of the company i.e. the members collectively.

4.8 The CLRC also noted that in respect to employees' interests, the Companies Act 1965 already contains provisions empowering company directors to establish and support various facilities calculated to benefit employees and past employees and their various dependents and to provide for pensions and benefits. On this point, the CLRC is inclined to adopt the approach advanced by the New Zealand Law Commission. The New Zealand Law Commission in its report recommended that social obligations such as looking after the environment and engaging in fair dealings with its customers should be imposed by particular statutes and not be reflected in the Companies Act 1965. This approach has been adopted by the New Zealand Companies Act 1993.

4.9 Thus, the CLRC is of the view that whilst company directors may consider the interests of stakeholders, for example, employees when managing and/or supervising the company's affairs, the recognition of employees' interest does not mean that a duty should be imposed on company directors to act in the best interest of employees. The CLRC is of the view that the relationship between a company and its creditors and employees are sufficiently dealt with and should not be regulated under the Companies Act 1965.".

[13] This is also found in paragraph 1.2 of the MCCG 2017.

is new, and not found in the earlier editions of MCCG issued in years 2000, 2007, 2012 and 2017.[14]

Though the MCCG 2021 is targeted at companies whose shares are listed on the Bursa Malaysia, non-listed entities including state-owned enterprises, public companies, and even small and medium enterprises are encouraged to embrace this code on corporate governance. According to paragraph 2.8, the objective in applying the practices in the MCCG 2021 is to enhance the business entities' accountability, transparency and sustainability.[15] It is in the members' interest that the company sustains and continues to grow. The long-term success of the company should be the goal and if so, directors should be permitted to take a wider view and not necessarily the one that would maximise profit in the short term.[16]

Nonetheless, the MCCG 2021 is a code of best practices. It has only a persuasive effect. It does not have the force of law unless implemented by other regulatory bodies such as the Bursa Malaysia in its Listing Requirements. Chapter 15 of the Listing Requirements, which was last revised on June 1, 2020, is dedicated to Corporate Governance, but does not include the directors' duties towards the company's stakeholders apart from members. Thus, we still have to fall back on the CA 2016, which S. 213 requires the directors to act in the best interest of the company. We will have to examine the other provisions in the Act which require, and in some provisions obligate directors to consider the interests of the company's stakeholders other than that of its members. While doing so, we must bear in mind that there is "a significant difference in the law allowing directors to consider stakeholders' interest and the law making this obligatory".[17]

Creditors

In *Multinational Gas and Petrochemical Co Ltd v Multinational Gas and Petrochemical Services Ltd*,[18] the court held that the directors were appointed to manage the affairs of the company and thus, stand in a fiduciary relationship to the company. They owe fiduciary duties to the company but not to the company's creditors, present or future, or to individual shareholders. This was affirmed by the Malaysian Court

[14] The closest is in Principle AI of the MCCG 2017. Practice 1.1 which prescribed that "the board should set the company's values and standards, and ensure that its obligations to its shareholders and other stakeholders are understood and met". Nonetheless, in Guidance 1.1, it still requires directors to "objectively discharge their duties and responsibilities at all times as fiduciaries in the interest of the company.".

[15] Paragraph 2.8 of the MCCG 2021.

[16] Walter Woon, *Companies Act of Malaysia: An Annotation 2020 Desk Edition* (Kuala Lumpur: LexisNexis Malaysia, 2020), 249.

[17] Aiman Nariman Mohd Sulaiman, and Effendy Othman, *Malaysia Company Law: Principles and Practices* (Kuala Lumpur: Commerce Clearing House (Malaysia) Sdn Bhd., 2021), 602.

[18] [1983] Ch 258.

of Appeal in *Dato' Abul Hasan bin Mohamed Rashid v Multi-Code Electronics Industries (M) Berhad & Anor.*[19]

However, there are cases which recognised occasions when it is important for directors to take into consideration the interests of creditors when the company is insolvent or on the verge of insolvency. In *Kinsela & Anor v Russell Kinsela Pty Ltd (In Liq)*[20] and *Colin Gwyer & Associates Ltd & Anor v London Wharf (Limehouse) Ltd & Ors*,[21] the courts held that in these situations, the directors must consider the interest of the company's creditors, which then becomes paramount. In *Kinsela*, the court held that when the company is insolvent, the members' approval or ratification of the act which has an effect on the availability of assets for distribution, is not sufficient. This is because when the company is insolvent, the interests of the company are those of the creditors, not that of the members.[22]

Actions like the giving of loans when the lender company itself is insolvent[23] or when the borrowers are insolvent,[24] and expropriating the company's assets[25] dissipates the company's assets, resulting in less available assets for distribution when the company is being wound up. They tantamount to misfeasance.[26] We will see below that S. 541 of the CA 2016 provides that in the course of the company's winding up, the court may order the director to contribute such sum to the company's assets by way of compensation in respect of the misfeasance.

There are also provisions in the CA 2016 which are aligned to the common law principle that directors must consider the interest of the company's creditors when the company is insolvent or on the verge of insolvency. The directors are required to consider the financial status of the company, failing which they may suffer dire consequences. These will be explained below.

When the Company is Insolvent

Foremost is the provision on wrongful trading found in S. 539(3). An officer of the company, which includes its director,[27] commits wrongful trading when he knowingly contracts a debt for the company at a time he has no reasonable or probable

---

[19] [2012] 5 MLJ 176.

[20] (1986) 4 ACLC 215.

[21] [2003] 2 BCLC 153.

[22] Aiman Nariman Mohd Sulaiman, and Effendy Othman, *Malaysia Company Law: Principles and Practices* (Kuala Lumpur: Commerce Clearing House (Malaysia) Sdn Bhd., 2021), 596.

[23] *CIMB Bank Berhad v Jaring Communications Sdn Bhd* [2016] MLJU 920.

[24] *Walker v Wimborne* (1976) 137 CLR 1.

[25] *Kinsela v Russell Kinsela Pty Ltd* (1986) 4 ACLC 215.

[26] Walter Woon, *Companies Act of Malaysia: An Annotation 2020 Desk Edition* (Kuala Lumpur: LexisNexis Malaysia, 2020), 252.

[27] S. 2(1) of the CA 2016 defines an officer to include, amongst others, a director, secretary or employee of the company.

ground of expectation that the company would be able to pay the debt. Upon an application made by the liquidator, any creditor or contributory of the company, the court may order the director who was convicted of the offence of wrongful trading to be liable for that debt or part thereof.[28]

It is noteworthy that the application to the court may be made in the course of winding up of a company or in any proceedings against a company. Thus, a director can be held liable for wrongful trading even in situations when the company is not being wound up. During the pandemic, many companies suffered cash flow issues. If such a company continued to trade or incurred further liability, then that officer who acted on behalf of the company could be held to be personally liable for that debt incurred. He owed a duty to the company's creditors not to cause the company to incur liabilities at a time when the company was not financially able. He would be liable if he was guilty of committing a breach of this duty.

An important principle in the stakeholder theory is that a company should not maximise shareholders value at the expense of the creditors. This principle can be seen to have motivated the enactment of the requirement for solvency statements for certain transactions. The CA 2016 requires the directors to declare the solvency status of the company before the company redeems its preference shares,[29] returns its capital to members without confirmation by the court,[30] finances the purchase of its shares,[31] and buys back its shares.[32] Before the company effects any of these transactions, the directors have to form the opinion that the company is solvent, and make a solvency statement to that effect. The various solvency tests are prescribed in S. 112 and the requirements for the statements are stated in S. 113. In general, the directors have to inquire into the affairs and prospects of the company and take into account all the liabilities of the company including contingent liabilities, and do a projection on whether the company could pay its debts. Section 114 provides that a director who makes the solvency statement without having reasonable grounds for the opinion expressed in the statement commits an offence.

When There is An Adverse Change in the Financial Position of the Company

For the redemption of preference shares and return of capital to members without confirmation by the court (herein this paragraph referred to as "the transaction"), the projection of the company's solvency is for at least 12 months that is, from the date of

[28] S. 540(2) of the CA 2016.

[29] S. 72 of the CA 2016.

[30] S. 117 of the CA 2016.

[31] S. 126 of the CA 2016.

[32] S. 127 of the CA 2016. This applies only to public listed companies.

the solvency statement to the date of the transaction[33] plus another 12 months from the date of transaction. However, if there is an intention to wind up the company within 12 months after the transaction, then the directors must project the company's solvency status for about 36 months. This is because the directors will have to project the company's solvency from the date of the solvency statement to the date of the transaction[34] and from the date of transaction to the date of commencement of winding up (which could be up to 12 months) plus an additional 12 months after the commencement of winding up.[35]

For share financing, the projection of the company's solvency is for about 24 months that is, from the date of the solvency statement to the date of the share financing[36] plus another 12 months from the date of financing. However, if there is an intention to wind up the company within 12 months after the share financing, then the directors must project the company's solvency status for about 36 months. This is because the directors will have to project the company's solvency from the date of the solvency statement to the date of the financing[37] and from the date of financing to the date of commencement of winding up (which could be up to 12 months) plus an additional 12 months after the commencement of winding up.[38]

However, for share buybacks, the forecast on the solvency of the company is for a shorter period. The directors are required to forecast the solvency status of the company immediately after each buyback. Since the solvency statement is effective for six months only, the directors have to make only a six months' projection.

Regardless of the duration of the forecast, there might arise a situation where there is a sudden unexpected change of event which negatively impacts the solvency status

[33] This is because the transaction will not be carried out immediately after the solvency statement is made. There will be a time gap between the declaration of solvency and the transaction. The directors make the solvency statement before the members pass the special resolution to reduce the share capital (S. 117(3) of the CA 2016). The resolution, solvency statement and notice of reduction must be lodged with the CCM after the passage of time prescribed in S. 119 of the CA 2016. Whereas, the exercise to redeem the preference shares can only be carried out after the company has lodged the solvency statement with the CCM (S. 72(6) of the CA 2016).

[34] This is because the transaction will not be carried out immediatly after the solvency statement is made. There will be a time gap between the declaration of solvency and the transaction. The directors make the solvency statement before the members pass the special resolution to reduce the share capital (S. 117(3) of the CA 2016). The resolution, solvency statement and notice of reduction must be lodged with the CCM after the passage of time prescribed in S. 119 of the CA 2016. Whereas, the exercise to redeem the preference shares can only be carried out after the company has lodged the solvency statement with the CCM (S. 72(6) of the CA 2016).

[35] This is following S. 112(1)(b)(i) of the CA 2016 which provides that if the company intends to commence winding up proceedings within 12 months from the date of transaction, the company must be able to pay its debts in full within 12 months after the commencement of winding up.

[36] This is because S.126(2)(e) of the CA 2016 provides that the company may give the share financing anytime within 12 months from the solvency statement.

[37] This is because S.126(2)(e) of the CA 2016 provides that the company may give the share financing anytime within 12 months from the solvency statement.

[38] This is following S. 112(1)(b)(i) of the CA 2016 which provides that if the company intends to commence winding up proceedings within 12 months from the date of transaction, the company must be able to pay its debts in full within 12 months after the commencement of winding up.

of the company. For example, no one foresaw the onslaught of COVID-19 and the damage it brought to the business community. Directors might have made a solvency statement before they fathomed the impact of COVID-19 on the company's affairs. The opinion expressed in the solvency statement was correct when it was made, but no longer holds due to a turn of events thereafter. The CA 2016 does not provide for such a situation. Nevertheless, it is submitted that the directors should not proceed with the proposed transaction if the solvency status of the company is in doubt. Further, the proposed transaction if carried out, will deplete the company's cash holding, bringing it deeper into insolvency. This surely acts against the best interest of the company, a duty required of the director under S. 213 of the CA 2016.

This position is aligned with the regulation on the distribution of company's profits. Section 131 reads that "a company may only make a distribution to the shareholders out of profits of the company available if the company is solvent". The payment of the dividends must be authorised by the directors,[39] who must be satisfied that the company fulfils the solvency test prescribed in S. 132(3). The company is regarded as solvent if the company is able to pay its debts as and when the debts become due within 12 months immediately after the distribution is made. The directors must conduct the solvency test as at the date the board authorises the distribution of profit. The directors must project the company's financials for more than 12 months (i.e. from the date of resolution to date of distribution[40] plus another 12 months after the distribution).

Whereas the provisions on the solvency statement for redemption of preference shares, return of capital to members, financing purchases of shares and share buyback do not provide guidance on the position of the directors when the solvency status of the company changes after the solvency statement was issued, S. 132(4) has done otherwise. It expressly clarifies that where the directors cease to be satisfied that the company will be solvent after the payment of dividend is authorised but before it is made, the directors should take all necessary steps to prevent the payment.

Treating Creditors Equally

We have seen above that a company may have different classes of members, and where an action impacts various groups of members differently, the directors must act fairly as among them. Similarly, there may be different classes of creditors such as secured creditors, preferential creditors and general creditors. The court in *GHLM Trading Limited v Anil Kumar Maroo*[41] held that where there are classes of creditors, the director shall take account of the interests of the creditors as a class. If he were

---

[39] S. 132(1) of the CA 2016.

[40] There will be a time gap between the date of the directors' resolution authorising the paying of dividend and the payment of the dividend.

[41] [2012] EWHC 61.

to act in the interest of one particular creditor only without believing the interest is also that of other creditors in that class, then he would have breached his duty.

Though the CA 2016 does not require the directors to act in the interests of creditors, the underlying principle for directors to take account of creditors as a class can be seen in the claw back provisions found in the Act. The claw back provisions in S. 528 and S. 529 allow a liquidator to recover assets which should have been part of the insolvent company's assets available for distribution. These assets are no longer available because the directors had disposed of them in favour of some creditors to give them preference over other creditors.

Section 528 requires a company to treat all its creditors of the same class equally when the company is insolvent. Subsection (1) defines insolvency as a situation where the company is unable to pay its debts, as the debts become due, from its own money.[42] In other words, when a company is suffering from cash flow insolvency, it should not give preference to any of its creditors.

Section 528 voids a transaction if it is made within six months before a specified event[43] leading to the company being wound up. The transaction is void if it is proven that the company is insolvent when the transaction is made. It must be noted that S. 528 applies not only to charges or securities created in favour of any creditor. This provision on undue preference also applies to transactions involving the transfer, mortgage, delivery of goods, payment, execution or other act relating to property made or done by or against a company, provided the transaction is in favour of any creditor or any person in trust for a creditor. Further, S. 528(3) also avoids a transfer or assignment by a company of all its property to the trustees for the benefit of all its creditors. This is despite no preference being given to a particular creditor.

The application of S. 528 is triggered only when the company is being wound up. A liquidator will be appointed to take possession of the company's assets, liquidate them and settle the company's creditors. He will go through the company's records. If there is a transaction made within the prescribed six months' period, then the liquidator can avoid the transaction by proving that the company was not able to pay its debts when the transaction was made. Once the liquidator has proven that, the transaction is void. The subject matter of the transaction reverts and forms part of the assets of the company.

---

[42] See also *Lian Keow Sdn Bhd v Overseas Credit Finance (M) Sdn Bhd* [1988] 2 MLJ 449.

[43] The events are specified in S. 528(2) of the CA 2016 as follows:

"(a) in the case of winding up by Court -

(i) the date of the presentation of petition; or.

(ii) where prior to the presentation of the petition a resolution has been passed by the company for voluntary winding up, the date upon which the resolution to wind up the company voluntarily is passed; and (b) in the case of voluntary winding up, the date upon which the winding up is deemed by this Act to have commenced.".

S. 441(1) of the CA 2016 prescribes the commencement date of voluntary winding up as follows:

"A voluntary winding up shall commence - (a) where an interim liquidator has been appointed before the resolution for voluntary winding up is passed, at the time when the declaration referred to in S. 440 is lodged with the Registrar; and (b) in any other case, at the time of the passing of the resolution for voluntary winding up."

However, to protect a creditor who acted in good faith, S. 528(4) provides that the transaction is not void where the transaction is made in favour of a person dealing with the company for valuable consideration and without any actual notice of the contravention. Section 528(5) defines "valuable consideration" to mean the consideration given by the creditor is a fair and reasonable money value in relation to the value of the property, or to the known or anticipated benefits of the contract. The provision also defines "notice" to include the creditor's knowledge of the company's inability to pay its debts or of the winding up proceedings against the company or the facts which are sufficient to indicate so. Thus, a creditor who wants to keep the benefits derived from the "undue preference" transaction has to prove that it gave valuable consideration to the company in the transaction and that it did not have actual knowledge that the company was insolvent when the transaction was made.

There is a specific provision on the effect of a floating charge created within six months before the presentation of the winding up petition or the passing of a resolution to wind up the company. Section 529 provides that the floating charge is only valid if it can be proven that the company was solvent immediately after its creation. Compared to S. 528, S. 529 is stricter because it provides that a floating charge is void if it was created within six months of the prescribed event. The liquidator is not required to prove the insolvency of the company when the floating charge was created. The general rule is that the floating charge is void unless one of the following two exceptions apply:

First, the floating charge is valid to secure only the amount released to the company at the time or after the charge was created. The interest for the loan which is secured against the floating charge is capped at 5% even though the agreement may have provided for a higher rate.

Secondly, the floating charge is valid for the whole amount secured (which can be more than the first exception above) if the creditor can prove that the company was solvent immediately after the floating charge was created.

Similar as in S. 528, S. 529 is triggered only when the company is being wound up. They do not apply if the company was solvent when the charge was created. However, the burden to prove the solvency of the company differs: For undue preference under S. 528, the transaction is presumed to be valid unless the liquidator proves the company was insolvent at the time the transaction was made. Whereas for the avoidance of floating charge pursuant to S. 529, the floating charge is presumed to be void unless the chargee proves that the company was solvent when the floating charge was created.

May Creditors Take Action Against Directors?

Though directors owe a duty to creditors when the company is insolvent or on the brink of insolvency, it must be stressed that the creditors cannot take direct action against the directors to recover their loan to the company. The company is a legal person and liable for its contractual obligations and hence it can be sued.[44] Further, the application of the doctrine of privity in Malaysia which prescribes that only parties to the contract can sue and be sued, ensures that the creditor can sue only the borrower company to recover the loan, not its directors unless they have guaranteed for the repayment of the loan. Further, the duty owed by the directors to consider the interests of the creditors, is not a direct one to the creditor.

Though the creditor cannot sue to enforce the duty,[45] there are provisions in the CA 2016 which allows a creditor to take action against the director. He can rely on S. 351 which confers on any person whose interest is affected or may be affected by the director's conduct which contravenes the Act, the right to apply to the Court for an injunction. The provision in S. 351 is very wide as it covers situations where the act had already been committed or yet to be committed.

Another provision which is of relevance is S. 541, which comes into play only when the company is being wound up. This section provides inter alia, that in the course of winding up, a creditor may apply to the Court to examine a director. If found guilty of breach of duty, the director may be required to pay compensation. However, such compensation will not be paid to the creditor, but will form part of the company's assets available for distribution to the company's creditors.[46]

Employees

Employees are one of the most valuable assets in a business. They are the face of the business, and are essential to produce the goods and services offered. Employees generate income for the business. Thus, it is important for a business to motivate their employees to improve their performance. The CA 2016 does recognise the role played by employees in the performance of the company. Section 253(3) provides that the directors' report to be attached to the company's financial statements may include a section on the business review of the company. The purpose of the business review is to provide an understanding of the development, performance and position of the company's business. It is suggested in Part II of the Fifth Schedule that the

---

[44] S. 20 of the CA 2016.

[45] *Spies v The Queen* [2000] HCA 43.

[46] S. 541(1) of the CA 2016 reads:

"If in the course of winding up it appears that—

(a) any person who has taken part in the formation or promotion of the company; or.

(b) any past or present liquidator or officer,

has misapplied or retained or become liable or accountable for any money or property of the company or been guilty of any misfeasance or breach of trust or duty in relation to the company, the Court may on the application of the liquidator or any creditor or contributory examine into the conduct of that officer and compel him to repay or restore the money or property or any part of the money with interest at such rate as the Court thinks just, or to contribute such sum to the assets of the company by way of compensation in respect of the misapplication, retainer, misfeasance or breach of trust or duty as the Court thinks just.".

business review may contain information about the company's employees and the company's policies in relation to employees.

However, despite the recognition given to the role of employees, the relationship between a company and its employees is not regulated under the CA 2016. There is no mention about considering the interests of the employees when making decisions. This is not an oversight but an intentional outcome. In the CLRC CD No 5, the CLRC debated whether the new Companies Act should empower directors to make provisions for the benefit of the company employees, or that the directors are allowed to consider employees' interest when exercising their powers. It held the view that the relationship between a company and its employees should not be regulated under the Companies Act. The reason given was that the matter was already sufficiently dealt with by other laws.[47] However, this may not be necessarily true.

During the pandemic, a company may find it necessary to scale down its operation or to close its loss making businesses. Employees who are made redundant, may have their services terminated. They are entitled to receive compensation according to the law. Currently, they are found in S. 60 J of the Employment Act 1955 and Regulation 6 of the Employment (Termination and Lay-Off Benefits) Regulations 1980. Unfortunately, the Employment Act 1955 applies only to categories of employees as stated in the First Schedule of the Act, and thus employees who are not covered may find themselves unprotected. Can the directors make provisions for employees other than those prescribed by law? Such provisions, which are *ex-gratia* in nature, would deplete the company's resources.

The case of *Parke v Daily News Ltd*[48] comes to mind. In this case, the company sold its business and the Board approved the payment of compensation to the company's employees for their loss of employment. The court found that the payment was not aligned to the interest of the shareholders. The company would not gain in any way, whether present or in the future, from the payment. Plowman J said,[49]

> In my judgement, therefore, the defendants were prompted by motives which, however laudable, and however enlightened from the point of view of industrial relations, were such as the law does not recognise as a sufficient justification. Stripped of all its side issues, the essence of the matter is this, that the directors of the defendant company are proposing that a very large part of its funds should be given to its former employees in order to benefit those employees rather than the company, and that is an application of the company's funds which the law, as I understand it, will not allow.

What about during better times? May the company directors provide employees with a good employee benefits and perks package to retain them? It is trite that most companies do provide benefits to employees to motivate them, and to retain them. The question is whether directors may approve benefits for the employees without breaching their duty. Are the employee benefits given in the interest of the company?

---

[47] Some of the Acts of Parliament that deal with the employer-employee relationships are the Employment Act 1955, Industrial Relations Act 1967, Workmen's Compensation Act 1952, Occupational Safety and Health Act 1994, and Employees' Social Security Act 1969.

[48] [1962] 2 All ER 929.

[49] [1962] 2 All ER 929, at p. 948.

Must such benefits be approved by the members? Notice may be drawn to the duties of a fiduciary. As per Millet LJ in *Bristol and West Building Society v Mothew (t/a Sapley & Co)*, a fiduciary may not act for the benefit of a third person without the informed consent of his principal.[50]

In the context of the CA 2016, we may refer to S. 224 and S. 225 which pertain to prohibition of loans to directors and persons connected with directors. Section 224 provides that a company may grant loans to its director who is a full time employee provided it is pursuant to a scheme which has been approved by company resolution. Similarly, S. 225 provides that a company may grant loans to a person connected with its director provided such person is its full time employee and the loan is given pursuant to a scheme which has been approved by company resolution. Both provisions require the employee benefit scheme to be approved by the company members before the director and person connected to the director who are in full time employment of the company, could enjoy the benefits.

Communities

The pandemic witnessed many haunting scenes. Hospitals overflowed with COVID-19 patients and make-shift wards were set. Many lost their jobs and white flags were flown outside homes to request for aids. Long queues were seen at food distribution centres. Could private hospitals do national service and treat patients at nominal fee? Could companies make contributions to help ease the sufferings of the people? Would the directors who authorised contributions to society be held liable for breaching their fiduciary duties? Such charitable acts might be seen as not done in the best interest of the company, as the company would not gain any profit from those acts, but instead reduce the profits of the company for distribution to its shareholders.

Under the Companies Act 1965 which was repealed when the CA 2016 came into force, S. 19(1) provided that the powers of a company included the power to make donations for patriotic or for charitable purposes. However, the same is not found in the CA 2016. Instead, the CA 2016 has enacted the directors' fiduciary duties in S. 213(1) as follows:

> A director of a company shall at all times exercise his powers in accordance with this Act, for a proper purpose and in good faith in the best interest of the company.

According to paragraph 4.16 of the CLRC CD No 5, the phrase "to act in the best interest of the company and to exercise powers for a proper purpose" requires a director to be aware that his conduct and decision must be made in the best interest of the company and that powers conferred on him must be exercised for a proper purpose. If he fails to adhere to this, he would be in breach of his duty even though there is no dishonest intent on his part.

---

[50] [1998] 1 Ch 1, at p.18. This view was endorsed by the Malaysian Federal Court in the case of *The Board of Trustees of the Sabah Foundation & Co v Datuk Syed Kechik bin Syed Mohamed & Anor* [2008] 5 MLJ 461.

According to the Federal Court in *Petra Perdana Berhad v Tengku Dato' Ibrahim Petra bin Tengku Indra Petra & Ors*,[51] the test whether the director has acted in the best interest of the company contains two elements namely the objective element and the subjective element:

- whether an honest and intelligent person in the director's position and facing a similar set of circumstances would have reasonably believed that the transaction was for the benefit of the company. This is the objective element.
- whether the director acted bona fide in what the director considers to be the best interest of the company. This is the subjective element.

Applying these tests, the questions to be asked are firstly, would another director reasonably believe that the donation or charity was for the benefit of the company; and secondly, did the director act in good faith for what he considered to be in the best interest of the company when he approved the donation?

Reinventing the Company

The pandemic had thrown a spanner on the operating wheels of many businesses. Due to the movement control orders, many could not go to work as usual. Working from the home became the norm, shopping online took on a new dimension. Businesses had to revamp to fit in with the new norm. We heard of hotels serving as quarantine centres, restaurants churning out meals for home delivery or setting up stalls outside the premises for takeaways, and airlines going into food delivery services. Their new ventures, though some humbling and a move down, are strategies to generate some income, though may not be at the pre-crisis level, but hopefully sufficient to sustain them during this difficult period.

In principle, such major business decisions and corporate strategies have to be approved by the Board. The directors, when voting on it, might have honestly believed that they acted in good faith and in the best interest of the company, but did they exercise their powers in accordance with the CA 2016 and for a proper purpose? This is crucial for a director may be acting in good faith in what he believes to be in the best interest of the company but yet breaches his fiduciary duty if he uses the power for the wrong purpose.[52]

Does the company have the capacity to venture into this new business? Though S. 21(1) of the CA 2016 provides that a company shall have the capacity to carry on or undertake any business or activity, this does not apply to a company which has a constitution and an objects clause in its constitution. Such companies are bound by S. 35(2) and thus, restricted from carrying on any business or activity that is not within its objects. Thus, a new business which is outside the company's objects clause, will

[51] [2018] 2 MLJ 177.

[52] Walter Woon, *Companies Act of Malaysia: An Annotation 2020 Desk Edition* (Kuala Lumpur: LexisNexis Malaysia, 2020), 247–248.

be in breach of S. 35(2). As the company has no capacity to enter into transactions for this new business, the transactions are *ultra vires* the company and consequently, void.

An issue is whether the company could take legal action against its directors for the decision to venture into a business which is outside the objects clause stated in its constitution. There is no specific provision in the CA 2016 on this aspect, but the company may rely on S. 213 which requires directors to exercise their powers for a proper purpose. But does authorising the company to venture into a business which is *ultra vires* the company's objects clause be said to be exercising their powers for an improper purpose?

In the case of *Re Lee, Behrens & Co Ltd*,[53] Eve J propounded the company's funds and assets can only be used for purposes reasonably incidental to the carrying on of the company's business. He laid down three pertinent questions to determine whether the transaction is *ultra vire*s the company:

(i) Is the transaction reasonably incidental to the carrying on of the company's business?
(ii) Is it a bona fide transaction?
(iii) Is it done for the benefit and to promote the prosperity of the company?

Though Eve J's approach was rejected by the courts in subsequent cases, the English Court of Appeal in *Rolled Steel Products (Holding) Ltd v British Steel Corp & Ors*[54] opined that these tests may be useful to determine whether the directors have abused their powers. Applying these tests, it would appear that authorising the company to venture into a business which is *ultra vires* the company's objects clause is tantamount to an abuse of power. The directors cannot be said to have exercise their powers for a proper purpose.

Though it is rare for a company to take action against its current directors for breach of duty, the directors should not take the risk as their term as directors is not perpetual. They can be removed as directors. Further, the provisions in S. 351 and S. 541 which confer a right on creditors to apply to the Court for an injunction or to examine a delinquent director, are also extended to a member of the company.

Thus, a company that wishes to carry on a business which is outside its objects clause in its constitution, is advised to include the new business in its objects clause. This can be done by altering the company's constitution following the procedure prescribed in S. 36. A special resolution is required, and during the pandemic, this might prove a challenge as will be seen in Chap. 6.

---

[53] [1932] 2 Ch 46, at p. 51.

[54] [1985] 3 All ER 52.

Conclusion

When the CA 2016 was drafted, the policy maker consciously took the stance that directors are to only act in the best interest of the company, and that the relationships between the company and its creditors and employees should not be regulated under the Act. They opined that the relationship with these stakeholders were already sufficiently dealt with. Thus, S. 213 of the CA 2016 which prescribes the fiduciary duty of a director, provides that a director shall at all times exercise his powers for a proper purpose and in good faith and in the best interest of the company. Company means the company's members as a whole. The interests of other stakeholders are not included.

Despite the exclusivity of S. 213(1), there are provisions in the Act which require directors to consider the interest of the creditors of the company, especially when the company is insolvent or on the verge of insolvency. In addition, directors are required to make a solvency statement before the company could carry on certain transactions such as returning capital to members without court's confirmation, financing the purchase of company's shares, buying the company's own shares and distributing dividends. These transactions, which deplete the company's resources, benefit the company's members but not its creditors. Thus, the requirement for solvency statements is a control placed to protect the interest of, among others, the creditors.

Employees are one of the company's greatest assets, but they are not in a favourable position. The CA 2016 does not contain any provision requiring or obliging the directors to take into account the employees' interest. There are statutes governing the relationship between an employer and its employees, but their applications are restrictive. For example, the Employment Act 1955 applies only to categories of employees stated in the First Schedule to the Act. The position of employees is precarious especially during bad times.

The policy makers have also made a conscious decision not to incorporate the social obligations of a company into the CA 2016. Even the provision empowering companies to make donations for patriotic or for charitable purposes found in the repealed Companies Act 1965, was omitted from the CA 2016. This gives rise to the issue whether directors may authorise donations without being called out for abusing their powers.

The COVID-19 pandemic may have laid bare the importance of stakeholder theory in the good governance of a company. Though the interest of the members is important, it must be balanced with the needs of other stakeholders such as creditors, employees, society and the communities in which the company conducts its business. The directors' fiduciary duty should thus be re-aligned to the principle propounded by the stakeholder theory, and not focused solely on maximising profits for members, at the expense of other stakeholders. To take a leaf from Nelson Mandela at his Inauguration as the State President of South Africa on May 10, 1994 "Let there be justice for all. Let there be peace for all. Let there be work, bread, water and salt for all."[55]

References

1. Companies Commission of Malaysia. CLRC Consultative Document No 5 Clarifying and Reformulating the Directors' Role and Duties. https://www.ssm.com.my/Pages/Publication/CLRC/Consultation_Documents/cd5%20(1).pdf.
2. Companies Commission of Malaysia. "Scope of the Corporate Law Reform Committee." Accessed on September 21, 2021. https://www.ssm.com.my/Pages/Publication/CLRC/Scope.aspx.
3. High Level Finance Committee. Report on Corporate Governance, 1999.
4. Loh, Siew Cheang. *Corporate Powers Accountability*. Petaling Jaya: LexisNexis, 2018.
5. Mohd Sulaiman, Aiman Nariman, and Effendy Othman. *Malaysia Company Law: Principles and Practices*. Kuala Lumpur: Commerce Clearing House (Malaysia) Sdn. Bhd., 2021.
6. Nelson Mandela at his Inauguration as the State President of South Africa on May 10, 1994. Accessed on September 21, 2021. http://db.nelsonmandela.org/speeches/pub_view.asp?pg=item&ItemID=NMS176&txtstr=inauguration.
7. Our World in Data. "Malaysia: What is the cumulative number of confirmed cases?" Accessed on November 28, 2021. https://ourworldindata.org/coronavirus/country/malaysia#what-is-the-cumulative-number-of-confirmed-cases.
8. Securities Commission Malaysia. Malaysian Code of Corporate Governance, 2017.
9. Securities Commission Malaysia. Malaysian Code of Corporate Governance, 2021.
10. Woon, Walter. *Companies Act of Malaysia: An Annotation 2020 Desk Edition*. Kuala Lumpur: LexisNexis Malaysia, 2020.

[55] http://db.nelsonmandela.org/speeches/pub_view.asp?pg=item&ItemID=NMS176&txtstr=inauguration.

Chapter 3
Directors' Duty to Exercise Due Care, Skill and Diligence

Usharani Balasingam

Abstract The chapter is interrelated and interconnected with the director's fiduciary duties. The focus here is on the statutory provision relating to the duty of care and skill and to act for proper purpose in the best interest of the company and the business judgment rule. Directors have to be continuously diligent and be informed in the matters of the company. This is magnified in the era of COVID-19, sustainability and regulatory provisions that have impacted businesses in many ways. Some companies in sectors of information technology may reap gains but others like those in sectors of tourism, airlines and constructions have a much more challenging time. All companies will be faced with the impacts of the COVID-19 pandemic and will need to strive to make business decisions for the best interest of the company and in certain situations the interest of creditors. Directors need to be aware of the regulatory requirements in various aspects in their dealings with stakeholders and the concessions made during the times of COVID-19 especially those adversely impacted in an attempt to weather the storm of COVID-19. The nature and mode of business undertaken, the impact of the digital and AI (IT) era on business, the impact on the human capital and the nature of work, the risk management in weighing risk and benefits, the financial impacts into the current and the future projections of the company are some of the challenges. All accounting reports and communication to the proper parties needs to be done in compliance with proper accounting standards without misprcsentations. The dire and opportunistic situations may allow for innovative creative solutions and options for some or detrimental effect to others. Companies may opt to innovate, restructure, merge or declare insolvency. The COVID-19 era ushered in abruptly the digital and AI age coupled with the sustainability age into transformative business platforms and human capital. These transformative changes are to be steered by directors given the COVID-19 onslaught which has ushered in not just medical emergencies but a transformation in the way in which businesses, work and lives operate. Directors are expected to diligently aspire to acquire skills and knowledge to be on top of such a curve which includes not least the embracing of the IT and sustainability era.

U. Balasingam (✉)
University of Malaya, Kuala Lumpur 50603, Malaysia
e-mail: usha@um.edu.my

L. Krishnan and W. M. Chan (eds.), *The Impact of COVID-19 on Corporations and Corporate Law in Malaysia*, https://doi.org/10.1007/978-981-19-5519-8_3

Introduction

Lockdowns for more than 50% of the earth population and resultant impacts severely disrupted the businesses, lives, consumption, mobility, unemployment rates and the economy in April 2020. Reduced trade and slump in general consumption was estimated at 10%. In the first six months of 2020, foreign direct investment was down 49% with the global economy estimated to have shrunken at 4.3% in 2020. This is six times more severe than that of the 2008–2009 world recession. The economic decline is comparable only to the Great Depression (August 1929 to June 1938). Current forecast suggests that the COVID-19 global recession will be the severest since World War II, with the largest fraction of economies suffering drops in per capita input since the 1870.[1]

There will be businesses that will not be able to survive the onslaught of slew of changes of the shut downs, restrictions, the financial collapse, the financial or digital demands of the pandemic crisis. There will be businesses that will manage to adapt, to seek opportunities, create new modes, ride on the wave of technology, to survive, rise and move beyond the crisis. The business landscape will be forever changed by the digital era. The pandemic has accelerated into various dimensions of businesses activities and in regulatory framework too aside from others aspects. The pandemic change is a common challenge foisted upon all directors and board of directors (term used interchangeably) who run companies. The challenges are also on the government and the regulators to ensure a right balance of rules, oversight, compliance and enablers are in place to delicately balance and to foster the survival, adaptation, productivity and interest of the all stakeholders involved.

On an incidental note, The World Economic Forum (WEF) in a 2016 study noted that 61% of CEOs had no social media presence (Facebook, Google, LinkedIn or Twitter) and others minimally considered it a distraction. The study has suggested that the most important skill for a CEO to have is a social digital skill. This improves work productivity and has multiple benefits.[2] It would seem the pandemic will drive in this virtual digitalisation and artificial intelligence changes faster than ever before.

The World Economic Forum (WEF) has forecasted the fallout for the COVID-19 as shown in the table below.[3]

[1] Martin Gelter, and Julia M. Puaschunder, "COVID-19 and Comparative Corporate Governance," *Journal of Corporation Law* 46, no. 3 (Spring 2021): 557–628.

[2] "Social CEO-Executives Tell All," Weber Shandwick, accessed October 1, 2021, https://www.webershandwick.com/uploads/news/files/Social_CEO-Infographic.pdf.

[3] "How the World Can Reset Itself After COVID-19: According to These Experts," World Economic Forum, accessed October 1, 2021, https://www.weforum.org/agenda/2020/06/covid19-great-reset-gita-gopinath-jennifer-morgan-sharan-burrow-climate?fbclid=IwAR3kaj9SVTBwhBYTregvrl-xDHXcDKrCqaAZ9XPUggzgNWyxWYlP_JkJkgU.

Table 1 Most likely fallout in the world

Prolonged recession of the global economy	68.6%
Surge in bankruptcies (big firms and SMEs) and a wave of industry consolidation	56.8%
Failure of industries or sectors in certain countries to properly recover	55.9%
High level of structural unemployment (especially youth)	49.3%
Tighter restrictions on the cross-border movement of people and goals	48.7%
Weakening of fiscal positions in major economies	45.8%
Protracted disruption of global supply chains	42.1%
Economic collapse of an emerging market or developing economy	38.0%
Cyberattacks and data fraud due to a sustained shift in working patterns	37.8%
Another global outbreak of COVID-19 or different infectious disease	30.8%
Additionally, unemployment from accelerated workforce automation	24.8%
Exploitation of COVID-19 crisis for geopolitical advantage	24.2%
Governmental retention of emergency powers and /or erosion of civil liberties	23.3%
Exacerbation of mental health issues	21.9%
Fresh surge in inequality and societal divisiveness	21.3%
Sharp increase in inflation globally	20.2%
Humanitarian crises exacerbated by a reduction in foreign aid	19.6%
Anger with political leaders and distrust of government	18.4%
Higher risk of failing to invest enough in climate resilience and adaptation	18.2%

The Malaysian Scenario

The picture is a daunting one. Malaysia has been in seclusion and suspension in varying degrees for almost a year and a half in September 2021. The Malaysian Government issued a Movement Control Order ("MCO") on March 16, 2020 pursuant to the Prevention and Control of Infectious Diseases Act 1988. It took effect on March 18, 2020. The purpose of the Order was to prevent the spread of an illness called COVID-19 which is caused by a novel Corona Virus-19.[4]

There is a recognition in early September 2021, that the pandemic is endemic.[5] The focus is the move towards easing up of restrictions fuelled with a recognition that livelihoods, businesses and economy need to be rejuvenated speedily. All sectors of businesses suffer but the more grievous burn perhaps is felt in the sectors such as airlines, shipping, tourism, hospitality and leisure, retail, projects and constructions. Education too but it can be seen that education players have adapted to online education where possible to minimise the impact on their business delivery and continuity.

---

[4] The Gazette of the MCO is PU(A) 87/2020.

[5] "COVID-19 Expected to Become Endemic in Malaysia by End of October, Says KJ". *The Star*, September 1, 2021. https://www.thestar.com.my/news/nation/2021/09/01/covid-19-expected-to-become-endemic-in-malaysia-by-end-of-october-says-kj.

The focus at hand is the impact of the pandemic on businesses. The Department of Statistics conducted a survey on the effects of the COVID-19 pandemic on Malaysian businesses. The following is the finding of the survey done during the period of April 10, 2020 to May 1, 2020.[6] A total of 4094 companies were surveyed. They comprised of large (7.2%), medium (9.1%) small (40.4%) and micro (43.4%) companies. Majority of respondents (67.8%) reported that they had no sales revenue during the MCO while some reported online sales (12.3%), physical (9.8%) and other (5.4%). The operation cost during the period was funded from business savings (68.9%), loan (19.8%) and capital injection (11.3%). Employees were working from home (33.5%), on reduced work hours, unpaid (16.5%) or terminated (4.3%). The duration of a company's ablility to survive with full or half pay to employees was reported to be less than one month (16.5%), one to two months (53.4%), three to six months (25 0.4%) and more than six months (4.7%). About 44.2% of the employees were on full or half paid leave. The three main issues facing businesses were salary payment (sole proprietor 62.5%, partnership 76.5% and private limited company 88.8%), rental payment (sole proprietor 60.5%, partnership 68.4% and private limited company 63.5%) and no customers. (sole proprietor 70.7%, partnership 68.8% and private limited company 63.2%). Two main assistances required were tax reductions (67%) and financial/subsidies assistance (83.1%). Estimated projected duration to recover were reported at more than six months (42.6%), four to six months (28.7%), two to three months (17.9%), less than two months (9%) and not expected to recover (1.9%).

The above is a reflection on the impact that the companies suffer as a result of the pandemic and the challenges faced in running companies and meeting obligations. Hence, funding and relief from pressing obligations are important.

Hence, a director needs to be aware of not only the business and affairs of the company but also the laws applicable or incentives that are available to lift the company from the pressures of the crisis. The same can be seemingly considered a reflection of reasonable care skill and diligence which will be dealt with in greater detail later. In the case of *Tan Ken Meng* v *HSL Plastics Sdn Bhd & Ors.*[7]

> [24] In the circumstances, in my view, the plaintiff's reliance on S. 213 is without basis as it was he who has not acted in the best interest of the first defendant. The sale of the assets of the first defendant in contravention of the statutory requirement of a company resolution indicated he was hopelessly incompetent as a director.

Hence, in this regard the following aspects in the topic below covered for an indicative but not exhaustive view of the reliefs available to a company in pandemic times.

[6] Department of Statistics Malaysia, "Survey on Effects of COVID-19," accessed September 26, 2021. https://www.dosm.gov.my/v1/index.php?r=column/cone&menu_id=RkJtOThJSlBJNStOV1liM1JsKzdZUT09.

[7] *Tan Ken Meng* v *HSL Plastics Sdn Bhd & Ors* [2019] 1 LNS 1291.

Statutes and Incentives

A company director and the board of directors (used interchangeably) need to be cognizant of the opportunities and the incentives that are available and to strategize how better to harness it. There are two major statutes to ease the difficulties and also certain exemption or relaxation given by regulatory bodies like the Securities Commission of Malaysian ("SC") and Companies Commission of Malaysia ("CCM") to lessen the compliance onus on companies. In order for directors to exercise skill and diligence, they are required to be in the know of the statutory and government packages to enable them to make decisions in the best interest of the company to steer the company out of the crisis. Hence this part is meant to highlight an overview of the measures in this regard.

Temporary Measures for Government Financing (Coronavirus Disease 2019 (COVID-19)) Act 2020[8]

Over time, there were packages provided for stimulus and protection. This covers the 6R Strategy Implementation Firmness, Endurance, Restart, Recovery, Empowerment, Restructuring. Packages include the Malaysian Prihatin (March 23, 2021), Prihatin PKS (April 6, 2021), Penjana (June 1, 2021) and Kita Prihatin (September 23, 2021).[9]

The Short Term Economic Recovery Plan (PENJANA) is an implementation plan to revive the national economy as a result of the COVID-19 global pandemic.[10] Immediate and proactive measures need to be devised to protect the people, support business and strengthen the country's economy to face this ongoing crisis. PENJANA outlines a short-term recovery plan, based on engagement sessions with the involvement of more than 100 stakeholders comprising both the public and private sectors. Collectively, a total of 40 initiatives worth more than RM35 billion have been designed to meet four main goals: enabling jobs & reducing unemployment; ensuring capability & providing liquidity; digitization & handling in new habits; and increasing consumer & investor confidence. The four main principles that drive it and refine it are based on priorities and needs. Coordinated public–private sector cooperation are not limited to Government-Linked Companies or Government Linked Investment Companies. Transparency and openness in publicizing all initiatives and results. A report on implementation status is to be done on a weekly basis by the Ministry of Finance.

---

[8] Temporary Measures for Government Financing (Coronavirus Disease 2019 (COVID-19)) Act 2020. Gazetted October 26, 2020.

[9] Ministry of Finance Malaysia, *Tinjauan Ekonomi* (Kuala Lumpur: Percetakan Nasional Malaysia Berhad). http://belanjawan2021.treasury.gov.my/pdf/ekonomi/2021/tinjauan-ekonomi-2021.pdf.

[10] Minsitry of Finance Malaysia, "Short Term Economic Recovery Plan," accessed October 3, 2021. https://malaysia.gov.my/portal/content/31148.

Each initiative is monitored to enable measures to be refined quickly as needed and to ensure assistance reaches directly to the targeted beneficiaries quickly and accurately. Data from 53 ministries and agencies were collected, analysed and shared with implementing agencies for the purpose of continuous improvement through the LAKSANA unit, the National Inter-Agency Economic Stimulus Implementation and Coordination Unit under the Ministry of Finance.

Temporary Measures for Reducing the Impact of Coronavirus Disease 2019 (COVID-19) Act 2020

Directors should be cognizant with the fact that there is an Act[11] "*to provide for temporary measures to reduce the impact of Coronavirus Disease 2019 (COVID-19) including to modify the relevant provisions in the Limitation Act 1953, the Sabah Limitation Ordinance, the Sarawak Limitation Ordinance, the Public Authorities Protection Act 1948, the Insolvency Act 1967, the Hire-Purchase Act 1967, the Consumer Protection Act 1999, the Distress Act 1951, the Housing Development (Control and Licensing) Act 1966, the Industrial Relations Act 1967, the Private Employment Agencies Act 1981, the Land Public Transport Act 2010, the Commercial Vehicles Licensing Board Act 1987, the Courts of Judicature Act 1964, the Subordinate Courts Act 1948 and the Subordinate Courts Rules Act 1955.*"

It is noteworthy that the inability to perform contractual obligation under the contracts specified under the schedule (construction work or consultancy contract or related contract, performance bond or like for construction or supply contracts, professional services, lease or tenancy of non-residential immovable property, tourism or tourism promotion contract and pilgrimage and related contracts) due to COVID-19 measures undertaken will not enable the other party to exercise his or her rights under the contract.[12] Disputes below RM500,000 are to be mediated under the COVID-19 Mediation Centre under the Prime Minister Office.[13]

There is extension of time in respect of filing of legal actions and court proceedings. The indebtedness to filing a bankruptcy action is RM100,000 for the period Oct 23, 2020 until August 31, 2021.[14]

---

[11] Temporary Measures for Reducing the Impact of Coronavirus Disease 2019 (COVID-19) Act 2020.

[12] S. 7 and Schedule 1 of the Temporary Measures for Reducing the Impact of Coronavirus Disease 2019 (COVID-19) Act 2020.

[13] S. 9 of the Temporary Measures for Reducing the Impact of Coronavirus Disease 2019 (COVID-19) Act 2020.

[14] S. 19 and 20 of the Temporary Measures for Reducing the Impact of Coronavirus Disease 2019 (COVID-19) Act 2020.

Securities Commission Malaysia (SC)

The SC like many other global regulators rose to the challenge to find ways to extend measures to assist companies to overcome challenges arising from the pandemic.[15] These included, among others, additionally measures to facilitate takeovers digitally[16] by application for listed issuers to conduct AGMs, adjusting onsite inspections, audit oversight requirements, providing flexibility on requirements related to AGM, as well as ensuring high quality financial reporting and disclosure obligations are maintained. On April 18, 2020, the SC issued a guidance note titled, Guidance and FAQs on the Conduct of General Meetings for Listed Issuers (Guidance Note).[17] Yet there was a need to ensure proper oversight and audit reporting is not compromised.[18]

Relief Measures on Fundraising by Securities Commission Malaysia

It is reported by SC that 47 companies sought fundraising and 389 companies received fee waivers. The relief measures can be found in the 2020 Annual Report of the SC.[19] There were also guidelines given to those in charge of corporate governance

[15] In 2020, Malaysia served as the Chair of the Asia-Pacific Economic Cooperation ("APEC") – the co-operative economic and trade forum with 21 members aimed at creating greater prosperity for the region. Themed 'Optimising Human Potential towards a Resilient Future of Shared Prosperity: Pivot. Prioritise. Progress', the APEC Finance Ministers' Meeting 2020 (APEC FMM 2020) was held virtually on September 25, 2020. CCM formed part of the delegation. COVID-19 economic implications were also part of the deliberations. See "2020 APEC Finance Ministers' Meeting," Asia- Pacific Economic Cooperation, accessed October 8, 2021, https://www.apec.org/Meeting-Papers/Sectoral-Ministerial-Meetings/Finance/2020_finance.

[16] Securities Commission Malaysia "Update on Flexibilities in Complying with Take-Over Offer Requirements under Capital Markets and Services Act 2007 and Rules on Take-Overs, Mergers and Compulsory Acquisitions," accessed October 8, 2021, https://www.sc.com.my/regulation/technical-notes-practice-notes-and-circulars/update-on-flexibilities-in-complying-with-take-overoffer-requirements-under-capital-markets-and-services-act-2007-and-rules-on-take-overs-mergers-and-compulsory-acquisitions.

[17] Securities Commission Malaysia "COVID-19 Related Announcements," accessed October 8, 2021, https://www.sc.com.my/covid-19.

[18] "AOB Communications to Auditors and Audit Committee," Securities Commission Malaysia, accessed October 8, 2021. https://www.sc.com.my/regulation/technical-notes-practice-notes-and-circulars/aob-communications-to-auditors-and-audit-committee; "SC'S AOB Emphasise the Need for High Quality Audit in Light of COVID-19," accessed October 8, 2021. https://www.sc.com.my/resources/media/media-release/scs-aob-emphasise-the-need-for-high-quality-audit-in-light-of-covid-19; "Stimulus Package Circular on Waiver of Fees and Charges," Bursa Malaysia, accessed October 8, 2021, https://www.bursamalaysia.com/sites/5d809dcf39fba22790cad230/assets/5e5e009639fba20b5c32a4f4/circular-on-waiver-of-fees-and-charges.pdf.

[19] Securities Commission Malaysia, "Relief Measures on Fundraising," in Securities Commission Malaysia Annual Report 2020 (Kuala Lumpur: Securities Commission Malaysia), 32–38. https://www.sc.com.my/api/documentms/download.ashx?id=e1c7eb21-53db-4f02-a8f8-55dc09f9ffff.

tied in to asset management and projections in reporting for financial statements. This includes to pay particular attention to when discharging their responsibilities during this challenging period namely to focus on assessing if assets are impaired, on the company's financial performance, the appropriateness of any past or current projected statements made, to factor in COVID-19 impact, to ensure audit quality is not affected by reporting deadlines, to make decision even after the report of any events that would require disclosures, to consider if a report is required to the auditor of any break in information flow between subsidiaries, associates and joint venture partners, to assess the impact on the internal risk management and internal reporting controls that may impact financial reporting controls to the auditors, to ensure proper assessment and sufficient disclosures are made with respect to assumption made by management in preparing the financial statements and that the auditor has sufficient evidence to collaborate the stated assumptions. Finally, to draft key audit matters with auditors so as to ensure that key issues are disclosed and addressed and if the same need to be in the Audit Report Committee to the shareholders.

Companies Commission Malaysia (CCM)

The Companies Commission Malaysia covers all business entities and private and public companies. There are many measures taken to assist companies that span from extension of timelines, virtual meetings and other measures. One of the most immediate and pressing was the increase of indebtedness of RM10,000 to RM50,000 to enable the commencement of a winding up action against companies which is anticipated to benefit 1500 companies.

An overview of the list of initiatives by CCM is accessible from the website.[20]

Duty of the Directors Under the Companies Act 2016

The COVID-19 pandemic has caused turbulence in the economy and in the pulse of businesses. The strain has been immense. The most affected sectors are perhaps airlines, shipping, tourism, hospitality and leisure, retail, education and projects and constructions. The companies' contractual obligations are impacted and financial reserves are taxed. Projections of future businesses and profits were strewn aside by the unforeseen advent of the pandemic. Board of directors and directors collectively were tested like never before in strategic and risk management, adaptability, resilience and innovative measures to weather the storm of the pandemic.[21] The directors need to

---

[20] "Companies Commission Malaysia, FAQs Related to Government's Movement Control Order to Contain COVID-19," accessed October 1, 2021. https://www.ssm.com.my/Pages/FAQ/FAQ-Covid19.aspx.

[21] Among innovative measures, see Tong See Kit, "How a Singapore firm in the printing business switched to making masks amid COVID-19," Channel News Asia. accessed October

Table 2 Initiatives by Companies Commission of Malaysia

Approval for Company Secretarial Firms to Operate Under Phase 1 and Phase 2 of the National Recovery Plan
Virtual General Meetings
Extension Of Time (EOT) For Circulation Of Financial Statements, Holding Of Annual General Meeting And Lodgement Of Financial Statements For Year Ending November 1, 2020 To 31 January 31, 2021
Register Ebiz Account during the mandatory movement restriction order
Extension Of Time (EOT) For Circulation Of Financial Statements, Holding Of Annual General Meeting And Lodgement Of Financial Statements For Year Ending April 1, 2020 To July 31, 2020
Express Filing Application For Customers During Of Movement Control Order (MCO)
Business Registration
CCM Counter Operations Post MCO
Compound Exemption for failure to lodge statutory documents
Remission of Late Lodgement Fee on Filing of Company Statutory Documents
Account Activation For MyCoID, MyLLP and SSM4U Portal Users During MCO
Company Limited By Guarantee ("CLBG"), Foreign Branch, Change Of Company's Name
Compound Reduction Incentive for Application to Strike Off Company Under S. 549/550 Companies Act 2016
Renewal Application of Practising Certificate Under S. 241 of the Companies Act 2016
Extension of Time ("EOT") for Circulation, Annual General Meeting and Lodgement of Financial Statements for Financial Year End January 1, 2020 to March 31, 2020
MBRS
Application for Company Information Update
Application for Registration of Charges
Extension of Time ("EOT") for the Holding of the Annual General Meeting ("AGM")
Compliance Campaign 2020 of Companies Act 2016
Application of Practising Certificate Under S. 241 of the Companies Act 2016
Increase to the Value of Indebtedness from RM10,000 to RM50,000 until December 31, 2020
Exemption from Obtaining Approval for Solicitation of Donation from the Public by Companies Limited by Guarantee ("CLBG")
Extension of Time ("EOT") for Lodgement of Financial Statements
Moratorium of Submission of Statutory Documents to CCM
AGMs and Filing of Document during the Movement Control Order

be conscious of the solvency status of the company as the duty of directors to creditors will arise in circumstances where there is insolvency or potential insolvency. Hence the duty is broader in this context not only to the shareholders but also to creditors

4, 2021. https://www.channelnewsasia.com/singapore/company-making-face-masks-diversify-printing-business-covid-19-634186.

of the company. As regards the employees the duty also arises to ensure that any termination must be done in a legal manner and in accordance with employment law with proper justifications or measures and the safety protocol at the premises according with the law.[22]

Section 210 provides that for S. 213, 214, 215, 216, 217, 218, 223 and 228, in addition to the definition of "director" in S. 2, "director" includes chief executive officer, chief financial officer, chief operating officer or any other person primarily responsible for the management of the company. This wider dimension of director will be applicable in the context under study here. This paper will be limited to scope of duty to exercise reasonable care skill and diligence under Companies Act 2016.[23] The directors here include executive and non-executive directors.[24]

It is made expressly clear beyond all doubt that the business and affairs of the company shall be managed by the Board of Directors ("the Board"). The Board has the powers to direct, manage and supervise the company subject only to the Act or provision of the constitution of the company. Further the provision in the Third Schedule shall govern Board proceedings subject to the constitution.[25] The need for directors to be proactive and have the continuing duty to acquire and maintain sufficient knowledge (and arguably acquire skills to meet the objective standard) to be able to carry out the task of director is stated in the case of *Balda Solutions Malaysia Sdn Bhd* v *Foo Wan Seng*.[26]

The director's duty of care is correlated to the responsibility to become and remain informed and attentive in making decisions and overseeing the corporation's business. The test to surmount is the objective expectation of a corporate director in the director's position of common sense, practical wisdom, rational and informed judgement with sufficient financial literacy. The special attributes and expertise of the director may be relevant too under the subjective elements. Directors are expected to have the drive and skills to being able to stay informed which includes reading financial reports, attending meetings, reading materials and otherwise preparing in advance of meetings; asking questions of management or advisors; requesting legal or other expert advice when appropriate for a board decision; and bringing their own knowledge, common sense, and experience to bear. Being proactive and in the know of the company business affairs and financial position, making needed inquiries and

---

[22] Some of the pertinent laws are found in the Prevention and Control of Infectious Diseases Act 1988 and the regulations thereunder, the Employment Act 1955 and the regulations thereunder and the Occupational Safety and Health Act 1994 and regulations thereunder.

[23] For a more comprehensive discussion, see Usharani Balasingam, "Director Duties: Foundation of Good Corporate Governance Part One," *Current Law Journal* 7 (2019): i-xx; Usharani Balasingam, "Director Duties: Foundation of Good Corporate Governance Part Two," *Current Law Journal* 9 (2019): xxxiii-xx.

[24] *Tanjung Offshore Bhd* v *Harzani Azmi & Ors* [2018] 1 LNS 1719.

[25] S. 211 and 212 of the Companies Act 2016 deal with the functions and proceedings of the board. See *Tengku Dato' Ibrahim Petra Tengku Indra Petra* v *Petra Perdana Bhd & Another* [2021] 7 MLJ 439.

[26] [2013] MLJU 1624.

dialogues so as to enable the director to steward the company to make business judgements.

The case related to a claim by the plaintiff company against the defendant, the former Chief Executive Officer ("CEO") and director of the plaintiff for the breach of duty of care and skill as CEO and director of the plaintiff. The court commented that the revised test introduced a subjective and objective standard of care to be applied and it was no longer possible to merely act honestly to escape liability. The director is to be judged on the knowledge, skill and experience reasonably expected of a director having the same responsibilities as well as any additional knowledge and skill the director actually has.

> In this regard, useful reference can be made to several propositions set out in the judgment in *Re Barings plc*, supra as follows (at p 489):
>
> (i) Directors have, both collectively and individually, a continuing duty to acquire and maintain a sufficient knowledge and understanding of the company's business to enable them properly to discharge their duties as directors.

The material sections for this part are reproduced here. This is with relation the statutory duty owed to the company, and the standard applicable under the Companies Act 2016.

> 213. (1) A director of a company shall at all times exercise his powers in accordance with this Act, for a proper purpose and in good faith in the best interest of the company. (2) A director of a company shall exercise reasonable care, skill and diligence with—(a) the knowledge, skill and experience which may reasonably be expected of a director having the same responsibilities; and (b) any additional knowledge, skill and experience which the director in fact has.

Good Faith and Proper Purpose

Good faith means more than acting honestly. A director who just accepts the view of another director may not be considered to be acting bona fide. Hence, due diligence by the director is expected and required. The directors are to be mindful of their fiduciary duties of loyalty and not to have conflict of interest (or self-dealing) with the company. In this regard, the purpose and best interest referred is that of the company. The context of proper purpose will not extend to breach of fiduciary duties. Hence the director's use of property of the company, information, position, opportunity or to engage in competition with the company is prohibited except where consent or ratification is obtained of the general meeting.[27]

[27] S. 218(1) of the Companies Act 2016.

Combined Test

Section 213(2) is very clear in that it combines an objective test expected of a director having the same responsibilities and added to that any special added knowledge and skill of the particular director. The same is seemingly applicable to both executive and non-executive directors.[28] The standard to be applied is fault based on the threshold of reasonable care, skill and diligence. The purpose for which the director exercises the power must be properly rooted in good faith for the best interest of the company.

The combined test has been applied in the case of *Tengku Dato' Ibrahim Petra bin Tengku Indra Petra* v *Petra Perdana Bhd & Another Appeal.*[29] The court applied the combined test stating the question is subjective in that the courts looked into the subjective intent or mind of the director to answer the question as to whether the director in exercising his discretion on the facts was acting bona fide (honestly without improper motive) in the best interest of the company. The objective element in the test relates to the court's supervision over directors not to replace the court's judgement or to act in hindsight but to ask the question if whether an intelligent and honest man in the position of a director of the company concerned could, in the whole of the existing circumstances, have reasonably believed that the transactions were for the benefit of the company.

Statutory Defence and Discharge of Duties for Directors

It is affirmed in the Federal Court case of *Tengku Dato' Ibrahim Petra bin Tengku Indra Petra* v *Petra Perdana Bhd & Another Appeal*[30] that the effect of the statutory business judgment rule reproduced below is a deeming provision that a director acted with due care and skill if the requisite elements stated below are fulfilled. The protective rule is to allow (and encourage) directors to discharge their role in the proper and dutiful manner without worry or fear (acting defensively) of unnecessary litigation.[31]

The Federal Court in *Tengku Dato' Ibrahim bin Petra Tengku Indra Petra* v *Petra Perdana Bhd & Another* Appeal decided that a balance must be kept between accountability and risk-taking as evident in the business judgment rule as follows.

---

[28] *Australian Securities and Investment Commission* v *Healey* [2011] FCA 717.

[29] [2018] 2 CLJ 641.

[30] *Tengku Dato' Ibrahim Petra Tengku Indra Petra* v *Petra Perdana Bhd & Another Appeal* [2018] 2 CLJ 641 paragraph 181.

See also *Pioneer Haven Sdn Bhd* v *Ho Hup Construction Company Bhd & Anor and Other Appeals* [2012] 5 CLJ 169.

[31] A comprehensive explanation on the safe harbour rule can be found in Pearlie MC Koh, *Pearlie MC Koh on Company Law* (Singapore: LexisNexis, 2009), 439; Rashidah Abdul Rahman and Mohammad Rizal Salim, *Corporate Governance in Malaysia* (Petaling Jaya: Sweet & Maxwell, 2010), 218.

[181] A related point is the statutory business judgment rule in s. 132(1B) of the Act (in pari materia with S. 214 CA 2016), which states as follows[32]:

A director who makes a business judgment is deemed to meet the requirements of the duty under subsection (1A) and the equivalent duties under the common law and in equity if the director:

(a) makes the business judgment in good faith for a proper purpose;

(b) does not have a material personal interest in the subject matter of the business judgment;

(c) is informed about the subject matter of the business judgment to the extent the director reasonably believes to be appropriate under the circumstances; and

(d) reasonably believes that the business judgment is in the best interests of the company.

[182] The statutory business judgment rule, which was added to the Act in 2007, provided a presumption that a director acted with due care and skill if the requisite pre-conditions are fulfilled.

S. 132(6) defines "business judgment" as "any decision on whether or not to take action in respect of a matter relevant to the business of the company"."

The now repealed S. 132(6) Companies Act 1965 is equivalent to S. 214 Companies Act 2016. In the case of *Symbion International Sdn Bhd* v *Mah Chez Yong*[33] the court applied the test and found that S. 214 was not applicable in the case as the director had personal interest in the subject matter. The director also admitted to poor day to day management and making wrong judgment on certain business aspects causing loss to the company.

[68] It can be noted that the instances wherein I found against the 1st Defendant have been instances wherein he had a personal interest in the subject matter of the business judgment, either by being involved as a shareholder and director himself or involving the 4th and 5th Defendants which are companies owned by his wife and mother-in-law who manage the companies pursuant to his instructions.

The case of *Balda Solutions Malaysia Sdn Bhd* v *Foo Wan Seng*[34] has this to state as to duty to act positively and proactively.

In this regard, useful reference can be made to several propositions set out in the judgment in *Re Barings plc*, supra as follows (at p 489):

In *Daniels v. Anderson*, supra, as well, the Supreme Court of New South Wales also outlined several important propositions with respect to the duty of care of directors as follows (from the headnotes): (a) Directors were required to take reasonable steps to place themselves in a position to guide and monitor the management of the company. (b) Directors must be allowed to make business judgments and business decisions in the spirit of enterprise untrammelled by the concerns of a conservative investment trustee. They could not safely proceed on the basis that ignorance and a failure to enquire were a protection against liability for negligence. (c) The directors' duty of care was not merely subjective, limited by the

[32] *Tengku Dato' Ibrahim Petra Tengku Indra Petra* v *Petra Perdana Bhd & Another Appeal* [2018] 2 CLJ 641 para 181. The in pari materia provision is set out as S. 214 of the Companies Act 2016.

[33] [2019] 1 LNS 1512.

[34] [2013] MLJU 1624.

> director's knowledge and experience or ignorance or inaction. Nor could a director rely blindly on the judgment of others.

Balada is a case where an executive director was held in breach of the statutory duty of care and skill against the company. The court considered the fact that he was an executive director with 17 years' experience. The terms of his contract with the company were also considered. With that in mind the court held his action as reckless and in breach of his duty of care. The defendant was the Chief Executive Officer (CEO) of the plaintiff who entered into a contract detrimental to the company due his actions. The defendant instruction was to reverse calculate the cost to suit Canon target price without considering the actual production cost. The actual cost was not used by the defendant in instructing the issuance of the quotation which he approved. The outcome was a loss to the plaintiff to the sum of RM 2.3 million. On the argument that he delegated and relied on two employees the court held that even if so, he had a duty to supervise them. However, the court held on facts there was no reliance but a top-down instruction given by the Defendant. This case is also relevant for consideration of the defence of reliance on information provided by others below.

Reliance on Information Provided by Others

This provision that was housed under the now repealed S. 132(1C) and 132(1D) Companies Act 1965 is now situated in *pari materia* under S. 215 Companies Act 2016. The *Kontena Nasional Berhad v Hood bin Osman ("Kontena")* case sets out the provision as follows:

> [33] S. 132(1C) of CA 1965 allows a CEO to rely on information, professional or expert advice, opinions, reports or statements prepared, presented or made by among others:
>
> (a) any officer of the company whom the CEO believes on reasonable grounds to be reliable and competent in relation to matters concerned; and
>
> (b) any other person retained by the company as to matters involving skills or expertise in relation to matters that the CEO believes on reasonable grounds to be within the person's professional or expert competence.
>
> [34] S. 132 (1D) of CA 1965 provides that the CE01's reliance made under subsection (1C) could only be deemed to be made on reasonable grounds if it was made (a) in good faith; and (b) after making an independent assessment of the information or advice, opinions, reports or statements having regard to the CEO's knowledge of the company and the complexity of the structure and operation of the company.

On the facts of the *Kontena* case the court noted that the defendant CEO's management style was dictatorial and autocratic. He was involved in the company's daily management and did not tolerate disagreement from his staff of his instructions which he gave for implementation as opposed to assessment. Hence, he could not pass the blame to his subordinates.[35]

---

[35] [2020] 1 LNS 1639 paragraph 25, 82 and 83.

The Court of Appeal case of *Soh Chee Gee* v *Syn Tai Hung Trading Sdn Bhd*[36] related to the acts of a CEO whom the court held to have breached his duties as CEO and a fiduciary of the plaintiff company. On the facts the court held that the CEO caused a loss to the company by permitting and signing off a financing scheme, for the benefit of Cosmo and to the detriment of the plaintiff company. His defence of relying on subordinates was rejected by the court. The court in this case held that the CEO cannot rely on delegation to subordinates to avoid being made accountable for the credit term and credit limit given as it was his decision to make.

The Federal Court case of *Tengku Dato' Ibrahim Petra Tengku Indra Petra* v *Petra Perdana Bhd & Another Appeal*[37] was an action against a director who was successful in invoking the provisions of S. 131(1)(C) and 131(1)(D) in relation to reliance on experts and senior management and an independent assessment of the same as indicator of the discharge of the duty of care, skill and diligence. In the case the decision to sell the PEB shares that was subject to contention was made after making independent assessment of advice from lawyers and financial consultants which included Affin Investment Bank and TA Securities Holding Bhd.

The guides as set out in the Australian cases were referred with approval in the High Court judgment of *Balda Solutions Malaysia Sdn Bhd* v *Foo Wan Seng*[38] as set out previously. The director has a duty to continuously acquire knowledge and make inquiries to steer the company.

The power of delegation and trust of the competence to others within the organisation does not mean there is no duty to supervise the discharge of the delegated function. Whether this duty is discharged is to be decided on the director role and the facts of each case. It arguably will be best practice not to blindly rely without inquiry on the judgment of others.

Delegation of Power to Act Under S. 216 Companies Act 2016

In the case of *Solaris Estate Sdn Bhd* v *Mat Shah bin Safuan* (Solaris),[39] the issue before the court was the plaintiff's application to remove the lawyers representing the 2nd Defendant on the ground that his appointment is by the General Manager and not the Director of the 2nd Defendant. The court held based on the authority of the Federal Court in *Ulimas Sdn Bhd* v *Hi-Summit Construction Sdn Bhd & Other Appeals* (Ulimas),[40] the authority to act must be from a resolution of the board or in the *Ulimas* case two out three directors who signed it and the third was held to have ratified by conduct. On the argument that given the meaning of S. 210 assigned to the Director as any other person primarily responsible for the management of the

[36] *Soh Chee Gee* v. *Syn Tai Hung Trading Sdn Bhd* [2019] 2 MLJ 279, paragraph 60.

[37] [2018] 2 CLJ 641, paragraph 85.

[38] [2013] MLJU 1624.

[39] [2020] 1 LNS 1693.

[40] [2017] 2 CLJ 636.

company (for purposes of S. 213–218, 223 and 228). The court also held that even if the argument was accepted, there has been no delegation of the power by the Board to the general manager in *Solaris* case. Hence, the plaintiff application was successful. The case is of importance to establish that where an authority to act is vested in the Board it should be exercised by the Board unless there is proper delegation of that authority.

Director's Responsibilities with Regard to Financial Statements and Reports Under the Companies Act 2016

This section focuses on the Companies Act 2016. The directors may be additionally liable for sanctions under other statutes including Capital Markets and Services Act 2007 which is incidental to and not the scope of this paper. One of the possibilities is the furnishing of false statements. The executive director of Linear Corporation Berhad at the time made a statement he knew was not true when he said that LCI Global Sdn Bhd, a wholly owned subsidiary of Linear Corporation Bhd, was awarded a RM1.6 billion construction project. He was sentenced on August 29, 2019 to seven months jail and a fine of RM100,000 after he pleaded guilty.[41]

There are important provisions as regards the financial pulse of the company that would come under scrutiny during these times. The directors are accountable and responsible to prepare financial statements on the effect of the pandemic on the business and also consider if director remuneration is to be impacted. The directors need to be especially vigilant in reporting the solvency status of the company and the annual reports of the company, the prediction and impact of COVID-19 on the current and future expectations for the company.[42] The non-mandated S. 253(3) and Part II of the Fifth Schedule allow all companies the discretion to include a business review of the company in the director's report which may also state the impact of COVID-19. It relates to sustainability of the company and information affecting stakeholder interest of the company. Some other provisions that applies to listed companies are the Code of Corporate Governance 2021 and SC regulations.

[41] S. 369(b)(B) of the Capital Markets and Services Act 2007. See also Bursa Malaysia, "Former Executive Director Sentenced and Fined for Furnishing False Statement to Bursa," Bursa Malaysia, accessed October 9, 2021. https://www.sc.com.my/resources/media/media-release/former-executive-director-sentenced-and-fined-for-furnishing-false-statement-to-bursa. See also insider trading and other breaches highlighted in Securities Commission Malaysia, "Actions," accessed October 9, 2021. https://www.sc.com.my/regulation/enforcement/actions.

[42] S. 244, 245, 248, 249, 252, 253, 257, 259 of the Companies Act 2016.

Special Considerations for Duty of Care in Light of the Pandemic

In the times of COVID-19 pandemic, the financial standings of most companies will be tested. In this regard, company tethering into insolvency there is a need to also consider the interest of the creditors. Directors of the company, as a general rule, do not owe a duty to the company creditors. However, a duty to consider the interest of creditors may be triggered when the company is near insolvency[43] or insolvent.[44]

The Hong Kong case of *Moulin Global Eyecare Holdings Limited* v *Olivia Lee Sin Mei*[45] indicates that the directors may be found wanting in care and skill if they ignore warning signals of the insolvency of the company. The defendant non-executive director was an experienced commercial solicitor and a member of the audit committee. It was held that the director had in cognizant of knowledge that should have prompted concern and further investigation. If this was done, the fraud would have been discovered. The finding was in the liquidator's favour with the director held in breach and personally liable for Moulin's losses and the relevant interest (approximately HK$464 million in total).[46]

The crisis of the pandemic requires proactive involvement of directors in all aspects of the business (product–related, supply chain stakeholder, employees, consumers, insider trading, communication (as opposed to misrepresentation), mergers, audit, risk management and financial records and balance sheet) in an innovative creative and opportunistic way. In this regard, the duty for oversight and ensuring internal control and measures are heightened.[47]

There is also the caution not to make representations in relation to the pandemic that are not supported by evidence. It may give rise to legal action. It is reported that there are lawsuits against public companies (primarily involved in health care, pharmaceutical, tourism and technology) in other jurisdictions by shareholders that

---

[43] *New Kok Ann Realty Sdn Bhd* v *Development & Commercial Bank Ltd* [1987] 2 MLJ 57; *Ng Pak Cheong* v *Global Insurance Co Sdn Bhd* [1995] 1 MLJ 64; *Nicholson* v *Permakraft (NZ) Ltd (In Liq)* [1985] 1 NZLR 242. In *Nicholson* v *Permakraft (NZ) Ltd (In Liq)*, the company adopted a reconstruction scheme when it was facing liquidity problems that had the effect of prejudicing its creditors. Somers J held: In the case of an insolvent company, at least in the sense that its liabilities exceed its assets, directors in the management of a company must have regard to the interest of creditors. That is because according to the order of the application of assets on a winding up, they are trading with the creditors money.

[44] *Kinsela* v *Russell Kinsela Pty Ltd (In Liq)* (1987) 10 ACLR 395. See also Hasani Mohd Ali, "Directors' Duties to Prevent Insolvent Trading: The Malaysian Fraudulent Trading Provisions Revisited," *Malayan Law Journal* 1 (2016): i-xx.

[45] [2019] HKCFI 1715.

[46] See Marcus O'Brien et al., "COVID-19 Insolvency: APAC Guide to Directors Duties and Insolvent Trading," *Clyde & Co*, April 15, 2020, https://www.mondaq.com/uk/operational-impacts-and-strategy/917302/covid-19-insolvency-apac-guide-to-directors39-duties-and-insolvent-trading.

[47] Jane Goldstein, Daniel Lim, and Kenneth Monroe, "Director Oversight Duties Amidst COVID-19," Harvard Law School Forum on Corporate Governance, May 8, 2020. https://corpgov.law.harvard.edu/2020/05/08/director-oversight-duties-amidst-covid-19/. See also *In re Caremark International Inc. Derivative Litigation Derivative Litigation*, 698 A.2d 959 (Del. Ch. 1996).

aver that companies have made overly optimistic statements, failed to disclose or concealed deficiencies and made false or misleading statements on the effect of the pandemic.[48] An example given is the suit against a cruise line for misreporting and concealing the handling of the pandemic inter alia in not disclosing that the increase in infections and the severity of the same on the company.

In the article *Director Oversight Duties Amidst COVID-19*,[49] the following points are mooted for directors to consider their oversight duties. This is namely financial impact and liquidity, dividend and shares repurchases, governmental assistance, health and safety, operations, employees and compensation, shareholder relations (shareholder activism, hostile takeovers, new investors, stock-drop litigation and other shareholder matters (including virtual meetings), public disclosures (public reporting and disclosure), investors and analysts (if in need of an update or a revision), internal disclosure controls, supply chain, customers and other external obligations (supply chain, customer and other external obligations, insider trading, IT infrastructure and cyber security, transactional and other business opportunities). Further it is recommended to have an efficient information and reporting system. This could include communication (regular board meetings, coordinated communication, online communication and cybersecurity,[50] standing committee and crisis management team), record keeping and contingency and succession plan.

In certain circumstances, the director may even need to consider if they need (where applicable) to amend existing constitution that may be restrictive to allow them to venture into other business like a case of a company changing track of business to face masks[51] and/or undertake mergers or acquisitions that may be beneficial for the company.[52]

---

[48] Jay Kasner, and Matthew Rosenthal, "Shareholder Litigation Over COVID-19: What Are the Risks Facing Directors?", *BRINK – Conversations and Insights on Global Business*, June 25, 2020. https://www.brinknews.com/shareholder-litigation-and-covid-19-risks-facing-directors-and-officers-of-public-companies-do-covid-claims-lawsuits/.

[49] Refer to footnote 43 above.

[50] Securities Commission Malaysia, *Guidelines on Management of CyberRisk SC-GL/2-2016* (Kuala Lumpur: Securities Commission Malaysia). https://www.sc.com.my/api/documentms/download.ashx?id=9aaddb2e-aa13-409a-a47f-8d0124afd229.

[51] "From Perfume to Hand Sanitizer, TV to Face Mask. How Companies are Changing Track to Fight Covid," World Economic Forum, accessed October 26, 2021, https://www.weforum.org/agenda/2020/03/from-perfume-to-hand-sanitiser-tvs-to-face-masks-how-companies-are-changing-track-to-fight-covid-19/.

[52] "COVID-19 Impact on Merger and Acquisition in Malaysia," Azmi & Associates, accessed October 26, 2021, https://www.legal500.com/developments/thought-leadership/covid-19-impact-on-mergers-and-acquisitions-in-malaysia/.

Corporate Rescue Schemes

Under the Companies Act 2016, the two new schemes introduced are the corporate voluntary arrangement[53] and judicial management.[54] The statutory scheme of compromise divided under moratorium scheme of arrangement and compromise scheme of arrangement has been maintained.[55] It is to be noted however that public companies are not allowed to apply for judicial management.[56] It is also noted that a judicial management order could only be given for six months and may be extended for another period of six months. Hence the total duration possible is 12 months on a literal reading of the statute. It has been recently decided in the High Court case of *Syed Ibrahim v Transfame Offshore Sdn Bhd* on a purposive reading of the statute that it is possible to apply afresh for a judicial management order against the same company. If the conditions are satisfied and the order granted, this will extend the time frame beyond 12 months.[57] The Companies Commission has a bill that proposed extension of judicial management to public companies and improvement on corporate rescue mechanisms as well other measures to ease the sting of the pandemic.[58]

Hence there are more options available to a company in distress to avail to avoid liquidation. These are options available to the Board of Directors to consider if it is in the best interest of the company if the situation warrants it and the requirements are satisfied. The case of *AirAsia X Bhd* under S. 366 of the Companies Act 2016 is evident of how a scheme of arrangement can be used to salvage an ailing company from liquidation with a scheme of arrangement with her creditors.[59] In the final recourse, winding up the company is also a recourse as seen in the *Genting Hong Kong* case, where due to inability to pay her creditors, the company opted for a

[53] S. 395 to 402 of the Companies Act 2016.

[54] S. 403 to 430 of the Companies Act 2016.

[55] S. 365 to 369 of the Companies Act 2016.

[56] The court dismissed an application by Scomi Group Berhad for judicial management. See "Application for Judicial Management Order for Scomi Group Bhd (SGB or the Company)," Bursa Malaysia, accessed October 4, 2021. https://www.bursamalaysia.com/market_information/announcements/company_announcement/announcement_details?ann_id=3197896.

[57] In regards to the case of, see "Lien Hoe Corporation Berhad ("the Company")—Macro Resources Sdn Bhd (Under Judicial Management)," Bursa Malaysia, accessed October 10, 2021. https://www.bursamalaysia.com/market_information/announcements/company_announcement/announcement_details?ann_id=3192386. See the case of *Syed Ibrahim & Co v Transfame Offshore Sdn Bhd* OS WA-28 JM -22-12/2021 decided by High Court Judge Nadzarin Wok Nordin June 16, 2022 that a fresh application for judicial management may be made and if satisfies the conditions be granted to extend the time frame of judicial management. (collectively beyond one year).

[58] Companies Commission of Malaysia, *Consultative Document on the Proposed Companies (Amendment) Bill 2020*, accessed October 10, 2021, https://www.ssm.com.my/Pages/Legal_Framework/Document/Consultative%20Document%20%26Companies%20(Amendment)%20Bill%202020%20(280720).pdf.

[59] *Airasia X Bhd* v *BOC Aviation Ltd & Ors* [2021] 1 LNS 188.

winding up.[60] The Companies Act 2016 under Part IV deals with compulsory and voluntary winding-up[61].

What Should Directors Be Doing?

There is a suggestion that these are steps directors should consider to include to have a business plan, to meet regularly to review ongoing financial performance in detail with a careful review of specific transaction that require special attention (eg those over a specific amount or outside the ordinary scope of business), to maintain regular minutes of meeting and rationale of decisions, to seek professional advice from specialist such as insolvency specialist where needed, to engage with funder or financiers, to liaise with supplier on contract terms on credit and to justify belief of the merits to continue to trade.[62]

Wrongful and Fraudulent Trading

In this regard, the provisions that are applicable under the Companies Act 2016 are S. 539(3) and S. 540(2). Section 540(1) CA 2016 deals with fraudulent trading. Wrongful trading attaches personal liability to an officer which includes director where in a proceeding against the company or in winding up action the officer was knowingly a party to contracting a debt when there was no reasonable or probable expectation that the company would be able to pay the debt commits an offence with a penalty of imprisonment not more than five years or a fine not more than RM 500,000 or both. Additionally, under S. 540(2), the court may upon application declare the person liable personally for a part or whole of the debt. Under S. 540(1) the liability is for fraudulent trading where there is intent to defraud in carrying out the business of the company, any person so doing may be made liable personally for all or any of the debts or other liabilities of the company as the Court directs.

---

[60] Weizhan Tan, "Cruise operator Genting Hong Kong Files to Wind Up Company as Cash Runs Out," CNBC, accessed January 18, 2022, https://www.cnbc.com/2022/01/19/genting-hong-kong-files-for-liquidation-amid-german-lawsuit.html.

[61] S. 431 to 535 of the Companies Act 2016 (Act 777).

[62] See Marcus O'Brien et al., "COVID-19 Insolvency: APAC Guide to Directors Duties and Insolvent Trading", Clyde & Co, April 15, 2020, https://www.mondaq.com/uk/operational-impacts-and-strategy/917302/covid-19-insolvency-apac-guide-to-directors39-duties-and-insolvent-trading. See also Jennifer F. Longhurst, "Directors Duties and Governance Best Practices in response to Covid-19," *Insights*, March 30, 2020, https://www.dwpv.com/en/Insights#/article/Publications/2020/COVID-19-Directors-Duties-and-Best Practices?utm_source = Mondaq&utm_medium = syndication&utm_campaign = LinkedIn-integration.

Hence under such circumstances directors must be conscious that they are not contravening the provision of wrongful or fraudulent trading more in the pandemic times when ability to pay debts may be compromised.

The Federal Court *Dato' Prem Krishna Sahgal* v *Muniandy Nadasan & Ors*[63] case is one where employees of a liquidated public listed company CNLT sued the appellant and the company to claim for statutory emoluments, arrears of salary and workers' compensation in the total sum of RM2,910,201.78. The appellant was the executive managing director of CNLT. The court held that the employees could fall under the definition of creditor under S. 304 Companies Act 1965 (equivalent to S. 540 Companies Act 2016) and that after they became creditors, the business of the company was carried out by the appellant with intent to defraud them. The director appellant would be held jointly and severally liable for the same.

The Court of Appeal case of *Wong Chu Lai* v *Wong Ho Enterprise Sdn Bhd*[64] illustrates how a director without the exercise of due care skill and diligence and/or motivated by other interests may be in breach of S. 304 and 305 Companies Act 1965 and be held accountable. The directors in the case were found to have conducted fraudulent trading. They siphoned off the company's monies by giving themselves loans or advances and pay out monies to related companies. The court held that on the balance of probabilities the company (suing by liquidator) has shown that there was intent to defraud its creditors and was in contravention of S. 304 and 305 and thereby attached personal liability on the defaulting directors. The directors are the directing mind of the company and continuing to trade in such circumstances warrant attachment of personal liability and the statutory exception to corporate veil.

Director's Duty to Act in the Interest of Employees

The company as an employer is subjected to statutory obligations under statutes aimed at employee protection and welfare. These obligations exist in all times even during the COVID-19 pandemic times. Termination and treatment of employees need to be in accordance with the Employment Act 1955 for those covered by the Act.[65] Section 101B Employment Act makes the director of a company, partner of a partnership, in case of society or trade union, the office bearer at the time of

---

[63] [2017] 10 CLJ 385, para 72.

[64] [2020] 4 CLJ 120. See also *see Aneka Melor Sdn Bhd* v *Seri Sabco (M) Sdn Bhd & Another Appeal* [2016] 2 CLJ 563 and *Chin Chee Keong v Toling Corporation (M) Sdn Bhd* [2016] 6 CLJ 666; [2016] 3 MLJ 479, para 20.

[65] Employees falling under the First Schedule of the Employment Act 1955. See Siti Suraya Abd Razak, Siti Fazilah Abdul Shukor and Ma Kalthum Ishak Teh Zaharah Binti Yaacob, "Employment Rights during the COVID-19 Pandemic: A Legal Analysis," *Journal of Muwafaqat* 4, no. 1 (2021): 29–40. See also "Malaysian Rights and Obligations under the Employment Contract During MCO and the Covid 19 Pandemic," Coventus Law, April 8, 2020, https://www.conventuslaw.com/report/malaysia-rights-and-obligations-under-the/. Employees not falling under the Act will be governed under contract of employment and may lodge claims for unfair dismissal or dismissal without just cause if the matter is not dealt with in a proper manner. In some cases, the defendant companies fail

commission of the offence deemed to have committed the offence and liable to be charged jointly. Section 46 of the Employees Provident Fund Act 1991 states that a director of the companies at the time of offence and at the time the action is taken can be held liable personally for non-contribution.[66] Likewise, under the Employees Social Security Act 1969,[67] S. 108A states that in the event of default of contribution, the directors of the company at the time the action is taken and the directors at the time of non-payment are jointly and severally liable alongside the company for the unpaid amount. Since the pandemic has raised health and safety issues, the other statute that would need the attention of directors in terms of compliance is the Occupational Health and Safety Act 1994 ("OSHA") and the related safety procedures and measures therein especially in relation to COVID-19. Section 52 of the OSHA provides that for any offence committed by the body corporate, the director, manager, secretary or officer at the time of commission of the offence may be charged jointly or severally.

It will be part of a director's duty of reasonable care and skill to ensure that the legal and regulatory provisions are adhered to. More so when they are at risk to be made personally liable in event of non-compliance under statutes. Whereas optional requirements under the S. 253(3) of the Companies Act 2016 of the business review plan will not attract penalties.

Conclusion

In their paper, Gelter and Puaschudner[68] observed three trends emerging from the pandemic. The three are the need for resilience, a growth of nationalist policies in corporate law and the move towards increased "stakeholder" interest. Resilience is a key factor with more long-term goals and the need to network with partners inter alia in terms of funding and IT platforms. Interaction with the workforce will also develop to have a healthy human capital.[69] Finally, a move toward sustainability issues will also propel and broaden the corporate purpose beyond shareholder to stakeholder's interest. In all these seats, the driver of any company remains the board of directors who are the stewards of the company in all weather and times. In the SC Corporate Governance Trends to watch for in 2021, cites trends like the evolving and increased role of oversight and risk management role, virtual meetings are here to stay, a heightened need for cybersecurity (seven of out 10 companies in

---

to appear in court. See *Patricia Kho Siew Woon* v *Reliance Shipping & Travel Agencies (Sarawak) Sdn Bhd* [2020] ILJU 263 and *Lau Ching Kui* v Flyglobal Charter Sdn Bhd [2020] ILJU 181.

[66] *Ong Kim Chuan & Anor* v *Lembaga Kumpulan Wang Simpanan Pekerja* [2009] 5 MLJ 807.

[67] *Pendakwa Raya (Perkeso)* v *Sapura Kencana Marine Sdn Bhd* [2020] MLJU 2473, where the need to comply with provision of the Act was highlighted.

[68] Martin Gelter, and Julia M. Puaschunder, "COVID-19 and Comparative Corporate Governance," *Journal of Corporation Law* 46, no. 3: 557–628.

[69] Zuraina Saieed, "The Hybrid Work Arrangement Option," *The Star*, October 9, 2021, https://www.thestar.com.my/business/business-news/2021/10/09/the-hybrid-work-arrangement-option.

Malaysia fear a cyberattack). Accountability to a wider range of stakeholders and not just shareholders and the need to direct focus to climate risk as 91% of Malaysian companies are also concerns highlighted.[70] The pace and vehicle of change and optimisation of intelligent technologies has transformed today and will continue to evolve to impact tomorrow. A director and the board of directors will need to ride the multiple waves of changes of digitalisation and optimize the opportunities it brings while downsizing the risks even beyond the term of COVID-19.

References

1. Abd Razak, Siti Suraya, Siti Fazilah Abdul Shukor, and Ma Kalthum Ishak Teh Zaharah. Yaacob, "Employment Rights during the Covid 19 Pandemic: A Legal Analysis." *Journal of Muwafaqat* 4, no. 1 (2021): 29–40.
2. Abdul Rahman, Rashidah, and Mohammad Rizal Salim. *Corporate Governance in Malaysia.* Petaling Jaya: Sweet & Maxwell, 2010.
3. "2020 APEC Finance Ministers' Meeting." Asia- Pacific Economic Cooperation. Accessed October 8, 2021. https://www.apec.org/Meeting-Papers/Sectoral-Ministerial-Meetings/Finance/2020_finance.
4. "Application for Judicial Management Order for Scomi Group Bhd (SGB or the Company)." Bursa Malaysia. Accessed October 4, 2021. https://www.bursamalaysia.com/market_information/announcements/company_announcement/announcement_details?ann_id=3197896.
5. Balasingam, Usharani. "Director Duties: Foundation of Good Corporate Governance Part One." *Current Law Journal* 7 (2019): i-xx.
6. Balasingam, Usharani. "Director Duties: Foundation of Good Corporate Governance Part Two." *Current Law Journal* 9 (2019): xxxiii-xx.
7. Companies Commission of Malaysia. "Consultative Document on the Proposed Companies (Amendment) Bill 2020." Accessed October 10, 2021. https://www.ssm.com.my/Pages/Legal_Framework/Document/Consultative%20Document%20%26Companies%20(Amendment)%20Bill%202020%20(280720).pdf.
8. Companies Commission Malaysia. "FAQs Related to Government's Movement Control Order to Contain Covid-19." Accessed October 1, 2021. https://www.ssm.com.my/Pages/FAQ/FAQ-Covid19.aspx.
9. "Corporate Governance Trends to Watch in 2021." Bursa Malaysia. Accessed October 10, 2021. https://bursasustain.bursamalaysia.com/droplet-details/corporate-governance/corporate-governance trends-to-watch-in-2021.
10. "Covid-19 Expected To Become Endemic in Malaysia by End of October, Says KJ." *The Star,* September 1, 2021. https://www.thestar.com.my/news/nation/2021/09/01/covid-19-expected-to-become-endemic-in-malaysia-by-end-of-october-says-kj.
11. "Covid 19 Impact on Merger and Acquisition in Malaysia." Azmi & Associates. Accessed October 26, 2021. https://www.legal500.com/developments/thought-leadership/covid-19-impact-on-mergers-and-acquisitions-in-malaysia/.
12. Department of Statistics Malaysia. "Survey on Effects of Covid-19." Accessed September 26, 2021. https://www.dosm.gov.my/v1/index.php?r=column/cone&menu_id=RkJtOThJSlBJNStOV1liM1JsKzdZUT09.

[70] Corporate Governance Trends to Watch in 2021," Bursa Malaysia, accessed October 10, 2021, https://bursasustain.bursamalaysia.com/droplet-details/corporate-governance/corporate-governance-trends-to-watch-in-2021.

13. "Former Executive Director Sentenced and Fined for Furnishing False Statement to Bursa." Bursa Malaysia. Accessed October 9, 2021. https://www.sc.com.my/resources/media/media-release/former-executive-director-sentenced-and-fined-for-furnishing-false-statement-to-bursa.
14. "From Perfume to Hand Sanitizer, TV to Face Mask. How Companies are Changing Track to Fight COVID." World Economic Forum. Accessed October 26, 2021. https://www.weforum.org/agenda/2020/03/from-perfume-to-hand-sanitiser-tvs-to-face-masks-how-companies-are-changing-track-to-fight-covid-19/.
15. Gelter, Martin, and Julia M. Puaschunder, "COVID-19 and Comparative Corporate Governance," *Journal of Corporation Law* 46, no. 3 (Spring 2021): 557–628
16. Goldstein, jane, Daniel Lim, and Kenneth Monroe. "Director Oversight Duties Amidst COVID-19." *Harvard Law School Forum on Corporate Governance*, May 8, 2020, https://corpgov.law.harvard.edu/2020/05/08/director-oversight-duties-amidst-covid-19/.
17. "How the World Can reset Itself After Covid-19: According to These Experts." World Economic Forum. Accessed October 1, 2021. https://www.weforum.org/agenda/2020/06/covid19-great-reset-gita-gopinath-jennifer-morgan-sharan-burrow-climate?fbclid=IwAR3kaj9SVTBwhBYTregvrl-xDHXcDKrCqaAZ9XPUggzgNWyxWYlP_JkJkgU.
18. Kasner, Jay, and Matthew Rosenthal. "Shareholder Litigation Over COVID-19: What Are the Risks Facing Directors?" *BRINK – Conversations and Insights on Global Business*, June 25, 2020. https://www.brinknews.com/shareholder-litigation-and-covid-19-risks-facing-directors-and-officers-of-public-companies-do-covid-claims-lawsuits/.
19. Koh, Pearlie M.C. *Pearlie MC Koh on Company Law.*Singapore: LexisNexis, 2009.
20. "Lien Hoe Corporation Berhad ("the Company") - Macro Resources Sdn Bhd (Under Judicial Management)." Bursa Malaysia. Accessed October 10, 2021. https://www.bursamalaysia.com/market_information/announcements/company_announcement/announcement_details?ann_id=3192386.
21. Longhurst, Jennifer F. "Directors Duties and Governance Best Practices in response to Covid-19." *Insights*, March 30, 2020. https://www.dwpv.com/en/Insights#/article/Publications/2020/COVID-19-Directors-Duties-and-Best Practices?utm_source=Mondaq&utm_medium=syndication&utm_campaign=LinkedIn-integration.
22. "Malaysian Rights and Obligations under the Employment Contract During MCO and the Covid 19 Pandemic." Coventus Law. April 8, 2020. https://www.conventuslaw.com/report/malaysia-rights-and-obligations-under-the/.
23. Ministry of Finance Malaysia. "Short Term Economic Recovery Plan." Accessed October 3, 2021. https://malaysia.gov.my/portal/content/31148.
24. Ministry of Finance Malaysia. *Tinjauan Ekonomi.* Kuala Lumpur: Percetakan Nasional Malaysia Berhad, 2021. http://belanjawan2021.treasury.gov.my/pdf/ekonomi/2021/tinjauan-ekonomi-2021.pdf.
25. Mohd Ali, Hasani. "Directors' Duties to Prevent Insolvent Trading: The Malaysian Fraudulent Trading Provisions Revisited." *Malayan Law Journal* 1 (2016): i-xx.
26. O'Brien, Marcus, et al. "Covid 19 Insolvency: APAC Guide to Directors Duties and Insolvent Trading." *Clyde & Co*, April 15, 2020. https://www.mondaq.com/uk/operational-impacts-and-strategy/917302/covid-19-insolvency-apac-guide-to-directors39-duties-and-insolvent-trading.
27. Saieed, Zuraina. "The Hybrid Work Arrangement Option." *The Star.* October 9, 2021, https://www.thestar.com.my/business/business-news/2021/10/09/the-hybrid-work-arrangement-option.
28. Securities Commission Malaysia. "Actions." Accessed October 9, 2021. https://www.sc.com.my/regulation/enforcement/actions.
29. Securities Commission Malaysia. "AOB Communications to Auditors and Audit Committee." Accessed October 8, 2021. https://www.sc.com.my/regulation/technical-notes-practice-notes-and-circulars/aob-communications-to-auditors-and-audit-committee.

30. Securities Commission Malaysia. "Covid-19 Related Announcements." Accessed October 8, 2021. https://www.sc.com.my/covid-19.
31. Securities Commission Malaysia, Guidelines on Management of CyberRisk SC-GL/2–2016. https://www.sc.com.my/api/documentms/download.ashx?id=9aaddb2e-aa13-409a-a47f-8d0124afd229.
32. Securities Commission Malaysia. "Relief Measures on Fundraising," In Securities Commission Malaysia Annual Report 2020. Kuala Lumpur: Securities Commission Malaysia, 2021. https://www.sc.com.my/api/documentms/download.ashx?id=e1c7eb21-53db-4f02-a8f8-55dc09f9ffff.
33. Securities Commission Malaysia. "SC'S AOB Emphasise the Need for High Quality Audit in Light of Covid-19." Accessed October 8, 2021. https://www.sc.com.my/resources/media/media-release/scs-aob-emphasise-the-need-for-high-quality-audit-in-light-of-covid-19.
34. Securities Commission Malaysia. "Update on Flexibilities in Complying with Take-Over Offer Requirements under Capital Markets and Services Act 2007 and Rules on Take-Overs, Mergers and Compulsory Acquisitions." Accessed October 8, 2021. https://www.sc.com.my/regulation/technical-notes-practice-notes-and-circulars/update-on-flexibilities-in-complying-with-take-over-offer-requirements-under-capital-markets-and-services-act-2007-and-rules-on-take-overs-mergers-and-compulsory-acquisitions.
35. See Kit, Tong. "How a Singapore Firm in the Printing Business Switched to Making Masks Amid COVID-19." Channel News Asia. Accessed October 4, 2021. https://www.channelnewsasia.com/singapore/company-making-face-masks-diversify-printing-business-covid-19-634186.
36. "Social CEO-Executives Tell All." Weber Shandwick. Accessed October 1, 2021. http: https://www.webershandwick.com/uploads/news/files/Social_CEO-Infographic.pdf.
37. "Stimulus Package Circular on Waiver of Fees and Charges." Bursa Malaysia. Accessed October 8, 2021. https://www.bursamalaysia.com/sites/5d809dcf39fba22790cad230/assets/5e5e009639fba20b5c32a4f4/circular-on-waiver-of-fees-and-charges.pdf.
38. Tan, Weizhan. "Cruise Operator Genting Hong Kong Files to Wind Up Company as Cash Runs Out." CNBC. Accessed January 18, 2022. https://www.cnbc.com/2022/01/19/genting-hong-kong-files-for-liquidation-amid-german-lawsuit.html.

Chapter 4
Auditors' Duties and Obligations in Light of COVID-19 Pandemic

Loganathan Krishnan

Abstract This chapter will discuss auditors' duties and obligations in light of COVID-19 pandemic. The discussion will show whether auditors are able to exercise their role effectively. This is due to the fact that movement control orders in Malaysia, would have either prohibited or restricted auditors from physically travelling to their client companies to carry out audits. Furthermore, employees of the client companies may not be available to provide the necessary documents and information as required by the auditors, especially in cases where the documents are at the physical premises of the company. This is so unless it is the practice of the companies to digitalise its documents. Even in that case, the question remains whether the employees have access to the documents using their own computers unless they are placed in the cloud storage. Furthermore, employees of the company will have to answer relevant questions raised by the auditors in relation to the documents which again may prove to be difficult in view of the movement control orders. Certain companies may not wish to store them in the clouds due to security issues. Thus, it can be observed that auditors face great challenges in carrying their audit. Consequently, the question will be whether the audit was compromised during these trying times. The chapter will examine the approaches taken by the audit profession and the guidelines issued by professional bodies in conducting audits in light of the pandemic. The guidelines are imperative in ensuring that client companies do not take advantage of the pandemic at the expense of the challenges faced by auditors. Additionally, guidelines by regulators will also be examined. Ultimately, effective auditing produces effective auditors as watchdogs.

Introduction

This chapter identifies the underlying issues governing auditors' duties and obligations. These issues form the crux of this entire chapter. The overriding objectives, justifications and implications to embark on this study will be discussed to show

L. Krishnan (✉)
Monash University, Selangor, Malaysia
e-mail: loganathan.krishnan@monash.edu

L. Krishnan and W. M. Chan (eds.), *The Impact of COVID-19 on Corporations and Corporate Law in Malaysia*, https://doi.org/10.1007/978-981-19-5519-8_4

the importance of this study. The subsequent discussions will provide the general setting to the current laws which govern auditors' duties and obligations in Malaysia. An evaluation will be made as to whether the legal principles which govern auditors' duties and obligations developed by case law are able to withstand the impact of COVID-19 pandemic. An examination will also be carried out as to whether the current statutory provisions which govern auditors' duties and obligations are able to do the same. Additionally, there will be a discussion as to whether the standards, guidelines and by-laws which govern auditors' duties and obligations issued by professional bodies address the impact of the pandemic. The ensuing section discusses the background of the enactment of the Companies Act 2016 ("CA 2016").

Background of Study

The Companies Act 1965 ("CA 2016") has been in existence for 51 years and there were 35 amendments made to the CA 1965. The amendments were not holistic.[1] Amendments were made as and when the need arises. Furthermore, the amendments were not in tandem with the approaches taken in developed countries[2] such as the United Kingdom, Australia and Singapore.[3] Be that as it may, the legislature realised that the CA 1965 is in need of a thorough reform as the CA 1965 looked messy. On January 31, 2017, the CA 1965 was replaced with a new Act. The Companies Act 2016 has taken into account some of the novel developments in other countries as they have been tested and tried in those countries.[4] In fact, the then Companies Commission of Malaysia's ("CCM") Chief Executive Officer, Datuk Zahrah Abd Wahab stated that the changes as reflected in the CA 2016 were necessary as it is crucial for businesses to remain relevant and competitive.[5] This is necessary if Malaysia wishes to be an attractive business hub locally, regionally and globally.[6] Thus, in 2003, the government formed the Corporate Law Reform Committee ("CLRC") to examine

---

[1] MAICSA Annual Conference 2006, Corporate Updates, Malaysian Association of Institute of Chartered Secretaries and Administrators, Kuala Lumpur, July 10–11, 2006.

[2] Adeline Paul Raj, "Companies Bill 2015 to Bring Major Reform," *The Edge Malaysia*, April 18, 2016, 24.

[3] MAICSA Annual Conference 2007, Challenges in Leading Governance, Malaysian Association of Institute of Chartered Secretaries and Administrators, Kuala Lumpur, July 16–17, 2007.

[4] Kenneth Poh Khean Foo, and Shih, Lee, (2017), *Companies Act 2016: The New Dynamics of Company Law in Malaysia,*(Ampang: CLJ, 2017).

[5] MAICSA Annual Conference 2014, Challenges of the Changing Corporate and Regulatory Landscape Malaysian Association of Institute of Chartered Secretaries and Administrators, Connexion @ Nexus, Kuala Lumpur, September 9–10, 2014.

[6] Malaysian Legal and Corporate Conference—Shifting Sands: Is the Law Reshaping Our Legal and Corporate Sectors? Current Law Journal Sdn Bhd and Malaysian Bar Council, Kuala Lumpur, July 3–4, 2013.

the CA 1965 and propose the necessary reforms.[7] The CLRC issued consultative documents for public views, comments and feedback. The CLRC then published a report titled "Review of the Companies Act 1965 – Final Report of the CLRC." The CLRC made a total of 188 recommendations out of which 183 were accepted. It was subsequently issued as 19 policy statements. The government gave its approval to the proposed amendments on June 18, 2010. In 2014, the CCM released an Exposure Draft (comprising 631 sections) for public consultation.[8] Hence, it took 13 years for the CA 2016 to materialise.[9] However, within a few years, the pandemic of COVID-19 hit the shores of the Malaysian waters. The uppermost question in mind is whether the CA 2016 is able to withstand the impact of the pandemic. The ensuing discussion provides a brief commentary on the various types of movement control orders issued by the Malaysian government and the duration.

Prevention and Control of Infectious Diseases (Measures Within the Infected Local Areas) Regulations 2020

In an effort to contain the outbreak of COVID-19, the Malaysian government issued the Prevention and Control of Infectious Diseases (Measures within the Infected Local Areas) Regulations 2020. The Regulations were issued under the Prevention and Control of Infectious Diseases Act 1988 and the Police Act 1967. Thus, under the Regulations, the government implemented a Movement Control Order ("MCO"). This was pursuant to S. 11 of the Prevention and Control of Infectious Diseases Act 1988 which imposed the MCO for 56 days i.e. phase 1 of the MCO was from March 18, 2020 till April 1, 2020, phase 2 was from April 1, 2020 till April 14, 2020, phase 3 was from April 14, 2020 till April 28, 2020 and phase 4 was from April 29, 2020 till May 12, 2020. Paragraph 3 of the Regulations prohibits the movement of individuals within an infected area unless they fall within the exceptions provided, such as providing for essential services.

The Conditional MCO ("CMCO") which was announced on May 1, 2020 ended on June 9, 2020. The Recovery MCO ("RMCO") was announced by the Government of Malaysia on June 5, 2020 and was effective from June 10 until August 31, 2020. On August 28, Prime Minister Muhyiddin Yassin announced the extension of the RMCO by a further four months until December 31, 2020. The second MCO which

[7] CCM National Insolvency Conference: Companies Bill 2015 – Modernising Corporate Insolvency Framework in Malaysia, Companies Commission of Malaysia, Sunway Putra Hotel, Kuala Lumpur, 11th October 2016.

[8] CCM National Conference 2014, Modernizing the Companies Act: Impetus for Business Transformation, Companies Commission of Malaysia, Connexion @ Nexus, Kuala Lumpur, June 3–4, 2014.

[9] Workshop on the New Companies Act, Corporate Securities and Financial Law and Regulation, Civil Law Department, Ahmad Ibrahim Kulliyah of Law, International Islamic University Malaysia, August 2–3, 2016.

was in January 2021 was implemented across a number of federal territories and states and the 3rd MCO was in June 2021.

During the time of MCO, CMCO and RMCO, companies carried on their businesses by implementing alternative arrangements to continue managing the affairs of their businesses in order to minimise the economic impact of the COVID-19. Meanwhile, companies wanted some form of legal solutions to address the challenges faced by them in managing their businesses. The ensuing section explores the legislation which was specifically enacted to address the pandemic.

Temporary Measures for Reducing the Impact of Coronavirus Disease 2019 (COVID-19) Act 2020

The Malaysian Government implemented a Movement Control Order ("MCO") commencing on March 18, 2020 and was extended until May 12, 2020.[10] In order to minimise the economic impact of the COVID-19 during the said period of time, businesses were carried out by implementing alternative arrangements.

Meanwhile various calls were made to enact a temporary COVID-19 Bill, similar to that which was passed in Singapore.[11] This means the legislators would have to go to the Parliament during the MCO. However, the government responded by stating that measures to help businesses would be presented in July 2020.

On October 23, 2020, the Temporary Measures For Reducing the Impact of Coronavirus Disease 2019 Act 2020 ("COVID Act 2020") was gazetted. The legislation is aimed to provide for temporary measures to reduce the impact of COVID-19 including to modify the relevant provisions in the Limitation Act 1953, the Sabah Limitation Ordinance, the Sarawak Limitation Ordinance, the Public Authorities Protection Act 1948, the Insolvency Act 1967, the Hire-Purchase Act 1967, the Consumer Protection Act 1999, the Distress Act 1951, the Housing Development (Control and Licensing) Act 1966, the Industrial Relations Act 1967, the Private Employment Agencies Act 1981, the Land Public Transport Act 2010, the Commercial Vehicles Licensing Board Act 1987, the Courts of Judicature Act 1964, the Subordinate Courts Act 1948 and the Subordinate Courts Rules Act 1955.

Section 1(2) of the COVID Act 2020 provides that except where the date of commencement and period of operation have been provided in respect of the respective Parts in this Act, this Act shall come into operation on the date of publication of this Act and shall continue to remain in operation for a period of two years from such date of publication. The COVID Act 2020 came into force on 23 October 2020.

[10] It was enforced under the Control and Prevention of Infectious Diseases Act 1988 and the Police Act 1967, and encompasses, among others, the closure of all government and private premises except those involved in essential services (water, electricity, energy, telecommunications, post, transportation, irrigation, oil, gas fuel, lubricants, broadcasting, finance, banking, health, pharmacy, fire prevention, prisons, ports, airports, security, defense, cleaning, food supply and retail).

[11] "Companies Need More Relief," *The Star*, May 11, 2020.

Nevertheless, it does not make any reference to the CA 2016. Hence, businesses and auditors would have to refer to guidelines issued by the CCM, Securities Commission ("SC"), Bursa Malaysia and the Malaysian Institute of Accountants ("MIA") in relation to the pandemic. The succeeding section explains the relevant auditors' duties and obligations under common law and the CA 2016.

Auditors' Duties and Obligations

Common Law Position

In *Re Kingston Cotton Mill Co (No 2),*[12] Lopes LJ observed that an auditor is a watchdog but not a bloodhound. Thus, auditors were not required to detect fraud. Nevertheless, in 1898, the duty to detect fraud was considered as one of the auditors' duties[13] although, as years pass by, the duty erodes. In later years, the approach taken by the courts changed as it was declared by Lord Denning in *Fomento (Sterling Area) Ltd* v *Selsdon Fountain Pen Co*[14] that auditors must approach their task with an inquiring mind suspecting that someone may have made a mistake somewhere and that a check must be made to ensure there has been none.

This includes the duty to report on any matter which is illegal or improper as pointed out in *Thomas* v *The Corporation of Devonport.*[15] If auditors are unable to obtain the full information on a company's accounts, they are obliged to make a qualified report as remarked in *Berg Sons & Co Ltd* v *Adams.*[16] Hence, auditors must be independent[17] and competent.[18] Thus, the management need not supervise or test auditors' work as observed by the court in *Dovey* v *Corey*[19] since auditors are professionals.

Additionally, the duty to give a true and fair view is more than merely forming an opinion. Romer J pointed out in *Re City Equitable Fire Insurance Co*[20] that audit will be an idle farce if auditors were allowed to rely on the statements by the management as the purpose of the audit is to check on the management. Audit will enable shareholders to exercise their supervisory powers on the directors i.e.

[12] [1896] 2 Ch 279, 288.

[13] Donald M Roberts, "Discussion of Auditing: Incentives and Truthful Reporting," *Journal of Accounting Research* 17, (1979):30.

[14] [1958] 1 All ER 11 at 23, [1958] 1 WLR 45 at 61 (House of Lords).

[15] (1900) 1 QB 16.

[16] [1993] BCLC 1045.

[17] Michael Sutton, "Auditor Independence: The Challenge of Fact and Appearance," *Accounting Horizons* 11, no. 1 (1997): 86.

[18] Paul Lyndon Davies, and Daniel Prentice, *Gower's Principles of Modern Company Law*, 6th ed. (London: Sweet & Maxwell, 1997), 538.

[19] (1901) AC 477.

[20] [1925] Ch 407, 481 [1924] All ER Rep 485: 133 LT 520.

to remove any director who committed a wrong. Thus, in *Re Westminster Road Construction & Engineering Co Ltd,*[21] the auditors were not entitled to rely on the figures supplied by the manager and the secretary without proper enquiries.

A company may have its internal system to detect deficiency, failures or shortcomings. Nevertheless, auditors should employ their own tests to determine whether the internal system is reliable. If auditors opine that the internal system is unreliable, they should make further inquiries *i.e.* a duty to take further steps. If there is a need, auditors should disallow the internal system as pointed out by the court in *Roberts* v *Hopwood.*[22]

If auditors uncovered certain wrongs which require them to take further steps, they should do so. Auditors must decide what should the steps be and how would the steps further assist them to unfold the wrongs committed by the management. Support for this can be found in *Re Kingston Cotton Mill Co (No 2)*[23] where the court stated that if there is anything calculated to excite suspicion, auditors should probe it to the bottom.

In *Thomas* v *The Corporation of Devonport,*[24] the court made it clear that if payments are made or sums are borrowed by a company, auditors should see that they are authorized and made in accordance with the company's constitution and the legislation.

In *Equitable Life Assurance Society* v *Roger Bowley,*[25] a claim for £2.6 billion was brought by Equitable Life Assurance Society, a company founded in 1762, against its auditors, *i.e.* Ernst & Young.[26] The auditors failed to warn the company of its financial liabilities from the sale of guaranteed annuity pension products during the 1990s. However, a settlement was reached and hence a solution is denied on the issue concerning auditors' duties.[27] Consequently this means that an opportunity to establish auditors' duties was lost.

In *Fomento (Sterling Area) Ltd* v *Selsdon Fountain Pen Co,*[28] the respondents agreed to the terms of full but non-exclusive sub-license to manufacture, use and sell writing instruments which were protected by patents. The agreement provides that the respondent undertook to give the appellant's auditors all such other information as may be necessary to enable the amount of royalties, payable to be ascertained. The auditors asked for further information but the respondent refused. Their Lordships held that the auditors were entitled to the information.

---

[21] (1932) unreported.

[22] [1925] AC 578, 605.

[23] [1896] 2 Ch 279.

[24] [1900] 1 QB 16 (CA).

[25] [2003] EWHC 2263.

[26] "Flawed Equitable Claims Heap More Misery on Chairman: Andrew Bolger and Nikki Tait on Yet Another Piece of Bad News That the Troubled Mutual Has to Report to Policyholders," *Financial Times*, February 11, 2003, 4.

[27] "Man v Freightliner Ruling Eases Auditors' Duty of Care Responsibilities," *The Lawyer,* November 7, 2005, 13.

[28] [1958] 1 All ER 11 at 23, [1958] 1 WLR 45 at 61 (House of Lords).

The Position Under the Companies Act 2016

By virtue of S. 266 (1) and (2), an auditor is required to prepare an auditor's report and give his true and fair view of the matters required by S. 248. If it is a holding company, auditors are required to report on the consolidated accounts. Furthermore, S. 266(3) provides that auditors must form an opinion on the matters specified therein and state the particulars of any deficiency, failure or shortcoming in respect of any of those matters. The reason for such requirements is to have an independent assurance that the financial information received from the management is reliable.[29] In fact, the credibility of the financial information is enhanced since it is audited.[30]

Additionally, S. 266(2)(a)(ii) and (iii) provides that auditors shall report whether the accounts have been properly drawn up in accordance with the provisions of the CA 2016 and applicable approved accounting standards respectively. This duty is equally applicable if it concerns consolidated accounts.

Section 266(2)(b) provides that if the auditor is of the opinion that the accounts were not drawn up in accordance with a particular applicable approved accounting standard, he shall report whether in his opinion the accounts would if drawn up in accordance with the approved accounting standards, have given a true and fair view of the matters required by S. 248. This duty shall also apply in relation to consolidated accounts. Notable, non-compliance with a single accounting standard triggers this provision. Auditors are also under a duty to report whether the accounting records, other records and registers are properly kept in accordance with the provisions of the CA 2016. If it is a holding company, auditors must also look into whether the subsidiary companies have done so.

Section 266(2)(c) provides that in the case of consolidated accounts, auditors must report which subsidiary companies they have not acted as auditors. Auditors must report whether they have considered the accounts and auditor's reports of all subsidiaries of which they have not acted as auditors being accounts that are included in the consolidated accounts. Furthermore, auditors must report whether they are satisfied that the accounts of the subsidiaries are in form and content appropriate and proper for the purposes of preparing consolidated accounts. They must also state whether they have received satisfactory information and explanations for those purposes. Finally, they must state whether the auditor's report on the accounts of any subsidiary was made subject to any qualification. The auditors of a holding company must be concerned with the accounts, registers and reports of subsidiary companies which is an extensive duty imposed on the auditors.

Section 266(8) provides that in carrying out auditing duties, if auditors discover that there has been a breach of the CA and it has not or will not be adequately dealt with by the report or the directors of the company, they are bound to report to the

---

[29] Pamela Hanrahan, Ian Ramsay, and Geof Stapledon, *Commercial Applications of Company Law*, 2nd ed (Sydney: CCH, 2000), 362.

[30] Greg Pound, John Willingham, and Douglas W Carmichael, *Auditing Concept and Methods* (Australia: The McGrawHill Companies Inc, 1997).

ROC. This is a watchdog function of the auditors[31] since the regulators are involved. Moreover, the provision requires auditors to review the steps taken by the directors in addressing the breach. However, it is a qualified duty as auditors are under such a duty only if they discover a breach of the laws and the auditors' report will not adequately deal with such a matter.

Section 266(9) provides that auditors of a public company are under a duty to report to the Registrar if auditors are of the opinion that a serious offence involving fraud or dishonesty is being or has been committed against the company or the CA 2016 by officers of the company.

The CA 2016 gives substantive powers to enable auditors to perform their duties effectively.[32] If auditors' hands are tied, they are not able to uncover any wrongdoings by the management.[33] Anyone who obstructs their duties is in breach of S. 266(12) of the CA 2016. Auditors have a right of access at all reasonable times to the accounting records and other records, including the registers of the company. They also have a right of access to the records of any subsidiary and may obtain information regarding a subsidiary for the purpose of reporting on group accounts as provided in S. 266(12(a) of the CA 2016. They are entitled to obtain from any officer of the company, such information and explanations as they require as provided by S. 266(12)(b) of the CA 2016.

In *Loh Yoon Thong* v *Malaysian Institute of Accountants,*[34] the appellant was a member of the respondent and was in practice as an auditor and an accountant for 25 years. The appellant was found guilty of a charge that he withheld the audited accounts of PIE Healthcare Sdn Bhd for the year ending 30 June, 1995. The court found that the primary reason the appellant could not release the auditors' report was because they failed to get the appropriate response from the company on the important information concerning the events subsequent to the balance sheet date as provided for under S. 174 of the CA 1965 which is now found in S. 266 of the CA 2016. The court emphasised the powers of the auditors under S. 174(4) and (5) of the CA 1965. Thus, the charge by the respondent is wrong in law and the auditors do have the powers to do so.

Challenges Faced by Auditors Due to COVID-19

Audit has not stopped by the presence of the pandemic. Auditors are still required to conduct auditing as per the CA 2016. Nevertheless, there are various challenges faced by auditors in carrying out their duties and obligations. The concern is whether auditors will be able to carry out their duties and obligations as required by S. 266 of

[31] Pamela Hanrahan, Ian Ramsay, Geof Stapledon, Aiman Nariman, and Aishah Bidin, *Commercial Applications of Company Law in Malaysia* (Singapore: CCH, 2002), 361.

[32] Siew Li, Kang. "Auditors Have Enough Powers" *New Straits Times*, August 18 2008, 34.

[33] Alix Adams, *Law for Business Students,* 7th ed (Harlow: Pearson, 2012), 521.

[34] [2001] 5 MLJ 596.

the CA 2016 regarding duty to report, provide a true and fair view of the company's affairs, report fraud, dishonesty or breaches of the CA 2016. One of the questions auditors have in mind is whether they are permitted to include in the auditors' report which enables them to make a modified opinion.[35] Consequently, this may mar the independence and judgement of the auditors.

Appointment at Annual General Meetings

Prior to the emergence of COVID-19 pandemic, annual general meetings were usually held in the physical presence of company's members and the management. However, due to COVID-19, companies had to either cancel or defer their meetings and conduct virtual meetings. Section 327(1) of the CA 2016 provides that a company may convene a meeting of members at more than one venue using any technology or method that enables the members of the company to participate and to exercise the members' rights to speak and vote at the meeting. The CCM issued a press release on March 17, 2020 that companies can apply for extension of period to hold AGM to a time period longer than six months from their financial year end.[36] The SC and Bursa Malaysia also announced that AGMs are allowed to be deferred as long as application was made to the CCM.[37] However, as AGM is not compulsory for private companies, they are not eligible to apply for this extension unless the constitution of the company requires it.

The re-scheduling of the AGM has an impact on the appointment of auditors.[38] Auditors are appointed at AGM and will hold office until the next AGM. Hence, auditors may remain in office for more than a year due to the pandemic although the audit only covers one year.

In view of the fact that there can be virtual general meetings, the notice may also be given by electronic form as provided by S. 319(1)(b) of the CA 2016 to the auditor. A notice given in electronic form shall be transmitted to the electronic address provided by the auditor.

---

[35] James Chan and Wai Lee, Kok. "Accounting and Audit Implications of COVID-19", *CROWE Insights*, May 21, 2020.

[36] Malaysian Institute of Accountants, COVID-19 Movement Control Order, March 17, 2020. See also Practice Directive No. 6/2020, Extension of Time for Annual General Meeting and Lodgement of Financial Statements, April 7, 2020 (Revised August 21, 2020), Practice Directive No. 6/2020, Extension of Time for Annual General Meeting and Lodgement of Financial Statements, April 7, 2020 (Revised October 22, 2020), Practice Directive No. 8/2021, Extension of Time for Circulation of Financial Statements and Reports, Holding of Annual General Meeting and Lodgement of Financial Statements for Companies Affected by the Implementation of Movement Control Order, June 1, 2021 issued by the Companies Commission of Malaysia.

[37] Securities Commission of Malaysia, Capital Market Regulators Grant Flexibility for Listed Issuers on AGMs and Issuance of Periodic Reports, March 17, 2020.

[38] See S. 267, 269, 271 and 273 of the CA 2016.

The SC issued a Guidance Note on the Conduct of General Meetings for public companies.[39] It provided that public companies shall only conduct fully virtual general meetings during MCO 1.0. There may only be eight individuals physically present at the main venue, which includes the Chairperson of the general meeting, Chief Executive Officer, Chief Financial Officer, company secretary, auditor and those providing audio-visual support. During the CMCO and RMCO, where safe distancing requirements remain, public companies may conduct their general meetings in a fully virtual or hybrid manner i.e. physical presence in the general meeting with the option of remote participation for shareholders. Nevertheless, the SC announced that a general meeting conducted in states or districts under CMCO shall be conducted in a fully virtual manner only where all shareholders are able to participate in the meeting online.[40] Despite the announcement made by the SC, from January 2, 2020 to April 17, 2020, only 85 general meetings have been conducted, representing a decrease of 23% compared to last year.[41]

During MCO 2.0, the SC announced that public companies should conduct fully virtual meetings in areas under MCO and CMCO. Hybrid or physical meetings may be conducted in areas under RMCO or areas not subjected to any movement restrictions.[42]

Remote Auditing

Due to the pandemic, auditors are faced with two challenges. Firstly, they are not able to go to their offices in order to conduct auditing. Secondly, they are not able to visit their client's office to conduct the auditing. This is because audit firms do not fall within the meaning of "essential services" during MCO 1.[43] However, audit firms were allowed to operate during the MCO 2.0 as it comes under the purview of the essential economic sector.[44] Nevertheless, only 30% of employees in the management group are allowed to be in the office. The number of support staff and employees directly involved in the provision of services will be determined by the audit firms. Under MCO 3.0, services of audit firms are allowed to operate physically under Phase

[39] Guidance Note, Securities Commission, April 18, 2020.

[40] Securities Commission of Malaysia, "Only Fully Virtual General Meetings to be Conducted in States Subject to Conditional Movement Control Order," October 13, 2020.

[41] Doreenn Leong, "Virtual AGM—A Necessary Reality," *Focus Malaysia*, April 20, 2020.

[42] Securities Commission of Malaysia, "MKN SOP for Capital Market and Securities Commission's Guidance on Virtual Meetings for Listed Issuers," January 18, 2021.

[43] Malaysian Institute of Accountants, "Updates on Finance—Essential Services Classification for MIA Member Firms under the COVID-19 Movement Control Order," March 18, 2020.

[44] Malaysian Institute of Accountants, "Essential Services Allowed to Operate in The Essential Economic Sectors Throughout the Period of Movement Control Order (MCO) In Selangor, Penang, Melaka, Johor, Sabah and The Federal Territories (Kuala Lumpur, Labuan, Putrajaya)," January 12, 2021.

1 of the National Recovery Plan with a capacity of 60%.[45] Hence, heavy reliance is placed on the technologies available to the auditors and the clients. In addition to that will be the know-how and skills required to use the technologies. In some cases, auditors will be required to use live camera feeds or web or mobile-based video conferencing. The concern is whether current audit standards permit remote auditing.

Digital Transformative Process

It is important for auditors to ensure that all processes are transformed to a digital format. Otherwise, in time of this pandemic which prohibits movement, auditing cannot be carried out. Large audit firms which have international presence may have achieved this much before the pandemic. Nevertheless, small or medium sized audit firms may still to some extent not fully adopt a digitalised process. It will require the technical skills and cost to do so which small and medium sized firms may not have. Nevertheless, in light of the ongoing pandemic, audits firms have no option but to adapt to a digitalised transformative process.

Evidence

Although, S. 266 (12) of the CA 2016 empowers auditors to obtain information, explanation and access to records, this could be a challenge as auditors need to be physically present at the client company's office. This will further cause delay in obtaining the records and documents.[46] This will certainly have an impact on the opinion of the company's financial affairs. In some cases, auditors may have to revisit their views and opinions. Some companies may not have digitalised their records and documents. This is more likely if it is a small company as opposed to larger companies. Even then, the question is whether the companies have digitalised all their records and documents. This could be a challenge since the pandemic hit the Malaysian shores without any warning. Businesses may not have been prepared to face a fully digitalised environment. Auditors may want the original documents. In some cases, the employees responsible for the documents may not be available. Be that as it may, current audit standards do not prescribe how the evidence is obtained as long as evidence is obtained.[47]

---

[45] Malaysian Institute of Accountants, Services of Professional Accountancy Firms Are Now Part of Essential Services Under the National Recovery Plan (NRP), 20th July 2021.

[46] "The Impact of COVID-19 on Audit and Assurance—Challenges and Considerations," ACCA Think Ahead.

[47] Bob Dohrer, "Auditing During COVID-19: 6 Areas to Focus on", *Journal of Accountancy*, 15 (May, 2020).

Going Concern

A company is said to be going concern, if it is financially stable and it is able to meet its obligations and continue its business. If the management of the company thinks otherwise they may wish to liquidate or cease trading in some cases. In any case, auditors will have to examine in depth the assumptions made by the management of the company as to the going concern of the company.[48] This is an area which requires much judgement on the part of the auditors. Auditors will have to be sceptical and careful in making its judgement. The auditor should inquire of management as to what information is available about the future, and determine whether this has been appropriately considered as part of management's assessment.[49] In view of the likelihood of liability attached to directors under S. 539(3) of the CA 2016 if they did not take reasonable steps to avoid the company from being in debt, directors may exercise caution to declare that the company is going concern especially in cases where the company is heading towards insolvency. Be that as it may, auditors have to make an independent judgement instead of relying on directors' judgement.

Security Issues

Auditors must ensure that all documents received and sent via web portal are secure and confidential. If it falls into the wrong hands, the auditors could be liable for breach of confidentiality. Any communications with the client via online platforms such as Zoom, Microsoft Team, Cisco Webex or Google Meet must also be secure and confidential. In light of the current pandemic and direction taken by many businesses, much information is stored in the clouds. The extent of security of such information is yet to be determined.

Regulatory Datelines

Auditors have to comply with the regulatory deadlines as required by the CA 2016. In cases where companies have applied for extension of time, this would provide a breathing space for audit firms. However, in cases where companies did not seek for extension, auditors have to comply with the deadlines as required by the CA 2016. This could prove to be a challenge if auditors were not able to complete their auditing due to the pandemic in order to submit auditors' reports. Furthermore, since

---

[48] Tan Khoon Yeow, "COVID-19 Impact on Audits of Entities Applying MPERS," *Accountants Today*, June 28, 2021.

[49] The Malaysian Institute of Certified Public Accountants, "Audit Considerations in Respect of Going Concern Due to the Impact of COVID-19."

the regulatory body has provided an extension of time, it will affect audit for the following year.

Written Resolutions

Written resolutions are only available for private companies as provided by S. 290(1)(a) of the CA 2016. In doing so, the procedures in S. 300 and 301 of the CA 2016 must be complied with. Section 297(1) of the CA 2016 states that it can be proposed by the Board of Directors or any member of the company. The percentage of votes required will depend on the type of resolution required by the CA 2016 as stipulated in S. 305(4) CA 2016. Fortunately, Digital Signature Act 1997 is already in place and it is useful since S. 62 allows for digital signatures. Section 279(1) of the CA 2016 enables a private company to appoint an auditor via written resolution. The good news for auditors will be that written resolutions cannot be used to remove auditors as provided in S. 297(2) of the CA 2016.

High Quality Audit

The Audit Oversight Board ("AOB") issued a circular[50] to auditors regarding the importance of ensuring high quality of audit on financial reports of public companies in light of the challenges posed by the COVID-19 pandemic. The audit quality should not be compromised. Hence, the AOB is watching the auditors very closely, on the quality of auditors' reports due to the pandemic. The AOB will conduct its inspection on audit firms after May 15, 2020. The implementation of Audit Transparency Report by large audit firms has been deferred to 2021.

Presumption of Insolvency

Section 465(1)(e) of the CA 2016 provides one of the circumstances whereby a company may be wound up by a Court, namely if the company is unable to pay its debts. A company shall be deemed to be unable to pay its debts if the company is indebted in a sum exceeding the amount as may be prescribed by the Minister and a creditor has served a notice of demand, requiring the company to pay the sum due and the company has for 21 days after the service of the demand neglected to pay the sum. Under the directive issued by the Minister, the amount is RM10,000.[51]

---

[50] Securities Commission of Malaysia, "AOB Communications to Auditors and Audit Committee, Impact of COVID-19 Pandemic on Financial Reporting of Public Interest Entities," April 7, 2020.

[51] P.U. (B) 58 issued on January 26, 2018.

However, in view of the pandemic, a new directive was issued. The Companies (Exemption) Order (No. 2) 2020 and the Direction of the Minister under S. 466(1)(a) CA 2016 were gazetted[52] and took effect from April 23, 2020 to December 31, 2020. Under the Exemption Order, the Minister of Domestic Trade and Consumer Affairs[53] has exempted all companies from the application of the presumption of insolvency provision under S. 466(1)(a) CA 2016.[54] The Directive increases the statutory threshold for presumption of insolvency from RM10,000 to RM50,000. Furthermore, the time period for a company to comply with a notice of demand was extended to six months from 21 days. This was seen to ease the burden of the business community resulting from the COVID-19 pandemic.[55] The effect of the Directive is that a creditor may only issue a statutory demand against a company for a debt which is more than RM50,000 and the company neglected it for more than six months. Due to the ongoing pandemic, another directive was issued to extend the period to March 31, 2021.[56] Another directive was then issued on March 22, 2021. Now the directive reads that it is effective from April 1, 2021.

Hence, auditors must be cognisant of this fact. Auditors should exercise due care in evaluating whether a company is insolvent. This will particularly be of importance when giving opinion on a company's status of going concern. As mentioned earlier, auditors should not rely on management's judgement in absolute terms on the solvency of a company.

Attendance at General Meetings

Section 285(1) of the CA 2016 provides that an auditor of a public company shall attend every AGM where the financial statements of the company for a financial year are to be laid. The objective is that he will be able to respond according to his knowledge and ability to any question relevant to the audit of the financial statements. Subsection 2 provides that in the case of a private company, if due notice is given to an auditor of the intention to move a resolution requiring the presence of the auditor at a general meeting of the company where financial statements of the company for any financial year are to be laid, the auditor shall attend that meeting. It can be observed that the duty is obligatory if it is a public company or private company. The only difference is that attendance at an AGM of a private company is dependent on whether due notice is given to the auditor as provided by S. 285(2) of the CA 2016. Section 285(3) provides that if the auditor fails to attend, it is an offence.

---

[52] On April 23, 2020.

[53] Datuk Alexander Nanta Linggi.

[54] Pursuant to S. 615(1) of the CA 2016.

[55] Rahmat Lim & Partners, "COVID-19 Response: Changes to the Presumption of Insolvency Provision under S. 466(1)(a) of the CA 2016," *Knowledge Highlights*, April 27, 2020.

[56] GN No. 21841 of 2020 which was issued on December 23, 2020.

However, a defence is provided under S. 285(4) of the CA 2016 in cases where (a) the auditor is prevented by circumstances beyond his control from attending the meeting; (b) the auditor arranges for another auditor with knowledge of the audit to attend and carry out the duties of the auditor at the meeting; (c) if the auditor is a partner of a firm, the person attending the meeting in place of the designated auditor is a partner of that firm; or (d) the auditor arranges for an agent authorized by the auditor in writing to attend and carry out the duties of the auditor at the meeting.

Hence, in view of the pandemic and the various MCOs, auditors may resort to S. 285(4)(a) of the CA 2016 in the event they are unable to attend the general meetings. Nevertheless, with the proliferation of online platforms and many companies resorting to virtual meetings, this defence cannot be relied upon. Hence, auditors should attend the general meetings. The only challenge is to ensure that internet connectivity is stable throughout the meeting. The recent meeting held by Maybank had to be cancelled due to technical glitch.[57] This will certainly affect the possibility of auditors attending the virtual meeting.

Conclusion

Audit standards prescribe what is auditing and what is required of auditors when conducting audit. Additionally, common law and the CA 2016 impose various duties and obligations on auditors to ensure auditors play an effective role of being a watchdog on a company's accounts. This will consequently place trust and confidence in their skills and judgments as auditors are professional and independent. Be that as it may, the pandemic of COVID-19 has certainly posed huge challenges to auditors in carrying out audits. Auditors would have to learn the norm and leave behind the shackles of the old school of doing things. The norms resulting from the COVID-19 pandemic are here to stay. Otherwise, auditors would face even more challenges and be left behind. Younger generations who are adept to technologies would transform the entire audit industry elevating it to greater heights. In any case, conducting an audit during these trying times isn't easy. Auditors would have to be more cautious in carrying out their duties and obligations. Otherwise, they could be liable for breach of duty, negligence or misrepresentation.

References

1. ACCA Think Ahead, "The impact of COVID-19 on Audit and Assurance – Challenges and Considerations," ACCA Think Ahead.
2. Adams, Alix. *Law for Business Students*. 7th ed. Harlow: Pearson, 2012.
3. Chan, James, and Wai Lee. Kok. "Accounting and Audit Implications of COVID-19." *CROWE Insights*, May 21, 2020.

[57] "Technical Issue Foil Maybank's AGM", *New Straits Times*, April 16, 2021, 17.

4. Companies Commission of Malaysia. Practice Directive No. 6/2020, Extension of Time for Annual General Meeting and Lodgement of Financial Statements, April 7, 2020 (Revised August 21, 2020).
5. Companies Commission of Malaysia. Practice Directive No. 6/2020, Extension of Time for Annual General Meeting and Lodgement of Financial Statements, April 7, 2020 (Revised October 22, 2020).
6. Companies Commission of Malaysia. Practice Directive No. 8/2021, Extension of Time for Circulation of Financial Statements and Reports, Holding of Annual General Meeting and Lodgement of Financial Statements for Companies Affected by the Implementation of Movement Control Order, June 1, 2021.
7. Davies, Paul Lyndon and Daniel Prentice. *Gower's Principles of Modern Company Law.* 6th ed. London: Sweet & Maxwell, 1997.
8. Dohrer, Bob Dohrer. "Auditing During COVID-19: 6 Areas to Focus on." *Journal of Accountancy* 15 (May, 2020).
9. "Flawed Equitable Claims Heap More Misery on Chairman: Andrew Bolger and Nikki Tait on Yet Another Piece of Bad News That the Troubled Mutual Has to Report to Policyholders." *Financial Times*, February 11, 2003.
10. Foo, Kenneth Poh Khean and Shih Lee. *Companies Act 2016: The New Dynamics of Company Law in Malaysia.* Ampang: CLJ, 2017.
11. Leong, Doreenn. "Virtual AGM – A Necessary Reality." *Focus Malaysia*, April 20, 2020.
12. MAICSA Annual Conference 2006, Corporate Updates, Malaysian Association of Institute of Chartered Secretaries and Administrators, Kuala Lumpur, July 10 - 11, 2006.
13. MAICSA Annual Conference 2007, Challenges in Leading Governance, Malaysian Association of Institute of Chartered Secretaries and Administrators, Kuala Lumpur, July 16 - 17, 2007.
14. MAICSA Annual Conference 2014, Challenges of the Changing Corporate and Regulatory Landscape Malaysian Association of Institute of Chartered Secretaries and Administrators, Kuala Lumpur, September 9 - 10, 2014.
15. Malaysian Institute of Accountants, COVID-19 Movement Control Order, March 17, 2020
16. Malaysian Institute of Accountants. "Essential Services Allowed to Operate in The Essential Economic Sectors Throughout the Period of Movement Control Order (MCO) In Selangor, Penang, Melaka, Johor, Sabah and The Federal Territories (Kuala Lumpur, Labuan, Putrajaya)." January 12, 2021.
17. Malaysian Institute of Accountants. "Services of Professional Accountancy Firms Are Now Part of Essential Services Under the National Recovery Plan (NRP)." July 20, 2021.
18. Malaysian Institute of Accountants. ""Updates on Finance - Essential Services Classification for MIA Member Firms under the COVID-19 Movement Control Order. March 18, 2020.
19. Malaysian Legal and Corporate Conference – Shifting Sands: Is the Law Reshaping Our Legal and Corporate Sectors? Current Law Journal Sdn Bhd and Malaysian Bar Council. Kuala Lumpur, July 3 - 4, 2013.
20. "Man v Freightliner Ruling Eases Auditors' Duty of Care Responsibilities." *The Lawyer*, November 7, 2005.
21. Pamela Hanrahan, Ian Ramsay, and Geof Stapledon. *Commercial Applications of Company Law.* 2nd ed. Sydney: CCH, 2000.
22. Pamela Hanrahan, Ian Ramsay, Geof Stapledon, Aiman Nariman, and Aishah Bidin. *Commercial Applications of Company Law in Malaysia.* Singapore: CCH, 2002.
23. Paul, Adeline Raj. "Companies Bill 2015 to Bring Major Reform." *The Edge Malaysia*, April 18 2016.
24. Pound, Greg, John Willingham, and Douglas W Carmichael, Douglas. *Auditing Concept and Methods.* Australia: The McGrawHill Companies Inc, 1997.
25. Rahmat Lim & Partners. "COVID-19 Response: Changes to the Presumption of Insolvency Provision Under S. 466(1)(a) of the CA 2016." *Knowledge Highlights*, April 27, 2020.
26. Roberts, Donald M. "Discussion of Auditing: Incentives and Truthful Reporting." *Journal of Accounting Research* 17 (1979): 30.

27. SC, AOB Communications to Auditors and Audit Committee, Impact of COVID-19 Pandemic on Financial Reporting of Public Interest Entities, 7th April 2020.
28. Securities Commission of Malaysia. "Capital Market Regulators Grant Flexibility for Listed Issuers on AGMs and Issuance of Periodic Reports." March 17, 2020.
29. Securities Commission of Malaysia. *Guidance Note*, April 18, 2020.
30. Securities Commission, MKN SOP for Capital Market and SC's Guidance on Virtual Meetings for Listed Issuers, January 18th 2021.
31. Securities Commission, Only Fully Virtual General Meetings to be Conducted in States Subject to Conditional Movement Control Order, October 13th 2020.
32. Siew Li, Kang. "Auditors Have Enough Powers." *New Straits Times*, August 18, 2008.
33. SSM National Conference 2014, Modernizing the Companies Act: Impetus for Business Transformation, Companies Commission of Malaysia, Connexion @ Nexus, Kuala Lumpur, 3rd – 4th June 2014.
34. SSM National Insolvency Conference: Companies Bill 2015 – Modernising Corporate Insolvency Framework in Malaysia, Companies Commission of Malaysia, Sunway Putra Hotel, Kuala Lumpur, 11th October 2016.
35. Sutton, Michael H. "Auditor Independence: The Challenge of Fact and Appearance. *Accounting Horizons* 11, no. 1 (1997): 86.
36. Tan, Khoon Yeow. "COVID-19 Impact on Audits of Entities Applying MPERS." *Accountants Today*, June 28, 2021.
37. "Technical Issue Foil Maybank's AGM." *New Straits Times*, April 16, 2021.
38. The Malaysian Institute of Certified Public Accountants, Audit Considerations in Respect of Going Concern Due to the Impact of COVID-19.
39. Workshop on the New Companies Act, Corporate Securities and Financial Law and Regulation, Civil Law Department, Ahmad Ibrahim Kulliyah of Law, International Islamic University Malaysia, 2nd – 3rd August 2016.

Chapter 5
Board Meetings, General Meetings and Shareholder Activism

Wei Fong Wong

Abstract The pandemic has changed the way meetings were held traditionally for most companies as physical meetings were the way of life till the world came to a stop. The technology innovators and providers have been plying their trade of using technology platforms for meetings. It was not until the pandemic that the technology platform was pulled from the back burner as a solution to hold virtual meetings when movement control order was in place. At the same time, the regulators have also been actively observing the development of the movement control order and issuing directives, guidance notes and frequently asked questions to help the companies during the pandemic. Securities Commission Malaysia had been instrumental in issuing guidance for the conduct of virtual meetings by public listed companies. The transformation was made possible as the Companies Act 2016 and Bursa Malaysia Securities Bhd's Listing Requirements were amended earlier prior to the pandemic but the real test was done during the pandemic.

Introduction

A company upon incorporation is a separate legal entity, having a legal personality separate from its members and officers.[1] The members being the owners of the company, would appoint directors to manage and supervise the company's business. Thus, arise the concept of corporate governance, a framework of control mechanisms that support the company in achieving its goals, while preventing unwanted conflicts[2] between the members and directors. There are many theories on corporate governance such as agency theory, stewardship theory and stakeholder theory.

According to the agency theory, one party hires another party to act on his behalf. The former is known as the principal and the latter his agent. In the context of a

[1] S. 9 of the CA 2016.

[2] Paragraph 1.1 of the Malaysian Code on Corporate Governance (2021).

W. F. Wong (✉)
Associate of MAICSA, Kuala Lumpur, Malaysia
e-mail: weifong.wong@yahoo.com

L. Krishnan and W. M. Chan (eds.), *The Impact of COVID-19 on Corporations and Corporate Law in Malaysia*, https://doi.org/10.1007/978-981-19-5519-8_5

company, the principal is the members of the company, whereas the agent is the directors and executives who manage the company. Where the company has few members, the members may be managing the company. However, in a company with many members, the members may not manage the company. They may engage other people to do so for them. Then, the interests of the principal and agent are not aligned. The principal, being the capital provider, will bear the risk of actions taken by the agents.

Thus, the legal framework of company law has set checks and balances. Indeed, paragraph 1.2 of the Malaysian Code on Corporate Governance (2021) ("MCCG") maintains that "proper corporate governance identifies the distribution of rights and responsibilities among different participants in the company and outlines among others the rules and procedures for decision-making, internal control and risk management."

The board of directors ("Board") and members of a company make decisions by passing resolutions. Companies which are incorporated under the Companies Act 2016 ("CA 2016") hold board meetings and company meetings by passing resolutions. The board of directors and members of private companies normally pass resolutions through written circular resolutions due to the size of the board of directors and members. Nevertheless, there are private companies that hold meetings regularly due to the provision of the constitution and shareholders' agreements particularly for joint venture companies. As for public companies, they are required under the CA 2016 to hold members' meetings to make decisions.[3] Companies holding meetings for their members have to observe the formality relating to passing such resolutions from the issuing of notices of meetings, period of notice, service to the day of meeting of having a chairman, requisite quorum and voting procedure. The CA 2016 also provides for the matters to be attended after the company meetings which require submission of statutory documents to the Companies Commission of Malaysia ("CCM") while for public listed companies, submission of compliance documents, where applicable, to Bursa Malaysia Securities Berhad ("Bursa Malaysia") to complete the process.

Board meetings are normally governed by the constitution of the companies. For those companies that did not adopt any constitution, they would have to refer to the Third Schedule of the CA 2016 for compliance in holding board meetings.[4] Board meetings are held regularly as compared with members' meetings especially for public listed companies, financial institutions and joint venture companies due to the respective requirements on the frequency of holding meetings. The principles for holding constituted board meetings from the serving of notice to the voting, apply to ensure that the decisions made are valid and effectual. Most companies hold quarterly meetings to present the quarterly reports and any other matters that require Board's deliberation and discussion.

[3] S. 297 of the CA 2016 provides for members' written resolution. The provision applies only to private companies.

[4] S. 212 of the CA 2016.

With the Coronavirus ("COVID-19") occurring in quarter 1 of year 2020, many companies have found themselves not being able to hold in-person meetings and gradually migrating to virtual meetings. The CA 2016 and most companies' constitutions provide for the holding of virtual meetings. In the past, most public listed companies would be holding members' meetings from the beginning of March onward for those with the financial year ended December 31 but in 2020, most meetings were held back, adjourned, deferred and postponed due to the lockdown situations and uncertainty of the recovery period from COVID-19. During this period, and the pandemic, the regulators like the CCM, Securities Commission Malaysia ("SC") and Bursa Malaysia had stepped in to guide the companies by issuing guidelines, directives and frequently asked questions so that the meetings of members are able to proceed under the new normal. The question is whether these guides were sufficient and timely to address the challenges faced by the companies during the unprecedented crisis.

Annual general meetings under the CA under the CA 2016 are for public companies and these are the meetings of the year where members meet the directors, management and auditors to raise questions on the performance of the companies and businesses of the meeting. Members are keen to understand how the companies are managed and they exercise their rights as owners of these companies which are known as shareholder activism. There have been more shareholder activism activities in recent years and more so with the involvement of Minority Shareholder Watch Group ("MSWG"), institutional shareholders, fund managers and major shareholders in muscling issues toward transparency of information and influencing change in management behaviour.

This chapter attempts to discuss the challenges faced by companies in holding company and board meetings during the COVID-19 pandemic. It will also examine shareholder activism in Malaysia during this testing period.

Board Meetings

Companies hold board meetings to discuss corporate matters and the frequency of holding these meetings would depend on the respective needs of the companies for these meetings. For public companies, board meetings may be held monthly, bi-monthly, quarterly or yearly basis while most private companies may not even hold board meetings at all. Public listed companies will normally hold meetings at least four times a year to approve the quarterly results and audited financial statements prior to releasing the announcements of these financial reports to Bursa Malaysia. Financial institutions which are regulated by Bank Negara Malaysia will hold bi-monthly meetings or more frequently as most matters are discussed and approved at meetings as opposed to passing resolutions by way of circular resolutions. For joint venture companies, due to the composition of the shareholdings, management will table the operations and financial reports to the non-executive directors and representatives of the members, depending on the provisions of the joint-venture agreement, normally on quarterly basis.

Bolts and Nuts of Virtual Meetings

At the onset of the pandemic, fully virtual board meetings were held and for Boards which were familiar with the virtual meetings, joining these meetings was a breeze. However, for the directors who are joining any virtual meetings for the first time, technical assistance was a call away to the company secretary and her assistants. The usual issues encountered are that the meeting link is not working, audio sound is soft or silent, visuals are missing, internet is weak, screen is frozen and screen sharing function is malfunctioning. The company secretary will normally conduct a headcount to ensure the directors have logged in and will contact those directors who have yet to log in, to remind them to join the meetings. For virtual board meetings, and they are normally conducted at the residence due to Movement Control Order ("MCO"), the considerations should be good internet connectivity, microphone and speaker are in working conditions, peace and quiet in a room, and physical or virtual background.

The board meeting dates are normally planned out for the year by the company secretary with the chairman of the Board. This aids in proper planning of board meetings and commits the time of the directors in advance.[5] For companies that prepare quarterly reports, and once the end of the quarter has passed, and the quarterly reports are expected to be ready, the meeting dates are then determined normally at least two weeks after the close of the preceding quarter. The Board would have agreed on the notice period and mode of sending the notice which during current technology age, via email while for some companies that adopt the electronic meeting platform, the directors will receive the notice in the electronic meeting platform together with the meeting papers. The directors are to receive complete and accurate meeting papers, within a reasonable period prior to the meeting.[6]

Statutory Reporting Woes

During the pandemic, even the best laid plans for board meetings do run awry. For the public listed companies, the preparation of the quarterly financial reports was an issue as the offices and factories were closed particularly for those companies which are categorised under the non-essential services and their records were still maintained in hardcopies. The public listed companies that were preparing for the audit of the financial statements hit a snag too as they were unable to provide the hardcopy of the documents to the auditors and conduct physical stock count due to the closure of the business premises during MCO. This had caused most public listed companies to delay issuing the quarterly reports and audited financial statements. During the pandemic with the active and conscious efforts of the regulators like SC, Bursa Malaysia and CCM, the public listed companies and other types of companies were

---

[5] Practice 5.5 of the MCCG.

[6] Practice 1.6 of the MCCG.

given an extension of time via guidelines and directives to issue the reports, financial statements and holding of annual general meetings, where applicable. The extension of time was a relief to many companies as this provided the grace period to finalise the financial reports. The audit during the pandemic required unprecedented action using desktop audit through electronic submission of documents and videoconferencing at the sites to view the stocks for companies that could arrange such an audit.

Keeping up with Technology

The company secretary will clear the notice and agenda of the meeting with the chairman prior to finalising and issuing the notice of meeting to the directors of the company. One of the key roles of the chairman[7] is to set the board agenda and to ensure that the directors receive complete and accurate information in a timely manner. The notice and meeting papers will be given to the directors based on the agreed mode of circulation which may be by email, delivery of hard copies or upload to an electronic meeting platform. In most constitutions or pursuant to Third Schedule of the CA 2016, the notice is given to every director and it includes the date, time and place of the meeting and the matters to be discussed.[8] A meeting of the Board[9] may be held in-person or by means of audio, or audio and visual, communication by which all directors participating constituting a quorum can simultaneously hear each other throughout the meeting. With COVID-19 situation, and the restriction in movement, in-person attendance at board meetings is replaced by virtual participation using the virtual meeting platforms like Microsoft Teams, Zoom, Webex and other acceptable similar platforms of which the directors, management and invitees are able to participate, talk, listen and see each other. The remote participation for a fully virtual board meeting is using a meeting link of the virtual meeting platform provided by the company secretary. She will host the meeting and admit the directors to join the meeting while the presenters are invited to join for specific agenda and leave after their sessions. This is similar to a physical meeting except that it is conducted on an electronic platform.

Meeting Bites for Properly Constituted Meetings

The notice of meeting is given based on the agreed period of notice. If any shorter period of notice is given due to emergency, the irregularity is waived if all directors entitled to receive notice of the meeting attend the meeting without objection to the

[7] Guidance 1.2 of the MCCG.

[8] Clause 4 of Third Schedule of the CA 2016.

[9] Clause 6 of Third Schedule of the CA 2016.

irregularity. The consent may be obtained in writing before the board meeting and recorded in the minutes for good governance.

A quorum[10] for a board meeting shall be fixed by the Board and if not so fixed, the quorum shall be a majority of the number of directors. In the absence of a quorum, no business may be transacted at a board meeting.[11] With the requisite quorum present, the company secretary will inform the chairman for him to call the meeting to order and proceed with the business of the meeting according to the agenda. During the pandemic, board meetings are mainly held virtually. The company secretary will check the names and visuals of the attendees on the virtual meeting platform or conduct a roll call to determine the attendance of the directors and requisite quorum. It is common that during board meetings, the participants may be disconnected and reconnected due to weak internet connectivity. This continued to pose a problem should any important part of the reporting or discussion was missed out due to the disconnection. The company secretary shall keep track of the maintenance of a quorum during the meeting. Subject to the provision of the constitution, the common rule is that a quorum should be present at all times during the meeting.[12] A constitution may provide for a quorum to be present at the time when the meeting proceeds to business only and not throughout the meeting.

The chairman of the board presiding the Board meeting will go through the agenda. For matters in the agenda that are tabled for approval by the Board, the chairman will put these matters to vote by the directors. Every director has one vote[13] while the chairman has a casting vote when there is equality of votes.[14] A resolution tabled at the board meeting is passed[15] when all the directors present at the board meeting have agreed without dissent or if a majority of the votes cast are in favour of the matter. In addition, a director who is present at a board meeting is presumed to have agreed to, and to have voted in favour of, a resolution of the Board[16] unless he expressly dissents from or votes to object against the resolution at the meeting. For any matters which may create any conflict, the director shall declare the fact and the nature, character and extent of the conflict at a meeting of the directors of the company.[17] The company secretary shall record the declaration in the minutes of the meeting.[18] The director concerned shall abstain from any discussion and shall not vote on the matter. He may leave the room so that the discussion can be carried out in his absence. The directors who are eligible to vote will normally vote by show of hands, voting through a virtual platform or verbally. The company secretary will

---

[10] Clause 7 of Third Schedule of the CA 2016.

[11] Clause 8 of Third Schedule of the CA 2016.

[12] Anthony David Lang, *Horsley's Meetings Procedure, Law and Practice* 6th ed. (Australia: Lexis Nexis Butterworth, 2010), 55.

[13] Clause 9 of Third Schedule of the CA 2016.

[14] Clause 10 of Third Schedule of the CA 2016.

[15] Clause 11 of Third Schedule of the CA 2016.

[16] Clause 12 of Third Schedule of the CA 2016.

[17] S. 221(6) of the CA 2016.

[18] S. 221(8) of the CA 2016.

inform the director who has left the meeting to rejoin the meeting after the decision has concluded. Likewise, during a virtual meeting, the director concerned will exit the meeting by logging out and logging in once the company secretary informs him to rejoin the meeting.

The company secretary will take notes of the proceedings of the board meetings and prepare the draft minutes accordingly. The company secretary may also be disconnected from the virtual meeting due to weak internet connectivity. She will need to recheck with the chairman on the missing discussions during her absence to ensure that the key discussions are included in the minutes. The company secretary will mark out the action items that have been deliberated during the board meetings so that these action items are attended by the relevant persons in charge.

General Meetings

Every public company is required to hold an annual general meeting during each calendar year to transact the business of laying of audited financial statements and the reports of the directors and auditors, the election of directors in place of those retiring, the appointment and the fixing of the fee of auditors and any resolution or other business of which notice is given in accordance with this Act or the constitution.[19] In addition, the annual general meeting shall be held within six months of the company's financial year end and not more than 15 months after the last preceding annual general meeting[20] while any other members' meetings are called extraordinary general meetings. The company secretary will work out a plan to convene an annual general meeting as there will be substantial work and time sensitive events involved. For a properly constituted meeting of members, it can be segregated into before meeting, during meeting and after meeting. Before the meeting, the company secretary will issue proper notice to all members with the agenda of the meeting. During the meeting, there should be a chairman of the meeting, requisite quorum present, transact the business as set out in the agenda and voting procedures for passing of proposed resolutions. After the meeting, the company secretary will prepare the minutes of the annual general meeting and attend to the statutory filing with the regulators.

These procedures are found in the CA 2016 and shall be complied with by all companies. Nevertheless, there are companies which have a constitution and the constitution may have prescribed a different regime. This is permissible so long as the constitution prescribed regime does not contravene with the provisions in the CA 2016.[21] For companies whose shares are listed on the stock exchange, they will have to also comply with the Listing Requirements issued by Bursa Malaysia. Parts H

[19] S. 340(1) of the CA 2016.

[20] S. 340(2) of the CA 2016.

[21] S. 32(2) of the CA 2016.

and I of Chap. 7 of the Listing Requirements provide for Meetings, and Voting and Proxies. These provisions will be explained in this chapter.

Pay Notice to the Days

Generally, the notice period varies with the type of company. It is prescribed that the notice period for a private company in calling for a meeting of members shall be 14 days.[22] For a public company, the notice period for calling of an annual general meeting shall be at least 21 days and in other meetings, at least 14 days. However, where there is motion to pass a special resolution, the minimum day of notice is 21 days.[23] In addition, the company's constitution may provide for a longer period.

A private company that holds an annual general meeting, will issue a notice of annual general meeting with at least 14 clear days (or longer period as specified in the constitution) before the meeting while a public company will issue a notice of at least 21 clear days (or longer period as specified in the constitution) before the meeting. For public listed companies, the Listing Requirements provide that 21 days' notice must be given to members too.[24] Nevertheless, the notice of meeting under MCCG is to be issued at least 28 days before the date of the holding of the meeting.[25]

The public listed companies are required to comply with the Listing Requirements to issue its annual report that includes annual audited financial statements together with the auditors' and directors' reports, to the Bursa Malaysia and shareholders within 4 months from the close of the financial year of the listed issuer.[26]

Bringing the CA 2016, MCCG and Listing Requirements together, for a public listed company with a financial year ending December 31, in summary, the annual report is issued by the last business day in April (due to the postal services for those companies that are sending out the hardcopies of annual reports, administrative notes, circulars to shareholders etc.), the notice period will be 28 days (taking the longer period between the CA 2016, Listing Requirements and MCCG) and the last day to hold the annual general meeting will be by June 30 (six months from the financial year end and 15 months from the last annual general meeting). For example, the financial year end was December 31, 2021, the last day to issue the notice and annual report for the annual general meeting will be April 29, 2022 (last business day) and the annual general meeting can be held on or after May 27, 2022 (at least 28 calendar days from date of notice). If the public listed company is unable to provide 28 days' notice period, it must still provide at least 21 days' notice due to the provision of the CA 2016 and Listing Requirements. The public listed company will then need to disclose

---

[22] S. 316(1) of the CA 2016.

[23] S. 292(1) of the CA 2016.

[24] Paragraph 7.15 of Bursa Malaysia Listing Requirements.

[25] Practice 13.1 of the MCCG.

[26] Paragraph 9.23 of Bursa Malaysia Listing Requirements.

in its next Corporate Governance Report that it departed from the practice.[27] The date of the annual general meeting is dependent on the finalisation of the audited financial statements. Bursa Malaysia had since the beginning of the pandemic, issued directives from time to time to assist the public listed companies in meeting their obligations. In this instance, Bursa Malaysia had allowed the holding of annual general meetings and related issues amidst COVID-19 breakout,[28] among others, the deferment of annual general meetings provided the application for extension of time was applied with the CCM and the flexibility to issue the annual report without the notice of the annual general meeting till a later date. Subsequently, when MCO was extended, Bursa Malaysia had issued another directive on the extension of time for submission of quarterly and annual reports,[29] allowing one month extension for issuance of those reports that were due by the prescribed timeline. This was in response to the extended MCO that might have caused operational difficulties and practical challenges to the public listed companies. Bursa Malaysia had proactively been issuing directives from time to time to ease the compliances during the pandemic.[30] The directives have assisted the public listed companies during MCO as seen from the announcements released for the financial reports and notices of annual general meetings that have utilised the extended period.

A notice of a meeting of members of a company shall state the place, date and time of the meeting and the general nature of the business of the meeting.[31] Notice of meeting of members may include the text of any proposed resolution and other information as the directors deem fit.[32] For public listed companies, the notice of any meeting called to consider special business shall be accompanied by a statement[33] at the footnote of the notice regarding the effect of any proposed resolution in respect of such special business. The notice of every general meeting must be advertised in at least one nationally circulated Bahasa Malaysia or English daily newspaper and in writing to each stock exchange upon which the company is listed.[34]

---

[27] Practice 13.1 of the MCCG.

[28] Bursa Malaysia Securities Bhd, "Holding of Annual General Meetings (AGM) and Related Issues Amidst COVID-19 Outbreak," March 17, 2021, accessed December 3, 2021. https://www.bursamalaysia.com/sites/5bb54be15f36ca0af339077a/content_entry5ce3b50239fba2627b2864be/5e70b50a39fba21f3032b53e/files/MainCircular-Covid19-v2.pdf?1584494155.

[29] Bursa Malaysia Securities Bhd, "Extension of Time for Submission of Quarterly and Annual Reports ..," March 26, 2020, accessed December 3, 2021. https://www.bursamalaysia.com/sites/5bb54be15f36ca0af339077a/content_entry5ce3b50239fba2627b2864be/5e7c954039fba20d9b0f2f82/files/MAINCircular26March2020CovidMeasures.pdf?1585222988.

[30] Bursa Malaysia's directives at its website https://www.bursamalaysia.com/regulation/listing_requirements/main_market/directives_clarifications.

[31] S. 317(1) of the CA 2016.

[32] S. 317(2) of the CA 2016.

[33] Paragraphs 7.15 and 8.27(3) of Bursa Malaysia Listing Requirements.

[34] Paragraph 7.15 of Bursa Malaysia Listing Requirements.

Notice Goes Electronic

With the advent of technology, the Act has provided for the electronic manner to give notice[35] and notification to be uploaded to the company's website[36] of which the company shall notify the members of the publication of the notice of the meeting of members on the website by serving the notification in hard copy or electronic form that it is a meeting of members, place, date and time of the meeting, statement to indicate annual general meeting (for public company). The notice of the meeting shall be available on the website of the company from the date of notice till the conclusion of the meeting. For public listed companies, if documents are sent by electronic means,[37] the Listing Requirements require the constitution to allow the use of electronic means, the electronic manner that it is to be used and the contact details of the members will be the last known address provided for the purpose of communication. In addition, if the public listed companies publish the documents on the website, there should be a separate and immediate notification to the members of the publication on the website and the designated website link or address of which a copy of the documents may be downloaded. There must be a proof of electronic delivery for documents sent by electronic mail. It was timely that when the pandemic hit, most of the constitutions of the public listed companies were amended by December 31, 2019[38] and contained the updated clause for the provision of electronic notification.

Though the public listed companies could proceed to issue the annual report by electronic means, they are still required to send the notification to the members.[39] The hardcopy of the notification had to be printed and posted to the members immediately the same day of the uploading of the annual report on the website. However, during the beginning of the pandemic, the printers were closed as only the essential services were allowed to operate. Subsequently when the MCO eased slightly, with the application for extension of time to hold annual general meeting approved by CCM, the audited financial statements finalised, the annual report ready and the notification printed, the public listed companies could proceed to hold their general meetings albeit the continuous changing of the restrictions and the risk of an adjournment, deferment or postponement of meeting due to the COVID-19 cases.

[35] S. 319 of the CA 2016.

[36] S. 320 of the CA 2016.

[37] Paragraph 2.19B of Bursa Malaysia Listing Requirements.

[38] Bursa Malaysia Securities Bhd, "Amendment to Bursa Malaysia Securities Bhd Main Market Listing Requirements Relating to Companies Act 2016 and Others ..," January 29, 2017, accessed December 3, 2021. https://www.bursamalaysia.com/sites/5bb54be15f36ca0af339077a/content_entry5ce3b50239fba2627b2864be/5ce3bf9c5b711a12d04fd89a/files/Circular_to_Main_PLC_29112017_fair.pdf?1570701439.

[39] Paragraph 2.19B(b) of Bursa Malaysia Listing Requirements.

To Attend or Not to Attend

A meeting of members is attended by members and if any member is not able to attend the general meeting but still wish to vote for the proposed resolutions, he may appoint a proxy pursuant to the provision of the constitution or the CA 2016. The CA 2016 allows a member of a company having a share capital to appoint another person or persons to be his proxy or proxies to exercise all or any of his rights to attend, participate, speak and vote at the general meeting of the company.[40] If the member appoints more than one proxy, the proportion of shareholdings to be represented by each proxy has to be specified.[41]

The executed proxy form and the power of attorney or other authority, if any, shall be deposited at the registered office of the company, or any such place in Malaysia as specified in the notice of the general meeting, not less than 48 hours before the time for holding the meeting or adjourned meeting[42] or otherwise, it would be invalid and the vote of the member would not be recognised. Generally, the notice of the general meeting and proxy form will provide the footnote on the rules for appointment of proxy, power attorney or other authority. The appointed proxy or proxies will participate in the general meeting and vote in accordance with the instruction of the member who appointed them unless the authority is terminated by the member by serving the notice of termination before the commencement of the general meeting or an adjourned general meeting.[43]

For a company which is a member of another company, it may consider executing a resolution to appoint a person or persons to be its representative or representatives at any general meeting of the latter company. There is no timeframe to deposit the resolution or form pertaining to the appointment of the corporate representative and it is as good as attending on the day of the general meeting. The submission of a proxy form or corporate representative form could be proceeded electronically and the procedures involved are guided by the administrative note for the meeting. This online facility had assisted the members to continue to lodge the forms safely at home while the companies or appointed share registrars were able to receive these forms without any physical interaction and exposure to the risk of COVID-19.

The pandemic has accelerated the use of technology platforms as an additional means of submitting a proxy or corporate representative form. The administrative note for the virtual meeting is provided to guide the members to register themselves with the appointed share registrar and submit a request to attend the general meeting remotely prior to the meetings to obtain the user identity and access code. This is only possible for members who have access to computers and are tech-savvy or being assisted with the process.

---

[40] S. 334(1) of the CA 2016.

[41] S. 334(2) of the CA 2016.

[42] S. 334(3) of the CA 2016.

[43] S. 338(1) of the CA 2016.

The Chairman who Chairs the Meeting

Every general meeting shall have a chairman of the meeting. Generally, the constitution will determine who shall be the chairman of the general meeting. If there is a chairman of the Board, he shall preside as the chairman of every general meeting and in the absence of the chairman of the Board or if the chairman is not present within 15 minutes after the time of the holding of the general meeting, or he is unwilling to act as the chairman of the general meeting due to his own reason, the members who are present at the general meeting shall elect one of their members to be the chairman of the meeting.[44]

The chairman of the meeting plays an important role in a meeting to ensure that the meeting is properly convened, the conduct of the meeting is observed, the business of the meeting is as stated in the agenda of the meeting, and maintain and preserve order. A detailed procedural script is prepared by the company secretary for the chairman to guide him during the proceeding of the annual general meeting. The chairman and company secretary will read out their respective sections from the prepared procedural script from welcoming the members to tabling of each agenda including the tabling of the audited financial statements and resolutions for voting by members and the declaration of the results of the voting.

The chairman of the meeting[45] is recommended to ensure that there should be a meaningful engagement during the meeting of members between the Board, senior management and members. The engagement is recommended to be interactive for which is to include robust discussion on the company's financial and non-financial performance which include the company's long-term strategies. Members are also provided with sufficient opportunity to pose questions during the general meeting and all the questions raised should receive a meaningful response from the chairman, Board and management. For virtual meetings of members, the members are allowed to submit their questions to the company before the day of the meeting of members. Minority Shareholder Watch Group ("MSWG") will submit questions to selected public listed companies on financial and non-financial matters with a request that the letter and the reply be read out at the meeting of members. The questions that are received through an email or technology platform prior to the annual general meeting will be dealt with at the beginning of the question and answer session leaving the live questions submitted via text messaging last. The Board and the chairman should ensure that the conduct of a virtual general meeting supports meaningful engagement between the Board, senior management and shareholders.[46] The shareholders' experience of a virtual meeting should be considered while a one-way monologue by the Board should be avoided.

[44] S. 329 of the CA 2016.

[45] Practice 13.4 of the MCCG.

[46] Guidance 13.5 of the MCCG.

The New Normal for Meetings

Virtual general meeting was a new normal during the pandemic. At the onset of the pandemic, even if there were willing public listed companies that braved the norm to hold virtual meetings, there were limited remote participation and voting facilitators available initially. The apprehension of the reliability of using a technology platform was another cause of concern to the chairman and Board members. With no end in sight of the pandemic, public listed companies slowly switched to virtual general meetings and conducted the meetings based on the guidance note issued by SC on the conduct of general meetings for listed issuers.[47] The notices of meetings for virtual meetings announced to Bursa Malaysia from April 2020 since then had increased. A dry run is held and attended by the chairman, directors, key management and company secretary to participate and familiarise themselves with the process of a virtual general meeting. The chairman would be looking into the camera, speaking from the procedural script and watching himself on the screen. He would not be able to see any remote participants of the general meetings during the live streaming. Other than the adoption of the technology platform, the role of the chairman at a virtual general meeting remained the same from the calling of the meeting to order, replying to questions, declaring the results and closing the meeting.

A quorum is required to be present for a meeting of members at the time when the meeting proceeds to business.[48] The requisite quorum is provided in the constitution of the company or the CA 2016 for the companies that do not adopt any constitutions. The company secretary will normally check and inform the chairman that the requisite quorum is present, the chairman of the meeting will call the meeting to order and proceed with the business of the meeting. For any companies that have a single member,[49] the single member shall constitute the quorum while for any other case, there shall be two members present in person or by proxy shall be considered to be the quorum subject to provision of the constitution which may require a higher number of members to form the quorum for a meeting.

With the availability of technology assisted devices for holding of virtual meeting, the members may participate in a meeting of members at more than one venue using technology,[50] for example, video conference, web-based communication, electronic or such other communication facilities or technologies available which would permit all members participating in the meeting of members to communicate and engage with each other simultaneously and instantaneously and to vote at such meetings. The constitution of a company will also provide that any meeting convened in using the communication facilities and attended by members shall be treated as presence in person and be counted as part of the quorum requirement notwithstanding that the

---

[47] "Securities Commission Issues Guidance on Virtual Meetings for Listed Issuers," *Securities Commission Malaysia*, April 18, 2021, accessed December 3, 2021. https://www.sc.com.my/resources/media/media-release/sc-issues-guidance-on-virtual-meetings-for-listed-issuers.

[48] S. 328(4) of the CA 2016.

[49] S. 328 of the CA 2016.

[50] S. 327 of the CA 2016.

person is not present physically at the venue of meeting and participating virtually and remotely.

Due to the COVID-19, SC had issued guidance notes and frequently asked questions for public listed companies that the quorum of a virtual meeting of members is determined by the number of members logged-in at the start of the meeting.[51] In addition, for a hybrid meeting of members, the quorum is determined by the number of physical presence of members, proxies, attorneys and corporate representatives at the meeting and members who logged-in at the start of the meeting. The public listed companies are to ensure that there is a proper mechanism to allow the members and proxies to participate at the meeting of members. The guidance note also provides the need for a proper audit trail for the purpose of recording of individual members or proxies participation at the meeting of members. With the guidance note issued by SC, the public listed companies continue to be guided to hold their meetings of members during each phase of the pandemic from full to partial lockdown as the number of COVID-19 cases changes over the period to meet the statutory obligations under the CA 2016. For public listed companies, the choice of physical meeting during the pandemic remained uncertain for the window for recovery phase was dependent on the bi-weekly announcement by the authorities on the state of MCO while the notice of meetings is normally planned for 28 days. The public listed companies are aware that there is still a chance that the physical meeting will be switched to a virtual meeting as seen from the amended notice of the meeting in the announcements released to Bursa Malaysia unless the location of the physical meeting is held in a green zone area. The companies were also required to follow the standard operating procedure ("SOP") issued by Majlis Keselamatan Negara ("MKN") to hold their meetings. MKN had imposed the age restriction to enter public premises that affected the presence of the chairman and directors who were over the age of 60 years at the broadcast venue of the meeting. In the absence of the chairman of the Board, subject to the constitution, the chairman of the meeting was appointed among the directors to preside at the annual general meeting.

Polling Day

A public listed company must ensure that any resolution set out in the notice of any general meeting, or in any notice of resolution which may properly be moved and is intended to be moved at any general meeting, is voted by poll.[52] The listed company is required to appoint at least one scrutineer to validate the votes cast at the general meeting.[53] The appointed scrutineer must not be interested in the proposed resolution

[51] Securities Commission Malaysia, "Guidance Note and Frequently Asked Questions on the Conduct of General Meetings for Listed Issuers," April 18, 2021, accessed December 3, 2021. https://www.sc.com.my/api/documentms/download.ashx?id=c5fbbbcd-3ab0-40ce-a22b-e8bb1d1fe0a8.

[52] Paragraph 8.29A(1) of Bursa Malaysia Listing Requirements.

[53] Paragraph 8.29A(2) of Bursa Malaysia Listing Requirements.

which is tabled for voting at the meeting of members and if he is, must refrain from acting as a scrutineer for that resolution.

SC has included the guidance note and frequently asked question on online voting that the members of public listed companies are allowed to cast their votes during the proceeding of the meeting of members.[54] The same frequently asked question also addressed the issue where the members who have no access to the internet to cast their votes online by appointing the chairman of the meeting to vote on behalf of the members.

The business of an annual general meeting of a public company shall include the laying of the audited financial statements and the reports of the directors and auditors, the election of directors in place of those retiring, the appointment and the fixing of the fee of auditors and any resolution or other business of which notice is given in accordance with the CA 2016 or the company's constitution.[55] These are considered as the ordinary business of the public company and any other business will be termed as special business for example, payment of dividend, directors fees and benefits, mandate for share buyback and others.

An ordinary resolution of the members is passed by a simple majority of more than half by the members who are eligible to vote and by proxies at the meeting of members.[56] On a poll, the ordinary resolution is passed at a meeting of members if it is passed by eligible members who represent more than half of the total voting rights of the members and proxies who are present and voting.[57] A special resolution of members is passed when the notice convening the meeting of members is served not less than 21 days with text clearly stating that it is a special resolution and a majority of not less than 75% of the members and proxies passed the resolution at the meeting of members.[58]

The CA 2016 provides for certain resolutions to be notified to CCM within a stipulated time frame from the date of passing the resolution at a meeting of members or written circular resolution of members. The company secretary will lodge such documents with CCM for example change of name of the company,[59] allotment of shares,[60] retirement of directors[61] and others. During the early period of MCO, CCM

---

[54] Securities Commission Malaysia, "Guidance Note and Frequently Asked Questions on the Conduct of General Meetings for Listed Issuers," April 18, 2021, accessed December 3, 2021. https://www.sc.com.my/api/documentms/download.ashx?id=c5fbbbcd-3ab0-40ce-a22b-e8bb1d1fe0a8.

[55] S. 340(1) of the CA 2016.

[56] S. 291(1) of the CA 2016.

[57] S. 291(3) of the CA 2016.

[58] S. 292(1) of the CA 2016.

[59] S. 28 of the CA 2016.

[60] S. 77 of the CA 2016.

[61] S. 58 of the CA 2016.

was closed[62] and online submission could proceed but over the counter lodgement of documents was not permitted. CCM had provided a moratorium period of 30 days from the end of the MCO to lodge the documents.[63]

Adjournment of Meeting

There are times when annual general meetings and meetings of members are not able to proceed to transact the business of the meeting due to lack of the requisite quorum or any event that may not allow the meeting to proceed of which case, such meeting will be adjourned later or to another day, date and time. In the event that a meeting of members is adjourned for 30 days or more,[64] the company will have to issue a notice of adjournment of the meeting and it shall be given according to the same manner as the original meeting. In addition, if within the appointed time to convene the meeting of members and the quorum is not present, the meeting will be dissolved if the meeting was requisitioned by the members or in any other case, the meeting shall stand adjourned to the same day in the following week at the same time and venue, or to such other day, time and venue as the directors may direct.[65] For any resolution which is passed at an adjourned meeting of members of a company, it shall be considered as having been passed on the date that it was in fact passed.[66]

The COVID-19 pandemic hit Malaysia in early 2020, and MCO was implemented throughout Malaysia in mid-March. Many public listed companies were affected by the untimely MCO for these companies were accustomed to convene their annual general meetings within three to six months after the financial year end. Some of the public listed companies had issued the notices of meetings of members before the announcement of MCO. The challenge faced by the companies was how they should proceed without breaching the timeline imposed by the CA 2016 and Listing

[62] "Penutupan Sementara Operasi SSM di Seluruh Negara," *Companies Commission of Malaysia,* March 17, 2020, accessed December 3, 2021. https://www.ssm.com.my/Lists/Press%20Release/DispForm.aspx?ID=172&Source=https%3A%2F%2Fwww%2Essm%2Ecom%2Emy%2FPages%2FPublication%2FPress%5FRelease%2FPress%2DRelease%2Easpx%3FPaged%3DTRUE%26p%5FID%3D181%26PageFirstRow%3D61%26%26View%3D%7BB0809F59%2DAD87%2D4B34%2D9117%2D1B0F28F9AF30%7D&ContentTypeId=0x010098952881AC48D34C9D9967E0232CDB0B.

[63] "SSM Umumkan Tujuh Inisiatif Untuk Kurangkan Beban Sektor Korporat Semasa Perintah Kawalan Pergerakan," *Companies Commission of Malaysia*, April 10, 2020, accessed December 3, 2021. https://www.ssm.com.my/Lists/Press%20Release/DispForm.aspx?ID=179&Source=https%3A%2F%2Fwww%2Essm%2Ecom%2Emy%2FPages%2FPublication%2FPress%5FRelease%2FPress%2DRelease%2Easpx%3FPaged%3DTRUE%26p%5FID%3D181%26PageFirstRow%3D61%26%26View%3D%7BB0809F59%2DAD87%2D4B34%2D9117%2D1B0F28F9AF30%7D&ContentTypeId=0x010098952881AC48D34C9D9967E0232CDB0B.

[64] S. 318 of the CA 2016.

[65] S. 328(5) of the CA 2016.

[66] S. 315 of the CA 2016.

Requirements, as well as the SOPs imposed to curb the spread of COVID-19. Continuing with the meeting as planned and then adjourning it, is not an option due to the uncertainty of the duration of the pandemic and the restriction of gathering of people and travel.

Another option is to postpone or defer the meeting, but neither the CA 2016 nor the Listing Requirements provide for it. Thus, reference has to be made to the company's constitution which may contain provisions on how the meetings are cancelled and postponed by setting out the procedures involved. Companies whose constitution did not provide for it were left in a bind. These companies have to wait out the MCO period and continue to monitor the timeline of the extension of time granted by CCM and Bursa Malaysia.

Virtual Meetings

It is noteworthy that both CCM and SC have leveraged on the provisions in the CA 2016 on virtual meetings and issued guidelines pertaining thereto. This has brought relief to the public listed companies and more annual general meetings were held virtually and also for those meetings that were adjourned, postponed or deferred earlier. Unfortunately, Bursa Malaysia was not as proactive even though it possessed a solution under paragraph 7.36 which provides as follows:

> (4) If the Listing Requirements require this constitution to contain a provision and it does not contain such a provision, this constitution is deemed to contain that provision.
>
> (5) If the Listing Requirements require this constitution not to contain a provision and it contains such a provision, this constitution is deemed not to contain that provision.
>
> (6) If any provision of this constitution is or becomes inconsistent with the Listing Requirements, this constitution is deemed not to contain that provision to the extent of the inconsistency.

Bursa Malaysia could have taken advantage of the effect of paragraph 7.36(4) and amended its Listing Requirements to provide for the postponement of meetings. By virtue of paragaph 7.36(4), such provision would become a deeming provision and included in the listed company's constitution.

With the lingering pandemic and increase of vaccination rate, and the situation normalises, it is expected that the public listed companies may consider convening their annual general meetings either fully physical, virtual or hybrid. The choice of holding the meeting of members will depend on the situation and during the pandemic, the meetings are held virtually due to safety reasons. When the situation improves, the meetings may revert to physical meetings or continue with virtual meetings or even hybrid meetings. Based on the survey conducted by SC on virtual meetings,[67] the key findings were that 17 out of 29 companies responded that they will continue to offer the option for virtual meetings in the future and several listed companies highlighted the substantial cost-saving from conducting a virtual meeting. There are risks involved for virtual meetings particularly a technical glitch that required an adjournment of the meeting as observed in Malayan Banking Bhd from April 15, 2021 to May 6, 2021.[68]

It is recommended that public listed companies should leverage on technology at the meeting of members for voting[69] which include voting in absentia and remote members' participation at such meetings too. In addition, there should be necessary steps taken to ensure good cyber hygiene practices which include data privacy and security to prevent cyber threats. During the pandemic, SC has guided the public listed companies on the holding of the meeting of members virtually. The public listed companies should consider reviewing their constitutions to ensure that once the pandemic is over, and the guidance by SC if withdrawn, they are still able to proceed to convene their meetings of members in accordance with the provisions in their constitutions for any change in the CA 2016 and/or Listing Requirements is still unknown. This is even more urgent for public listed companies that need to amend their existing constitutions that provide only physical general meetings to include virtual general meetings.

Minutes of meetings are important as they are records of the formal proceeding of the decisions made by the members of the company. For public listed companies, the minutes of the meeting of members will be uploaded to the website within 30 business days.[70]

Shareholder Activism

In 2000, the MSWG was formed as an initiative of the government with the objective to protect the interests of minority shareholders through shareholder activism.[71] It is an avenue to foster good governance amongst public listed companies with the objective of raising shareholder value over time and holding the directors of the companies accountable. MSWG advises on voting at general meetings of public listed companies and is seen as the first step towards encouraging shareholder activism without recourse to the courts. Since its establishment, MSWG has been actively participating at meetings of members of public listed companies and posing questions

[67] "Virtual General Meetings - Malaysia's Experience" in the *Securities Commission of Malaysia Annual Report 2020*, accessed December 3, 2021. https://www.sc.com.my/api/documentms/download.ashx?id=963a5bb2-fd8a-48d6-b3ea-60dcdff5fdc1.

[68] "General Meetings: Notice of Meetings," *Bursa Malaysia Securities Bhd*, April 21, 2021, accessed December 3, 2021. https://www.bursamalaysia.com/market_information/announcements/company_announcement/announcement_details?ann_id=3150192.

[69] Practice 13.3 of the MCCG.

[70] Practice 13.5 of the MCCG.

[71] Refer to MSWG's website https://www.mswg.org.my/who-we-are.

on operations, financial performance and corporate governance as well as providing its opinion on corporate governance matters. It also educates the retail investors in making informed decisions on investments and understanding the risks involved. MSWG allows the registration of investors to access its website for information of the general meetings of the public listed companies and the queries posed by MSWG to these companies.

The landscape of the listed companies has shifted with members in recent years being unhappy with the Board having actively requisitioned to remove directors and replacing them with new directors (for example NWP Holdings Bhd[72]) and in other instances, saying "No" to paying fees and benefits to the directors (for example FGV Holdings Bhd[73]). The votes and proxy fights to achieve the winning votes are dependent on the passing of the proposed resolutions which are ordinary resolutions and require a majority of the votes of those present and voting. Retail members have also been active by participating in meetings and raising questions during the meetings as seen at the adjourned annual general meeting of Malayan Banking Bhd in year 2021 which took about six hours[74] of which the chairman and the Board dealt with the questions posed by the members. With the requirement for public listed companies to publish the key pertinent questions and answers on the websites and the recent MCCG practice of publishing the minutes of the general meetings, these documents are now transparent and readily accessible by the members, analysts, investors and public. MSWG had issued a media release on the appointment of independent moderators at virtual meetings[75] for the purpose of improving and enhancing transparency of the question and answer sessions as questions may not be addressed by the public listed companies.

---

[72] "General Meetings: Notice of Meeting," *Bursa Malaysia Securities Bhd*, May 24, 2021. accessed December 3, 2021. https://www.bursamalaysia.com/market_information/announcements/company_announcement/announcement_details?ann_id=3159755.

[73] "General Meetings: Outcome of Meeting," *Bursa Malaysia Securities Bhd*, June 25, 2019, accessed December 3, 2021. https://www.bursamalaysia.com/market_information/announcements/company_announcement?keyword=&cat=GM%2CMECO&sub_type=&company=5222&mkt=&alph=&sec=&subsec=&dt_ht=&dt_lt.

[74] "Minutes of the 61st Adjourned Annual General Meeting," *Malayan Banking Bhd*, May 3, 2021, accessed December 3, 2021. https://www.maybank.com/iwov-resources/corporate_new/document/my/en/pdf/agm-egm/2020/Minutes-of-AGM-2021.pdf.

[75] "MSWG Urges PLCs to Appoint Independent Moderators at Virtual General Meetings," *Minority Shareholder Watch Group*, June 18, 2020, accessed December 3, 2021. https://www.mswg.org.my/sites/default/files/Media%20Release%20-%20Time%20to%20appoint%20independent%20moderators%20at%20virtual%20general%20meetings.pdf.

Malaysian Code for Institutional Investors

In 2014, the Malaysian Code for Institutional Investors was launched jointly by the Securities Commission Malaysia and MSWG.[76] This code was developed as one of the recommendations of the Corporate Governance Blueprint 2011 with the objective to strengthen the accountability of institutional investors and as these institutional investors have substantial shareholdings in the investee companies, their presence can influence good corporate governance practices in delivering long term sustainability for the shareholders. This code is a voluntary code setting out the broad principles of effective stewardship by institutional investors. There are six principles of the code and one of them being the publication of a voting policy. In line with this policy, the institutional investors namely, Kumpulan Wang Simpanan Pekerja, Perbadanan Nasional Berhad and others would clearly indicate in their voting policy on certain matters for example the tenure of the independent non-executive director, the payment of fees and benefits to the directors, general mandate for allotment of shares, allotment of shares to the directors and others. Their roles are important in the corporate governance ecosystem when most of the public listed companies are dominated by the major shareholders that control the voting rights and having these institutional investors which are mostly substantial shareholders not only augur well for these companies with their presence but also instill good corporate governance practices.

Conclusion

The pandemic tested the companies and the regulators when movement was restricted and technology platforms were the means to access to everyone from home while meeting the legal obligations. Meetings are important as they provide the communication platform for the members of the Board or company to discuss matters prior to passing the resolutions to approve such matters. With the availability of technology for meetings to be conducted online and the participants to log in from anywhere, attendance of meetings has become better for as long as a person is able to access the internet. The companies have accelerated the use of technology to hold meetings particularly during the pandemic to adapt to the new normal. Virtual meetings are without doubt not flawless as the technology platform will encounter technical glitch. Companies would need to be prepared for a technical glitch with supplemental procedural script for the chairman and a holding statement for announcement to Bursa Malaysia. Minutes of the meetings should provide the discussions, dissenting views and decisions of the matters and these are kept at the registered office. There are formal procedures that the companies must comply strictly with the CA 2016, constitution and Listing Requirements (for public listed companies) in holding any

---

[76] Institutional Investors Council Malaysia, *Malaysian Code for Institutional Investors*, June 27, 2014, accessed December 3, 2021. http://www.iicm.org.my/malaysian-code-for-institutional-investors/.

meetings. In recent years, the shareholders have been active in their investee companies and corporate tussles have surfaced with intense actions during the general meetings. The Boards are beginning to be aware that keeping their shareholders happy goes beyond paying dividends and becoming more transparent about their own doing or the continuous enhancement of the MCCG and Listing Requirements particularly for the public listed companies.

References

1. "About Us." *Minority Shareholder Watch Group.* Accessed December 3, 2021. www.mswg.org.my/who-we-are
2. Bursa Malaysia. "Amendment to Bursa Malaysia Securities Bhd Main Market Listing Requirements Relating to the Companies Act 2016 and Others..." Accessed December 3, 2021. www.bursamalaysia.com/sites/5bb54be15f36ca0af339077a/content_entry5ce3b50239fba2627b2864be/5ce3bf9c5b711a12d04fd89a/files/Circular_to_Main_PLC_29112017_fair.pdf?1570701439
3. Bursa Malaysia. *Corporate Governance Guide 4th ed.* Accessed December 3, 2021. https://bursa-malaysia.s3.amazoaws.com/Binder-Bursa-CG-Guide.pdf.
4. Bursa Malaysia. "Extension of Time for Submission of Quarterly and Annual Reports ..." March 26, 2020. Accessed December 3, 2021.https://www.bursamalaysia.com/sites/5bb54be15f36ca0af339077a/content_entry5ce3b50239fba2627b2864be/5e7c954039fba20d9b0f2f82/files/MAINCircular26March2020CovidMeasures.pdf?1585222988
5. Bursa Malaysia. "Holding of Annual General Meetings (AGMs) and Related Issues Amidst COVID-19 Outbreak." March 17, 2020. https://www.bursamalaysia.com/sites/5bb54be15f36ca0af339077a/content_entry5ce3b50239fba2627b2864be/5e70b50a39fba21f3032b53e/files/MainCircular-Covid19-v2.pdf?1584494155.
6. "General Meetings: Notice of Meeting Malayan Banking Berhad." *Bursa Malaysia*, April 21, 2021. Accessed December 3, 2021.www.bursamalaysia.com/market_information/announcements/company_announcement/announcement_details?ann_id=3150192
7. "General Meetings: Notice of Meeting NWP Holdings Berhad." *Bursa Malaysia*, May 24, 2021. Accessed December 3, 2021.www.bursamalaysia.com/market_information/announcements/company_announcement/announcement_details?ann_id=3159755
8. Institutional Investors Council Malaysia. *Malaysian Code for Institutional Investors.* Accessed December 3, 2021. www.iicm.org.my/malaysian-code-for-institutional-investors/
9. Lang, Anthony David. *Horsley's Meetings Procedure, Law and Practice* 6th ed. Australia: Lexis Nexis Butterworth, 2010.
10. "Minutes of the 61st Adjourned Annual General Meeting." *Malayan Banking Berhad*, May 3, 2021. Accessed December 3, 2021. www.maybank.com/iwov-resources/corporate_new/document/my/en/pdf/agm-egm/2020/Minutes-of-AGM-2021.pdf
11. "MSWG Urges PLCs to Appoint Independent Moderators at Virtual General Meetings." *Minority Shareholder Watch Group*, June 18, 2020. Accessed December 3, 2021.www.mswg.org.my/sites/default/files/Media%20Release%20-20Time%20to%20appoint%20independent%20moderators%20at%20virtual%20general%20meetings.pdf
12. "Penutupan Sementara Operasi SSM Di Seluruh Negara." *Companies Commission of Malaysia.* March 17, 2020. Accessed December 3, 2021. www.ssm.com.my/Lists/Press%20Release/DispForm.aspx?ID=172&Source=https%3A%2F%2Fwww%2Essm%2Ecom%2Emy%2FPages%2FPublication%2FPress%5FRelease%2FPress%2DRelease%2Easpx%3FPaged%3DTRUE%26p%5FID%3D181%26PageFirstRow%3D61%26%26View%3D%7BB0809F59%2DAD87%2D4B34%2D9117%2D1B0F28F9AF30%7D&ContentTypeId=0x010098952881AC48D34C9D9967E0232CDB0B

13. Securities Commission Malaysia. *Corporate Governance Monitor 2021*. Accessed December 3, 2021. https://sc.com.my/api/documentms/download.ashx?id=aa1a0385-f2fe-473e-8499-5876a1ad85ea.
14. Securities Commission Malaysia. *Malaysian Code on Corporate Governance 2021*. Accessed December 3, 2021. https://www.sc.com.my/api/documentms/download.ashx?id=239e5ea1-a258-4db8-a9e2-41c215bdb776.
15. "Securities Commission Issues Guidance on Virtual Meetings for Listed Issuers." *Securities Commission Malaysia*, April 18.2020. Accessed December 3, 2021. www.sc.com.my/resources/media/media-release/sc-issues-guidance-on-virtual-meetings-for-listed-issuers
16. Securities Commission Malaysia. "Guidance Note and Frequently Asked Questions on the Conduct of General Meetings for Listed Issuers." April 18, 2020. Accessed December 3, 2021.www.sc.com.my/api/documentms/download.ashx?id=c5fbbbcd-3ab0-40ce-a22b-e8bb1d1fe0a8
17. "SSM Umumkan Tujuh Inisiatif Untuk Kurangkan Beban Sektor Korporat Semasa Perintah Kawalan Pergerakan." *Companies Commission of Malaysia*. April 10, 2020. Accessed December 3, 2021. www.ssm.com.my/Lists/Press%20Release/DispForm.aspx?ID=179&Source=https%3A%2F%2Fwww%2Essm%2Ecom%2Emy%2FPages%2FPublication%2FPress%5FRelease%2FPress%2DRelease%2Easpx%3FPaged%3DTRUE%26p%5FID%3D181%26PageFirstRow%3D61%26%26View%3D%7BB0809F59%2DAD87%2D4B34%2D9117%2D1B0F28F9AF30%7D&ContentTypeId=0x010098952881AC48D34C9D9967E0232CDB0B
18. "Virtual General Meetings - Malaysia's Experience." In *Securities Commission of Malaysia Annual Report 2020*. Accessed December 3, 2021. www.sc.com.my/api/documentms/download.ashx?id=963a5bb2-fd8a-48d6-b3ea-60dcdff5fdc1

Chapter 6
Compliance with Statutory Requirements During the COVID-19 Pandemic

Li Chen Mah and Wai Meng Chan

Abstract The Companies Act 2016 ("CA 2016") requires companies to lodge certain documents with the Companies Commission of Malaysia ("CCM"). Failure to meet the respective prescribed deadlines will subject the company to a penalty. Further, companies may have to call for meetings of board of directors or members to deliberate and decide on matters. For public companies, they are required to hold their annual general meeting once in every calendar year. When COVID-19 arrived on the shores of Malaysia, lockdowns were declared to curb the spread of the virus. One pertinent issue is how did the companies fare in meeting these statutory requirements. The CA 2016 has provisions on the use of technology to facilitate online meetings and communication, however companies have to ensure that their constitutions do not impede the application of those provisions. In addition, the regulatory bodies issued directives and provided guidelines to companies on compliance with some of the statutory requirements. Moratoriums and extensions of time were granted. There are also plans to amend the CA 2016 to address some of the weaknesses revealed by the pandemic such as the CCM may extend the time for lodgement of documents as well as to any action required by the Act, without any application from the company on certain circumstances which is just and in the interest of the public.

Introduction

In 2003, the Companies Commission of Malaysia ("CCM") established the Corporate Law Reform Committee ("CLRC"), which was tasked to carry out an extensive review of the company law framework in Malaysia. The then Companies Act was enacted in 1965 ("CA 1965"). Though it was amended more than 30 times during its lifespan of more than 50 years, many of its provisions were archaic and did not meet

L. C. Mah (✉)
Secretaries Inc Sdn Bhd, Kuala Lumpur, Malaysia
e-mail: lichenmah711@gmail.com

W. M. Chan
University of Malaya, Kuala Lumpur, Malaysia

L. Krishnan and W. M. Chan (eds.), *The Impact of COVID-19 on Corporations and Corporate Law in Malaysia*, https://doi.org/10.1007/978-981-19-5519-8_6

the needs of the business environment. Thus, the CLRC's mission was to modernise the company law framework and in doing so, it was to take into account, among others, the advances made in information and communication technology ("ICT").[1] The culmination of the CLRC is the Companies Act 2016 ("CA 2016"), which came into force on January 31, 2017.

Three years later, COVID-19 arrived on the shores of Malaysia, and created an upheaval in the lives of her people and business community. Lockdown was imposed in March 2020. Social distancing was the call of the day, resulting in no gathering of people. As no physical meetings were allowed, virtual meetings came to the fore. During this time, ICT played a vital role in communication and was heavily relied upon to disseminate and provide access to information.

The CA 2016 requires companies to lodge certain documents with the CCM. Failure to meet the respective prescribed deadlines will subject the company to a penalty. Further, companies may have to call for meetings of board of directors or members to deliberate and decide on matters. For public companies, they are required to hold their annual general meeting once in every calendar year.

Despite the lockdown, the clock continued to tick and companies had to comply with the deadlines imposed by the CA 2016. Could the companies meet these statutory requirements? In Malaysia, companies are regulated mainly by three bodies, namely the CCM, the Securities Commission Malaysia ("SC") and if the company's shares are listed on the stock exchange, Bursa Malaysia Securities Bhd ("Bursa Malaysia"). Did these regulators facilitate the compliance of these statutory requirements?

It is coming to almost two years at the time of writing since the COVID-19 pandemic first hit Malaysia, and it is timely to undertake a study on the above issues raised. We shall first examine the law and procedure pertaining to the lodgement of documents with the CCM and company meetings. This will be followed by a walkthrough of two annual events which are crucial to a company, namely the filing of Annual Return, and the preparation and filing of financial statements with the CCM. These events are chosen, as they would comprehensively cover the aspects of two statutory requirements imposed by the CA 2016, namely the lodging of documents and the conduct of meetings.

Lodgement of Documents With CCM

The traditional way to lodge documents with the CCM is by way of submitting the hardcopy to the CCM office. The CCM would then scan the documents and make them available to the public. With the advent of ICT, the Companies Act 1965 was amended in 1998 and 2007 to, among others, recognise electronic lodgement of

[1] See "Scope of the CLRC," Companies Commission of Malaysia. https://www.ssm.com.my/Pages/Publication/CLRC/Scope.aspx.

documents with the CCM. Currently, the provision pertaining to electronic lodgement of documents is found in S. 604 of the CA 2016.

Concurrently with the coming into force of the CA 2016 on January 31, 2017, the CCM issued Practice Directive 1/2017 on "Documents under the Companies Act 2016, the Lodgement Requirements and Related Matters" ("PD 1/2017"). The PD 1/2017 identifies the documents which are required to be lodged electronically using the MyCoID 2016 portal and those over the counter at the CCM office. They are listed in Schedules A and B respectively.[2] According to paragraph 5 of the PD 1/2017, all other lodgements must be made at the CCM office. This gives rise to issues which were flagged out when lockdown was implemented to fight the COVID-19 pandemic.

There are many documents required to be lodged with the CCM. Some are to update the records, for example, notification of change in the company's registered office,[3] notification of change in the Register of Director, Manager and Secretary,[4] and return on allotment of shares.[5] However, there are some instances where the lodgement is a prerequisite to another matter. For example, in the context of a company secretary, S. 237(2) of the CA 2016 allows the company secretary to resign if he cannot communicate with all directors of the company at their respective last known residential addresses. The secretary is to give a notice to the CCM, and he shall then cease to be the secretary of the company on the expiry of 30 days from the lodgement of the notice.[6] The notice is listed in Schedule B and has to be given over the counter.

Another form of concern is the "Statement of Particulars to be Lodged with Charge". According to S. 352, a charge created by a company is required to be lodged with the CCM within 30 days by the company or any person interested. The failure to do so brings about severe consequences, i.e. the charge is void against the company's liquidator and creditors,[7] and the money secured shall immediately become payable.[8] Thus, the chargee is a person interested, and it is the norm that the chargee will handle the lodgement of the "Statement of Particulars to be Lodged with Charge" with the CCM. Only after the document is lodged, would the chargee release the loan secured by the charge.

[2] Currently, only six documents are required to be lodged using the electronic means, namely:

- Application for registration;
- Application for availability of names and reservation;
- Lodgement of constitution (for the incorporation of new companies);
- Notification of change in the Register of Members;
- Return on allotment of shares; and
- Notification of appointment of first secretary.

[3] S. 46 of the CA 2016.

[4] S. 58 of the CA 2016.

[5] S. 78 of the CA 2016.

[6] S. 237(3)(b) of the CA 2016.

[7] S. 352(2) of the CA 2016.

[8] S. 352(3) of the CA 2016.

At the initial stage of the MCO, the CCM offices were closed and no registration over the counter was allowed. This resulted in delay in the drawdown of loans. Further, after the lapse of the 30-day period, the Statement could not be registered unless with a court order for extension of time. In this connection, on October 2, 2020, the CCM issued "Guidelines for Application to Extend Time for Registration of Charge, Rectification and/or Amendment of Information of Charge (including Cancellation of Charge) under S. 361 of the Companies Act 2016". It provided guidance on the filing of an application to the court for extension of time, even provided the template for the application.

We have seen in Chap. 2 of the risk of committing wrongful or fraudulent trading if debts are being contracted at a time when the company is facing insolvency.[9] Directors may want to avoid liability and take steps to wind up the company by making a Statutory Declaration of the company's inability to continue business[10] and calling for members and creditors meetings. Section 441(1)(a) provides that the voluntary winding up of the company will commence after the Statutory Declaration is lodged with the CCM, and thereupon the directors will appoint an interim liquidator.[11] This document is not listed in Schedule A for lodgement via the MyCoID 2016 online platform, and thus has to be lodged over the counter at the CCM office.

Compared to the over the counter services which are available only during office hours, the services on the MyCoID 2016 online platform are available 24/7. Payment can also be made online. Though it is indicated that the submissions will only be processed during office hours, practitioners have received emails from the CCM on the approval of filings via MyCoID 2016, in particular the return on allotment of shares, during weekends.

Irrespective of whether the lodgement is to be done electronically or over the counter, it must be done within the time stipulated in the CA 2016. If the Act does not state the deadline, S. 609(1) provides that the document is then required to be lodged within 30 days from the time the requirement of lodgement arises. Late lodgement penalty will be imposed on any lodgement exceeding the deadline stipulated in the CA 2016. Nevertheless, paragraph 17 of PD 1/2017 provides an administrative grace period of seven days, for which no late lodgement penalty is imposed for any lodgement within those seven days after the due date.

Application for Extension of Time

Despite the blanket administrative grace period of seven days given for the lodgement of documents with the CCM, there are occasions when a company is unable to meet even the extended deadline. The company will then be required to apply to

[9] S. 539(3) and 540 of the CA 2016.

[10] S. 440(1) of the CA 2016.

[11] S. 440(1) of the CA 2016. One pre-requisite for a voluntary winding up is members resolution. See S. 439(1).

the CCM for extension of time. Section 609(2) empowers the CCM to extend the deadline subject to terms and conditions as he deems fit. On July 26, 2018, the CCM issued Practice Note No 3/2018 on "Clarification on Application for Extension of Time Under the Companies Act 2016" ("PN 3/2018"). Paragraph 7 provides that lodgement of documents within the approved extended deadline is deemed to be lodgement within the prescribed period. It will thus not attract any late lodgement penalty. Nevertheless, there is a fee of RM100 charged for an application to the CCM for extension of time.[12]

The PN 3/2018 also prescribes the deadline for the application for extension of time.

PN 3/2018 specifically mentions the lodgement of audited financial statements and reports ("AFS") by a public company. We will see below that a public company is required to hold its annual general meeting ("AGM") once every calendar year within a prescribed timeframe. One of the agenda of the AGM is the tabling of the company's AFS. Section 259(1)(b) requires a public company to lodge the AFS with the CCM within 30 days from its AGM. It follows that if the company delays its AGM, it will also delay the lodgement of those documents. Paragraph 22 of PN 3/2018 provides that in such a situation, the company must also apply to extend the time for lodgement of the AFS. The application must be made at least 30 days before the last day to hold its AGM.

Movement Control Order

In response to the COVID-19 pandemic, the Malaysian government announced on March 16, 2020 that a national lockdown would be implemented from March 18 to 31, 2020 to curb the spread of COVID-19.[13] This lockdown, known in Malaysia as the Movement Control Order ("MCO"), was subsequently extended until May 12, 2020.[14] During this period, only essential services were allowed to operate. The counters at the CCM offices were closed, resulting in companies not able to access CCM's services including the lodging of documents over the counter.

Subsequently, when the MCO was implemented again in January 2021, the CCM facilitated the lodgement of documents by introducing two other methods.[15] It

---

[12] See item 40 of the Schedule to the Companies Regulations 2017.

[13] Ashley Tang, "Malaysia Announces Movement Control Order After Spike in COVID-19 Cases," *The Star*, March 16, 2020.

[14] "MCO Extended Another Two Weeks to May 12—Muhyiddin," Bernama, April 23, 2020, accessed on November 10, 2021. https://web.archive.org/web/20200424030524/https:/www.bernama.com/en/general/news.php?id=1835248.

[15] See Companies Commission of Malaysia, "Frequently Asked Questions CCM Counter Operations During MCO, CMCO & RMCO Starting 13th Until 26th January 2021," January 14, 2021, accessed on November 10, 2021. https://www.ssm.com.my/Documents/FAQ%20PASCA%20PKP.pdf.

provided Dropbox services from 8.30am to 2pm on weekdays (except public holidays). It placed the Dropbox at the main entrance or lobby of the CCM office and it was supervised by an officer. Another method was by sending the documents to the CCM office by registered post. On May 13, 2021, the CCM introduced a third method. It opened its counter for lodgement of documents by appointment.[16] As at the date of writing, the counter services at the CCM offices have resumed operations under a new normal.

It is noteworthy that the CCM took cognisance of the unintended non-compliance of statutory requirements during the lockdowns implemented in Malaysia and the after effects. On November 5, 2021, the CCM issued a notice giving companies more time to fulfil its statutory obligations to lodge documents with the CCM. It gave companies 30 days starting from December 1 to 31, 2021 to lodge all statutory documents required to be lodged with the CCM during the MCO, without any late lodgement penalty. Late lodgement penalty will be imposed from January 1, 2022. The statutory documents could be submitted at/through: (a) Service counters; (b) Dropbox; (c) Malaysian Business Reporting System ("MBRS")[17]; and (d) MyCoID 2016 online platform.[18]

However, though the moratorium was good for the companies generally, it did not bring comfort to persons who wanted to lodge documents urgently to activate a particular event. An example which was discussed above is S. 352(2) which requires the lodgement of the "Statement of Particulars to be Lodged with Charge" with the CCM within 30 days of its creation to validate the charge.

Members' Meetings

The above section discusses the importance of lodging documents with the CCM. Some of the documents pertain to decisions and actions taken by the company. For example, when the company makes decision by passing a resolution to increase its share capital[19] and when the company changes its name.[20] Such resolutions may need to be passed by members at a general meeting.

---

[16] See CCM's…—Suruhanjaya Syarikat Malaysia (Laman Rasmi) | Facebook.

[17] Malaysian Business Reporting System ("MBRS") refers to the platform based on the eXtensible Business Reporting Language ("XBRL") format used to submit certain statutory documents to the CCM. The documents are the company's Annual Return ("AR"); Financial Statements and Report ("FS"); and. exemption applications related to the FS and AR.

[18] See Companies Commission of Malaysia, "Frequently Asked Questions Moratorium 30 Days for Lodgement of Statutory Documents under the Companies Act 2016 and the Limited Liability Partnership Act 2012," November 8, 2021, accessed on November 10, 2021. https://www.ssm.com.my/Documents/FAQ%20BI%20MORATORIUM%20AS2016%20APLT2012.pdf.

[19] S. 76 and 78 of the CA 2016.

[20] S. 28 of the CA 2016.

Members at a general meeting and the board of directors ("Board") are the two organs in a company. Though the general power to manage the company is vested in the Board,[21] the CA 2016 recognises the importance of checks and balances.

First, the Board does not have power to approve certain transactions such as issue of new shares,[22] approve or ratify the use of the company's property by a director or officer of the company,[23] approve substantial value transaction,[24] approve home loan to directors,[25] approve transaction of requisite value involving a director or substantial shareholder,[26] and remove an auditor.[27] Instead, the authorisation is vested with the members at a general meeting.[28]

General meetings are an important component in the governance of the company. It is a way to check the excesses of management; it is during a general meeting when members may query the directors on the operations and affairs of the company. In this chapter, the terms 'general meeting' and 'members' meetings' are used interchangeably. Members may also make binding recommendations to management.[29] Due to its importance, a public company is mandated to hold at least an AGM in every calendar year.[30] Members may also convene a meeting by complying with the procedure in S. 310, or require directors to convene a members' meeting by following the procedure in S. 311. Members of both public and private companies may avail themselves to these rights.

Venue

Traditionally, meetings are held in a venue where the persons are physically present. They meet face to face to discuss and make decisions. In the context of a company, the formal decisions of members or directors are known as resolutions. However, as early as in the late nineteenth century, the English court said that the directors need not gather together to make decisions. Sir James VC in *Re Bonelli's Telegraph Co Collie's Claim*[31] said that, "it is not necessary that whatever is done by directors should be done under some roof, in some place, where they are all there assembled".

[21] S. 211 of the CA 2016.

[22] S. 75(1) of the CA 2016.

[23] S. 218 of the CA 2016.

[24] S. 223 of the CA 2016.

[25] S. 224 of the CA 2016.

[26] S. 228 of the CA 2016.

[27] S. 276 of the CA 2016.

[28] For private companies, S. 297 of the CA 2016 permits the members to approve transactions by passing a written resolution unless it is on the removal of a director or auditor before the expiration of his term of office.

[29] S. 195 of the CA 2016.

[30] S. 340 of the CA 2016.

[31] (1871) LR 12 Ex 246, at 258.

What is important is that there is "combined wisdom.. that they must all be of one mind". In other words, a meeting is a meeting of minds.[32]

Subsequent cases recognised meetings using technology, such as in the case of *Byng v London Life Assurance*,[33] where the court said that modern technological advances permit members to debate and vote on matters affecting the company "without all the members coming face to face; without being physically in the same room they can be electronically in each other's presence so as to hear and be heard and to see and be seen."

In 2007, the CA 1965 was amended to include S. 145A to expressly permit the use of technology by facilitating members' meetings at more than one venue. However, it had its limitations, i.e. all the venues of the meeting must be in Malaysia. This was reformed under S. 327 of the CA 2016 which provides that only the main venue shall be in Malaysia and the chairperson shall be present at the main venue. Thus, the other venues may be located outside of Malaysia so long as all the venues are connected by technology.

An issue that arises is the scope of this provision in view of the phrase "subject to the constitution" appearing in S. 327.[34] According to Chen and Chen,[35] this is a presumptive provision and applies by default. However, Loh[36] and Cheah et al.[37] hold the opposite view. They opine that a company cannot take advantage of S. 327 to hold virtual meetings unless the company's constitution provides for it. If so, this is a setback, for some companies might not have reviewed their constitution to align it with the change of times.

The Guidance Note issued by the SC on April 18, 2020 and subsequently revised[38] in line with the changing lockdown status and Standard Operating Procedures ("SOPs") issued by the authority ("SC Guidance Note"), took the stand of Chen and Chen. One of the questions posted in the Frequently Asked Questions section is "Can a listed issuer conduct its general meeting online e.g. remote shareholders' participation, live broadcasting?"[39] The SC takes the view that by default, a company

[32] Siew Cheang Loh, *Corporate Powers and Accountability* (Petaling Jaya: LexisNexis, 2018), 1047.

[33] [1989] 1 All ER 560.

[34] The provision is stated as follows: (1) Subject to the constitution, a company may convene a meeting of members at more than one venue using any technology or method that enables the members of the company to participate and to exercise the members' rights to speak and vote at the meeting. (2) The main venue of the meeting shall be in Malaysia and the chairperson shall be present at that main venue of the meeting.

[35] Thim Wai Chen, and Siew Thong Chen, *The Company Constitution* (Subang Jaya: Sweet and Maxwell, 2018), 134.

[36] Siew Cheang Loh, *Corporate Powers and Accountability* (Petaling Jaya: LexisNexis, 2018), 1060.

[37] Foo Seong Cheah, Philip Tong Ngee Koh, and Xin Yi Ooi, *Company Meetings and Resolutions* (Subang Jaya: Sweet & Maxwell, 2019), 3.

[38] As at October 13, 2021, it was revised 11 times.

[39] Question 2.4 of the SC Guidance Note. The response is as follows:

may conduct its members' meetings virtually unless the company has a constitution and the constitution requires a physical meeting.

The SC Guidance Note explains the four modes of conducting a members' meeting. First, a fully virtual meeting where all the participants including the chairperson and directors, participate in the meeting online. Second, a virtual meeting where only essential persons are physically present at the broadcast venue. Essential persons may include the chairperson, directors, senior members of the management team, auditor, company secretary and those providing audio and visual support. The shareholders are not physically present at the broadcast venue. Instead, they participate in the meeting online.

The third mode is hybrid meeting. The meeting is held at a physical venue. The meeting is also streamed live and thus, members have the option to attend the meeting either at the physical venue or online. The fourth mode is the traditional physical meeting, where all the participants are present at the physical venue. It is not streamed live.

On June 15, 2021, the then Prime Minister Tan Sri Muhyiddin Yassin introduced a four-phase National Recovery Plan ("NRP") to transit the nation from the COVID-19 pandemic.[40] There are four phases, with Phase 1 akin to total lockdown. States were gradually moved from one Phase to the next Phase, based on the number of new COVID-19 cases, people requiring ICU treatment, and vaccination rates. Nevertheless, an area with a surge in COVID-19 cases can still be put under Emergency Movement Control Order ("EMCO").

In line with this, on July 16, 2021, the SC updated its Guidance Note on the mode of conducting a general meeting based on the respective phases. For states in Phase 1 and areas under EMCO, only fully virtual general meetings were allowed. This was because physical gathering irrespective of size was prohibited in these states and areas. For states in Phases 2, 3 and 4 other than areas under EMCO, the company could conduct a hybrid or physical meeting provided compliance of the relevant SOPs applicable to the location of the meeting. Nevertheless, companies in these states were still encouraged to conduct fully virtual meetings.

The next issue is on the determination of the main venue of the meeting. Following the requirement in S. 327(2) of the CA 2016 that the main venue of members meeting shall be in Malaysia, it is crucial that the virtual meeting is held on an online platform located in Malaysia. The CCM addressed queries posed on the identification of the main venue of the meeting. In its "Frequently Asked Questions on Virtual General

---

S. 327 of Companies Act 2016 allows the use of technology for the conduct of general meetings unless the listed issuers' constitution requires the general meeting to be organised at a physical venue.

The listed issuer should ensure that the –

(a) technology used enables members to exercise their rights to speak and vote at the meeting;
(b) main venue of the meeting is in Malaysia; and.
(c) Chairperson of the meeting shall be present at the main venue of the meeting.

[40] "PM to deliver special address on National Recovery Plan at 5 pm today," *The Star*, June 15, 2021.

Meetings" issued on June 8, 2021 ("CCM FAQ of June 8, 2021"), the CCM said that the virtual meeting service provider's ("VMSP") online platform domain must be situated in Malaysia.[41] The CCM has issued guidelines that the main venue shall be deemed in Malaysia if the domain name is registered with MYNIC Bhd ("MYNIC"), which is the sole administrator for web addresses that end with ".my" in Malaysia. Alternatively, it has to be the physical address of the registrant in Malaysia. In other words, for domain names which are not registered with MYNIC, there must be proof that the registrant's physical address is located in Malaysia.[42]

As the company is required to state the main venue of the meeting in the notice convening the meeting, the CCM FAQ of June 8, 2021 also provided guidance to companies in this aspect. In view of the requirement in S. 327(2) that "the main venue of the meeting shall be in Malaysia and the chairperson shall be present at that main venue of the meeting", obviously the notice can give the physical address of the chairperson during the meeting as the main venue. However, due to the MCO, the chairperson might be homebound and he might not want to reveal his home address to the members and other recipients of the notice. Under such circumstances, the CCM provides guidance that the company could state the domain name registered with MYNIC or the physical address of the registrant of the Uniform Resource Locator ("URL") as the main venue of the members meeting. Whether the main venue provided is the chairperson's location, domain name registered with MYNIC or the registrant's physical address, the details of the online meeting platform i.e. the URL of the web address must be made available to the members to access and participate in the meeting.[43]

As regards the question whether the chairperson is deemed present at the main venue of the virtual meeting, CCM responded in the affirmative.[44] It is immaterial that the meeting is broadcasted from a venue in Penang and carried out via an online platform provided by a virtual meeting service provider but the chairperson is using the computer from his home in Kuala Lumpur so long as two conditions are fulfilled: First, the online platform is located in Malaysia; and second, the chairperson is physically present in Malaysia.[45]

In order to prove the online platform is located in Malaysia, again we fall back on the guidance by the CCM that it could be proven by using the domain name registered with MYNIC and if the domain name is not registered with MYNIC, the evidence that the registrant's physical address is located in Malaysia.[46]

[41] See the response to question 6 in the CCM FAQ of June 8, 2021.
[42] See the response to question 3 in the CCM FAQ of June 8, 2021.
[43] See the response to question 2 in the CCM FAQ of June 8, 2021.
[44] See the response to question 5 in the CCM FAQ of June 8, 2021.
[45] See the response to question 4 in the CCM FAQ of June 8, 2021.
[46] See the response to question 6 in the CCM FAQ of June 8, 2021.

Quorum

Section 328(4) of the CA 2016 provides that no business shall be transacted at any members meeting unless a quorum is present at the time when the meeting proceeds to business. In other words, there must be a quorum when the members meeting commences. Subsection (2) provides that the quorum is one member if the company has only one member. For a company with more than one member, the default quorum is two members personally present or by proxy unless the company's constitution specifies a higher number.

The issue on how to count the number of members present at a fully virtual, virtual or hybrid general meeting to determine quorum was dealt with by the SC in its Guidance Note as follows[47]: Where the meeting is either fully virtual or virtual general meeting, the quorum may be determined by the number of members logged-in at the start of the meeting. And for hybrid meetings, the quorum can be determined by the number of members attending the meeting at its physical location and members logged-in at the start of the meeting. It is crucial that the company ensures there is a proper audit trail to record the attendance of members at the meeting.

Right to Speak

The mode chosen to carry out the general meeting must enable the members to participate and to exercise their rights to speak and vote at the meeting. This is aligned with S. 71 which provides that members enjoy statutory rights such as, the right to attend, participate and speak at meetings and the right to vote. The SC in its Guidance Note reinforces this and requires public listed companies ("PLC") to use a reliable infrastructure which allows the members to exercise their statutory rights.[48] This should apply to all companies as well, for S. 327 dictates it.

In the conventional physical meeting, a member may participate at a meeting by speaking out. The number of members who can speak at any one time can be controlled through various strategies such as placement of a limited number of microphones. However, at a virtual meeting, unless the function is disabled, all members could unmute their microphones to speak. It would be chaotic if many members were to do so simultaneously. Thus, the SC Guidance Note also provides that the PLC gives guidance to its members on the requirement and method of participating in the meeting.[49] Participation is not limited to verbal communication but may also use other modes such as pre-meeting as well as real time submission of typed texts. In order to further enhance inclusivity, the questions and comments posted should

[47] See the response to question 2.16 in the SC Guidance Note.

[48] See the response to question 2.9 in the SC Guidance Note.

[49] See the response to question 2.9 in the SC Guidance Note.

be visible to all participants of the meeting.[50] The chat window function which is available in the online platform, could be employed to meet this requirement.

Right to Vote

Unless the member is holding a non-voting share,[51] or he has not paid the calls or other sums presently payable by him in respect of the shares,[52] he has a right to vote on the motions tabled at the meeting. It is thus important that where the meeting is held virtually, there must be a mechanism in place to support "in time" voting during the proceeding.[53] Apart from personally casting his votes, he may also do so by appointing a proxy to vote on his behalf. In this connection, it shall be noted that the appointment of a proxy is also a statutory right conferred on a member,[54] and S. 335 requires the notice of meeting to draw this right to the attention of members.

Section 330(1) provides that a member's resolution could be decided on a show of hands where a member has one vote each irrespective of his shareholding. However, before or on the declaration of the results of the show of hands, a poll may be demanded. A vote on a poll is more equitable as the number of shares held determines the number of his votes. Generally, one share carries one vote.

A PLC is obligated to comply with the Bursa Malaysia Listing Requirements. Where the company's shares are listed on the stock exchange in Malaysia, paragraph 8.29A of the Listing Requirements states that the voting on resolution must be on poll, and not on a show of hands. The company is required to appoint a scrutineer to validate the votes casted at the meeting. The SC Guidance Note confirms that this applies too in a virtual meeting. A PLC must "appoint at least one scrutineer to validate the votes cast at the general meeting whether on-site or remotely. Similar to the validation process at a physical general meeting, the scrutineer must ensure that the votes cast are validated accordingly."[55]

---

[50] See the response to question 2.7 in the SC Guidance Note.

[51] S. 90(2) of the CA 2016.

[52] S. 293(2)) of the CA 2016.

[53] See the response to question 2.17 in the SC Guidance Note. According to footnote 7 in the Guidance Note, "In time voting" refers to the ability for members to cast their votes remotely or contemporaneously (live) during the proceeding of the general meeting.

[54] S. 334(1) of the CA 2016.

[55] See the responses to questions 2.19 and 2.20 in the SC Guidance Note.

Financial Statements

One of the items on the agenda of the members' meetings, specifically at the company's annual general meeting, is the laying of the company's audited financial statements ("AFS"). Section 248 of the CA 2016 provides that the directors of the company have the responsibility to prepare the financial statements. In order to ensure that the reported financial statements reflect the true and fair view of the company's financial position and performance, the CA 2016 requires every company to appoint an auditor to audit the statements. Nevertheless, S. 267(2) empowers the CCM to exempt certain private companies from audit.[56]

The AFS will then be circulated to every member of the company, every person who is entitled to receive notice of the general meetings, every auditor of the company and every debenture holder of the company on a request being made to the company.[57] Thenceforth, the statutory requirements and deadlines imposed on a public company and a private company with regards to AFS diverge.

For a public company, the AFS must be circulated at least 28 days before the company's AGM,[58] tabled at the AGM,[59] and then lodged with the CCM within 30 days of the AGM.[60]

As a private company is not mandated to hold an AGM unless its constitution requires it,[61] the deadline on the circulation of the AFS is referenced to its financial year end. Section 258(1)(a) provides that a private company is to circulate the AFS within six months of its financial year end. Further, the company is required by S. 259(1)(a) to lodge the AFS with the CCM within 30 days from the day the AFS are circulated pursuant to S. 257(1).[62] These deadlines apply to a private company which is exempted from audit too. It will then circulate and file its unaudited financial statements, which must have been prepared in accordance with the applicable approved accounting standards.[63]

During the lockdown period, many, if not all companies, found it a challenge to meet the deadline in the preparation of the financial statements for lodgement with the CCM. For companies which were not exempted from audit, the challenge was shared and faced by the appointed auditors too. For public companies, the mandated

[56] In 2017, the CCM issued Practice Directive 3/2017 to confer audit exemption to three classes of private companies. They are namely, dormant companies, zero revenue companies and threshold qualified companies.

[57] S. 257(1) of the CA 2016.

[58] S. 258(1)(b) of the CA 2016.

[59] S. 340(1)(a) of the CA 2016.

[60] S. 259(1)(b) of the CA 2016.

[61] S. 340 of the CA 2016 on the requirement for annual general meeting specifically applies to only public companies.

[62] The financial statements are not only circulated to members but auditors (if the company's financial statements are audited) and debenture holders, upon request.

[63] This is confirmed by paragraphs 14 and 15 of the Practice Directive 3/2017.

AGM which requires the tabling of the AFS as one of its agenda,[64] increased the pressure on the company and its auditors. This is because failure to prepare the AFS, lodgement with the CCM and holding of the public company's AGM within the prescribed time are offences.

A director who fails to prepare the financial statements, circulate the AFS to members and table them at the AGM commits an offence.[65] Failure to lodge the documents with the CCM is also an offence committed by the officers[66] of the company.[67] Whereas the failure by a public company to hold an AGM is an offence imputed on both companies and officers.[68] The consequences of being convicted are far reaching; S. 198(1)(b) provides that a person who has been convicted of an offence relating to the management of a corporation is disqualified from being a director. He cannot also be involved directly or indirectly in the management of any company. Thus, an officer who is convicted of one of the aforementioned offences will suffer financial setbacks as well as disqualification from being a director or managing any company.

In order to avoid such severe consequences, provisions are put in place for the application for extension of time. This was explained above and with regard to AGM and lodgement of the financial statements with the CCM, S. 340(4) and S. 259(2) provide that the company may apply to extend the respective deadlines.

Automatic Extension of Time of 90 Days Upon Application

The CCM realising the challenges faced by companies and auditors during these unprecedented times, was proactive and issued Practice Directive 6/2020 ("PD 6/2020") on April 7, 2020[69] and Practice Directive 8/2021 ("PD 8/2021") on June 1, 2021 to enable companies to comply with the relevant statutory obligations including preparing financial statements, holding AGM, completing relevant statutory documents, as well as to enable audit firms to complete delayed assignments in a more reasonable timeframe. The effect of these two Practice Directives was that companies were given an extension of time of 90 days to circulate its financial statements to members, and lodgement of the said documents with the CCM and for a public company, an extension of time to hold its AGM. Nevertheless, the extension of time was not automatic. As required by the respective provisions in the CA 2016, the company is required to make an application to the CCM. The fee for the application was waived during this unprecedented time.

---

[64] S. 340(1) of the CA 2016.

[65] S. 248 of the CA 2016.

[66] See S. 2(1) of the CA 2016 on the scope of the term "officers" which include directors, secretary and employees of the company.

[67] S. 259 of the CA 2016.

[68] S. 340(6) of the CA 2016.

[69] PD 6/2020 was revoked on June 1, 2021 when PD 8/2021 came into effect.

As further guidance to companies, the CCM issued various Frequently Asked Questions ("FAQs").[70] The latest as at the date of writing is the one issued on June 1, 2021. These FAQs gave illustrations to guide companies. For example, the FAQ of June 1, 2021 on "Extension of Time (EOT) for Circulation of Financial Statements, Holding of Annual General Meeting and Lodgement of Financial Statements for Year Ending November 1, 2020 to January, 31 2021" provided four examples. We shall extract two of the examples, one each for private and public company.

Example 1: Private company with Financial Year Ending on November 30, 2020		
Event	Expiry date under the CA 2016	Extension of time (90 days)
Circulation of financial statements	May 31, 2021	August 29, 2021
Lodgement of financial statements	June 30, 2021	September 28, 2021

Example 2: Public company with Financial Year Ending on November 30, 2020		
Event	Expiry date under the CA 2016	Extension of time (90 days)
Circulation of AFS	May 10, 2021	August 8, 2021
Annual General Meeting	May 31, 2021	August 29, 2021
Lodgement of AFS	June 30, 2021	September 28, 2021

The FAQ provided that the fee for the application of time to circulate and lodge the said documents and the holding of AGM would be waived.[71] Possibly expecting an avalanche of applications, applications which complied with the procedure prescribed in PD 8/2021 and which contained correct information were considered as approved. An extension of 90 days from the original expiry date was given. On the other hand, applications that did not meet the requirements set in PD 8/2021 were not approved and no email notification would be sent. Thus, it was crucial that an email copy of the application for extension of time be kept as "proof of application and approval."

In addition, as highlighted above, the CCM had on November 5, 2021 granted another moratorium for 30 days starting from December 1, 2021 to December 31, 2021 to companies. Companies could submit all statutory documents required to be lodged, but not lodged with the CCM during the MCO, without any late lodgement penalty. Late lodgement penalty would be imposed from January 1, 2022. Thus, companies could use this opportunity to lodge the overdue financial statements. Nevertheless, this extension of time did not apply to the circulation of the financial statements and the holding of AGM. Companies would still need to apply to the CCM for the extension of time for these two events.

[70] FAQs were issued on March 18, 2020, July 28, 2020, November 7, 2020, and June 1, 2021.

[71] The CCM waived the fees by exercising its powers under Regulation 8(5) of the Companies Regulations 2017. The usual fee per application for extension of time is RM100 (item 40 of the Schedule to the Companies Regulations 2017).

A Walkthrough

In this section of the chapter, we will walk through selected annual events of a company, namely the preparation and filing of Annual Return, the preparation and circulation of financial statements, the auditing of financial statements and the preparation of annual general meetings.

Annual Return

Under S. 68 of the CA 2016, a company must lodge its Annual Return with the CCM every calendar year within 30 days from the anniversary of its incorporation date. Though lodgement could be done online on the Malaysian Business Reporting System ("MBRS") platform, preparing the document might prove an issue especially where the company did not digitalise their records. This is because the information required in the Annual Return, among others, comprise a summary of the company's shareholding structure, total amount of its indebtedness, and list of members.[72] During the lockdown period, offices were not allowed to be opened unless they were in the essential services sector and had obtained the necessary approvals. The company officers would not be able to prepare the Annual Return if they could not access the necessary records.

It is observed that Annual Return was not one of the documents listed in PD 6/2020 and PD 8/2021. Thus, the company was not able to apply for extension of time to lodge the Annual Return under the directives. However, it could enjoy the moratorium issued by the CCM on the lodgement of statutory documents and if the company missed the deadline given in the moratorium, the company would have to apply for extension of time under S. 609 of the CA 2016.

Financial Statements

Section 248 of the CA 2016 provides that it is the responsibility of the directors to prepare the financial statements. The timeframe given to the directors is as follows: The first set of financial statements must be prepared within 18 months from the date of the company's incorporation and the subsequent ones within six months of its financial year end. The timeframe applies to public and private companies. Unless the company is exempted from audit, S. 248(2) also requires the accounts to be audited before they are sent to the members.

[72] S. 68(3) of the CA 2016.

Preparation

In order to facilitate the preparation of true and fair accounts, S. 245(1) requires the directors, the company and its manager to ensure the company's accounting and other records are kept sufficiently well to explain the transactions and financial position of the company. Section 252 also requires the directors to prepare a directors' report to be attached to the financial statements. The report shall be approved by the Board and signed on behalf of the Board by at least two directors. Where it is a private company with only one director, it will be signed by the sole director. These documents must subsequently be lodged with the CCM.

During the MCO, only companies providing essential services were allowed to open for operations provided with the Ministry of International Trade and Industry's approval and with the restricted movement allowed. Many companies could not operate as their offices were closed. As a result, the preparation of financial statements was hampered unless that information was digitised and could be accessed online by the preparer.

Audit

Even assuming that the company could prepare the financial statements, the accounts must be audited unless the company was exempted from audit.[73] We have seen in Chap. 4 the role of an auditor and his challenges during the COVID-19 pandemic. As an auditor has to give his opinion whether the financial statements give a true and fair view of the company's affairs, he would have to view documents relevant to sampled transactions. However, the client company might not be able to supply them as the office was not opened. The staff would not be able to retrieve the documents for the auditor. Even assuming that the company was in the essential services sector, and the staff could attend office, the auditor could not attend. This is because auditing did not form part of the essential services sector until May 31, 2021.[74]

Another challenge faced by auditors was the lockdown had resulted in a backlog of audit work. Though the CCM has extended the time for circulation and lodgement of the AFS under PD 8/2021, there was a spill-over effect from the backlog. Auditors had to play catch up with audits on those companies falling within the extension of time allowed under PD 8/2021 (for companies with financial year end from November 1, 2020 to January 31, 2021) and those whose financial year end was after January 31, 2021. As a result, many companies, though granted extension of time under PD 8/2021 had to apply under S. 259(2) for further extension of time beyond what was allowed under PD 8/2021. The audits of companies whose financial year ended after January 31, 2021 were also affected as they were pushed down the queue. Thus, these

[73] S. 248(2) of the CA 2016.

[74] Malaysian Institute of Accountants, "Circular to Members No. MF22/2021. Further Updates On The Operation Of Firms During Total Lockdown.".

companies had to also apply to extend the deadlines for circulation and lodgement of their AFS and to hold their AGM.

Nevertheless, companies could also enjoy the moratorium issued by the CCM on the lodgement of statutory documents. However, if a company missed the deadline given in the moratorium for lodgement of the financial statements and directors report, the company would have to apply for extension of time for lodgement under S. 609 of the CA 2016. It is to be noted that the moratorium applied only to the lodgement of statutory documents. It did not apply to the circulation of the financial statements to the members or the holding of the AGM. The company would still have to apply for extension of time if it was unable to circulate the financial statements or hold the AGM within the prescribed time.

Signing

The financial statements and director's report require the signature of directors. Though S. 196 of the CA 2016 provides that a private company shall have at least one local resident director and a public company to have a minimum of two local resident directors, a situation may arise where the directors were overseas when the lockdown was declared and the borders were closed. If they could not return to Malaysia in time, the financial statements and directors report could not be signed. In addition, the offices of Commissioner for Oaths were also not essential services and therefore not opened. The attestation of the signature of a director or an officer who was primarily responsible for the financial management of the company during the MCO could not be performed and this further exacerbated the situation. Consequently, the documents could not be circulated to members and lodged with the CCM within the prescribed time.

Circulation of Financial Statements and Reports

Section 257 requires copies of the financial statements and reports to be sent to the last known address of every member of the company, every person who is entitled to receive notice of general meetings, every auditor of the company as well as every debenture holder of the company on a request being made to the company. If an email address has not been provided, the company will have to send a printed copy of the documents to them. However, the printer was not an essential service and thus, many companies particularly public listed companies due to large number of members, faced difficulty in getting the documents printed and organising the circulation of the documents.

Annual General Meeting

Section 327(1) allows a company to conduct its members' meetings online unless the company's constitution provides otherwise. Thus, if the company's constitution specifically mentioned that only physical meetings were allowed, the company would not be able to carry on its AGM during the lockdown period. On the other hand, where the company did not have a constitution or its constitution did not restrict virtual meetings, the company could proceed to hold its AGM on an online platform during the lockdown period. However, this was not without any problem as technical glitch could happen during the meeting. Lack of technology knowhow among the members and other participants at the meeting might also impede the smooth running of the meeting.

Moving Forward

We have seen above that the CA 2016 stipulates the deadlines for lodgement of documents with the CCM. The failure to lodge within time is an offence and will attract late lodgement penalty imposed under the CA 2016. In addition, the CCM may also impose administrative penalties not exceeding RM5,000 under S. 20E(2)(b) of the Companies Commission of Malaysia Act 2001 among other actions the CCM is empowered to take thereafter. Nevertheless, companies may apply for extension of time, and S. 609(2) of the CA 2016 provides that the CCM has the power and upon payment of the prescribed fee extend the period to such further period as the CCM deems just and expedient. Nonetheless, the CA 2016 does not empower the CCM to grant blanket automatic extension. A company that requires extension of time must initiate it, as the CCM may grant the extension only upon application from the company.

The pandemic resulting in the lockdown, reveals that there may arise occasions where it might be necessary for the CCM to grant a blanket extension to all companies to lodge documents with it. On July 29, 2020, the CCM released a consultative document seeking feedback on the proposed Companies (Amendment) Bill 2020. The Bill proposed to insert a new provision in the CA 2016 to the effect that the CCM may extend the time for lodgement of documents as well as to any action required by the Act, without any application from the company on certain circumstances which is just and in the interest of the public.

Further, it is observed that the MBRS is the platform for the lodgement of financial statements and Annual Return, whereas MyCoID 2016 is the platform to lodge other documents. However, the latter is limited in its application. There are statutory documents which are not included in the MyCoID 2016 platform such as the Notice of Intention to Vacate the Office of Secretary under S. 237(2). In addition, there are documents which require lodgement to give effect to a transaction such as the "Statement of Particulars to be Lodged with Charge" under S. 352(2). It had been taken for granted that the CCM offices would be opened to accept lodgement of documents but the COVID-19 pandemic showed that CCM counter services could be unexpectedly closed for months. This caused an upheaval in the business community. Thus, it is crucial for the portal for lodgement of documents to CCM to be fully digitalised. This might obviate the need for companies to do any physical lodgement to CCM. It is therefore very crucial now that CCM has its end-to-end digital filing system in place sooner than later.

In addition, it is timely for the authority to review the list of documents which are to be submitted to the CCM. For example, every company must lodge its Annual Return with the CCM within 30 days from the anniversary of its incorporation date.[75] The question is whether the Annual Return is necessary as most information contained therein are either lodged with the CCM as and when there are changes,[76] or in the company's financial statements and directors' report.[77] In the former, the information is "live" as the company has to update the information with the CCM. Thus, the CCM records would have the latest information.

The authority may also review the work process for the lodgement of the AFS with the CCM. It could be done by the company directly into the MBRS upon the completion of the audit. We have seen that where the company is a public company, the AFS is lodged with the CCM within 30 days from the company's AGM and for a private company, within 30 days from the day the documents are circulated to its members. There is no requirement for the members' approval and thus, there is no need to reference the date of lodgement to the date of AGM or circulation, as the case may be.

The pandemic has also pushed companies to explore the virtue of virtual meetings. The SC in its Guidance Note on the conduct of general meetings during the pandemic encourages PLCs to continue to leverage on technology to conduct their general meetings, as well as to facilitate communication and engagements with shareholders. The "advice" given by the SC should apply not only to PLCs. Even companies whose shares are not listed on the Bursa Malaysia should consider making virtual meetings a norm as it saves time, money and resources.

Conclusion

The CA 2016 was enacted to modernise the company law framework in Malaysia, taking into account the advances made in information and communication technology. It was tested when the COVID-19 pandemic hit Malaysia in 2020. Though it

[75] S. 68 of the CA 2016.

[76] For example, when the company changes its registered office, S. 46(3) of the CA 2016 requires the company to notify the CCM within 14 days; changes in the shareholder (S. 51 of the CA 2016); and changes in directors, managers and secretaries (S. 57 of the CA 2016).

[77] For example, the nature of its business and place of business; and the total amount of its indebtedness.

may be concluded that the CA 2016 has provisions on the use of technology to facilitate online meetings and communication, we have seen that the use of technology to facilitate meetings and communications are not mandated. In fact, companies have to ensure that their constitutions do not impede the application of those provisions.

The pandemic has shown that technology is the way to go, and everyone has to adapt and adjust to move forward. The CA 2016 has provisions to facilitate the use of technology, and it is up to the users to take advantage of them. As Bill Gates said at an interview,[78] "the advance of technology is based on making it fit in so that you don't really even notice it, so it's part of everyday life".

References

1. Cheah, Foo Seong, Philip Tong Ngee Koh, and Xin Yi Ooi. *Company Meetings and Resolutions*. Subang Jaya: Sweet & Maxwell, 2019.
2. Chen, Thim Wai, and Siew Thong Chen. *The Company Constitution*. Subang Jaya: Sweet & Maxwell, 2018.
3. Companies Commission of Malaysia. "FAQ on Virtual General Meetings." June 8, 2021. Accessed on November 10, 2021. https://www.ssm.com.my/Pages/Legal_Framework/Document/FAQs_VIRTUAL%20GM%20_.pdf
4. Companies Commission of Malaysia. "Frequently Asked Questions Moratorium 30 Days for Lodgement of Statutory Documents under the Companies Act 2016 and the Limited Liability Partnership Act 2012." Accessed on November 10, 2021. https://www.ssm.com.my/Documents/FAQ%20BI%20MORATORIUM%20AS2016%20APLT2012.pdf
5. Companies Commission of Malaysia. "Frequently Asked Questions SSM Counter Operations During MCO, CMCO & RMCO Starting 13th Until 26th January 2021." January 14, 2021. Accessed on November 10, 2021. https://www.ssm.com.my/Documents/FAQ%20PASCA%20PKP.pdf
6. Companies Commission of Malaysia. "Practice Directive 3/2017. Qualifying Criteria For Audit Exemption For Certain Categories Of Private Companies."
7. Companies Commission of Malaysia. "Practice Directive 6/2020. Extension of Time for Annual General Meeting and Lodgement of Financial Statement."
8. Companies Commission of Malaysia. "Practice Directive 8/2021. Extension of Time for Circulation of Financial Statements and Reports, Holding of Annual General Meeting and Lodgement of Financial Statements for Companies Affected by the Implementation of Movement Control Order."
9. Companies Commission of Malaysia. "Scope of the Corporate Law Reform Committee." Accessed on December 16, 2021. https://www.ssm.com.my/Pages/Publication/CLRC/Scope.aspx.
10. Exclusive Interview of Bill Gates by Sarah on December 7, 2011. Accessed on November 10, 2021. http://news.bbc.co.uk/cbbcnews/hi/club/your_reports/newsid_1697000/1697132.stm
11. Loh, Siew Cheang. *Corporate Powers and Accountability*. Petaling Jaya: LexisNexis, 2018.
12. Malaysian Institute of Accountants. "Circular to Members No. MF22/2021. Further Updates On The Operation Of Firms During Total Lockdown."
13. "MCO Extended Another Two Weeks to May 12 - Muhyiddin." *Bernama*, April 23, 2020. Accessed on November 10, 2021. https://web.archive.org/web/20200424030524/https:/www.bernama.com/en/general/news.php?id=1835248.

[78] Exclusive Interview of Bill Gates by Sarah on December 7, 2011, accessed on November 10, 2021. http://news.bbc.co.uk/cbbcnews/hi/club/your_reports/newsid_1697000/1697132.stm.

14. "PM to Deliver Special Address on National Recovery Plan at 5pm Today." *The Star,* June 15, 2021.
15. Securities Commission Malaysia. "Guidance and FAQs on the Conduct of General Meetings for Listed Issuers." Accessed on September 21, 2021. https://www.sc.com.my/api/documentms/download.ashx?id=c5fbbbcd-3ab0-40ce-a22b-e8bb1d1fe0a8
16. Tang, Ashley. "Malaysia Announces Movement Control Order After Spike in COVID-19 Cases." *The Star,* March 16, 2020.

Chapter 7
State Intervention to Oblige Corporations' Measures to Prevent COVID-19 Diffusion: A Truly Justified Matter?

Yusramizza Md Isa and Anis Shuhaiza Md Salleh

Abstract Global labour and organisations were threatened by CoV-2's SARS-like virulence. Governments worldwide have developed workplace preventative and regulatory measures like corporate commitment. Mandatory safety and health regulations are considered as a management strategy to prevent health risks and disease at workplaces, including virus transmission. States have enforced isolation, quarantine, mask wear, and social separation to combat COVID-19 in the workplace. Malaysia employs a number of rules and regulations for the control of COVID-19 transmission. The most important are the Prevention and Control of Infectious Diseases Act 1998 and the Occupational Safety and Health Act 1994 ("OSHA"). By employing these statutes, the state intervenes to mandatorily impose certain preventive measures on the company to prevent the spread of COVID-19, thereby obliging the company to impose them on its employees. The state's engagement in the corporations' management of the COVID-19 outbreak has also been criticised. It was suggested that making certain preventive measures obligatory or making particular individuals in a corporation responsible for violating government-issued regulations or norms is a rigorous approach and not justifiable. Beginning with a philosophical discussion of the justifications of public health and criminal law in disease prevention and control, this chapter would address the state's intervention in corporations to require COVID-19 prevention measures under public health and criminal law, followed by a discussion of how corporations could be regulated to prevent disease spread. The following section of this chapter discusses governments' implementation of obligations on corporations to adopt preventive steps against COVID-19 transmission in the workplace.

Y. Md Isa · A. S. Md Salleh (✉)
Universiti Utara Malaysia, Sintok, Malaysia
e-mail: shuhaiza@uum.edu.my

L. Krishnan and W. M. Chan (eds.), *The Impact of COVID-19 on Corporations and Corporate Law in Malaysia*, https://doi.org/10.1007/978-981-19-5519-8_7

Introduction

The COVID-19 pandemic has profoundly altered practically every area of human life around the world. Its ramifications are far-reaching and substantial. As a result of the virus SARS-rapid CoV-2's evolution, new variations emerged which endangered worldwide public health. More than 200,000 deaths were projected among 3,059,642 COVID-19 cases in 212 countries by April 30, 2020, with a range of 1.0–18.8% among the top ten nations.[1] Since then, environments that were once considered safe for working, meeting, worshipping, gathering, and other activities appear to be no longer safe, as they may have become one of the most contagious areas for COVID-19. Significantly, the pandemic disrupted and jeopardised labour and organisations all across the world. In February 2021, approximately 61% of new massive cluster infections in the Republic of Korea were confirmed from under ventilated and overcrowded workplaces.[2]

Due to the disease transmission between workers and their families and friends at their homes and neighbourhoods, workplaces are alleged to be common venues for catastrophic infectious disease crises.[3] The findings of a study of COVID-19 exposure risk in various occupational contexts and demographics in Qatar suggest an extremely high rate of COVID-19 infections at work, particularly in the construction and related industries, as well as retail and wholesale trade. A total of 201,006 people were tested between March 1, and July 31, 2020, with 59,175 of them testing positive. This results in an overall positive rate of 29.4%. Employees in the private sector are more likely to be positive than those in the government.[4]

Nonetheless, it is found that the principal COVID-19 strategies in the majority of nations appear to concentrate on community infection prevention. While efforts to limit COVID-19 transmission in the workplace have largely been abandoned,[5] evidently, research revealed that some workplaces, such as meat-processing plants in the United States, Germany, Ireland, and Canada, call centres in the Republic of the Philippines, as well as nursing homes were identified as significant locations at

---

[1] Committee for the Coordination of Statistical Activities, "How COVID-19 is Changing the World: A Statistical Perspective; 2020," accessed July 2, 2021. https://unstats.un.org/unsd/ccsa/documents/covid19-report-ccsa.pdf.

[2] "About 61% of New Mass Cluster Infections Occurred in Workplaces," The Hankyoreh, March 1, 2021, accessed November 2, 2021, http://www.hani.co.kr/arti/society/health/984971.html.

[3] Sasaki N., Kuroda R., Tsuno K., Kawakami N. Workplace Responses To COVID-19 Associated with Mental Health and Work Performance of Employees in Japan. *J. Occup. Health.* 2020;62: e12134. https://doi.org/10.1002/1348-9585.12134.

[4] Mohamed Ghaith Al Kuwari, Asma Ali Al-Nuaimi, Jazeel Abdulmajeed, Sandy Semaan, Hamad Eid Al-Romaihi, Mujeeb Chettiyam Kandy, and Selvakumar Swamy, "COVID-19 Infection Across Workplace Settings in Qatar: A Comparison of COVID-19 Positivity Rates of Screened Workers from March 1st Until July 31st, 2020", *Journal of Occupational Medicine and Toxicology*, 16, no. 1 (2021): 1–9.

[5] Derek Miller et al., "Overview of Legal Measures for Managing Workplace COVID-19 Infection Risk in Several Asia-Pacific Countries," *Safety and Health at Work*,12, no 4, (December 2021): 531, https://doi.org/10.1016/j.shaw.2021.08.003.

the centre of COVID-19 outbreaks.[6] As far as Malaysia is concerned, it was reported that workplace clusters have emerged as a key source of COVID-19 infection with hundreds of cases drawn from private companies and government agencies.[7] Until the middle of September 2021, out of 282,729 cases reported to the Malaysian Ministry of Health (MOH), there were 2839 workplace COVID-19 clusters, mainly from factories, palm oil plantations, learning institutions, and wholesale markets.[8]

Impact of COVID on Workplace

Changes have been made in this regard for workers, workplaces, and work habits as a result of emerging clusters in the workplace. In order to manage the crisis, governments all over the world have implemented a range of preventive and controlling measures at workplaces, including mandatory commitment on the part of corporations. Public health interventions such as policies and legal tools have been strengthened in order to reduce the risk of transmission of COVID-19 in the workplace. COVID-19 has also been specifically designated as an occupational disease in nations such as Canada and South Africa, where occupational exposure is suspected. COVID-19 has been considered an occupational disease in Germany and Italy, but exclusively in the health sector.

Further, the implementation of mandatory safety and health standards as outlined by public health laws in many states is seen as one of the management tools that address general behaviours and procedures to reduce health risks and illness at workplaces, including virus transmission. Just to name a few, among the laws are the United Kingdom Health and Safety at Work Act 1974, the United States Occupational Safety and Health Act of 1970, the Republic of the Philippines' Mandatory Reporting of Notifiable Diseases and Health Events of Public Health Concern Act and the New Zealand COVID-19 Public Health Response Act 2020.

Apparently, like other jurisdictions around the globe, the government of Malaysia has the legal basis to interfere in its people's businesses through the enabling provision of laws, particularly when issues come under the purview of public health and safety. These statutes, if applicable, may govern not only the actions and omissions of individuals, but also the actions and omissions of corporations. In relation thereto, many countries around the world, including Malaysia, Australia, Singapore, the Philippines, Vietnam, Thailand, Japan, Hong Kong, and China, have imposed responsibility and obligation on employers to create a disclosure rule requiring employees to

---

[6] Derek Miller et al. "Overview of Legal Measures," 531.

[7] Ministry of Health, "Workplace clusters are key source of COVID-19 infections in Malaysia", New Straits Times. January 23, 2021, https://www.straitstimes.com/asia/se-asia/workplace-clusters-are-a-key-source-of-covid-19-infections-in-malaysia.

[8] "ANNEX 25: COVID-19 Management Guidelines for Workplaces", Last Modified October 8, 2021 https://covid-19.moh.gov.my/garis-panduan/garis-panduan-kkm/.

disclose if they are a "risk-factor" to the employer.[9] Stronger restrictions on mandatory isolation, quarantine, use of face masks, and social distancing are among the measures taken by states in the fight against COVID-19 at workplaces.

Background of Study

Several statutes and regulations are used in Malaysia to enforce the control of COVID-19 diffusion. The most crucial is the Prevention and Control of Infectious Diseases 1988, also known as the 342 Act. Initially, the Act was designed with the contemplation of an epidemic situation in mind, which was about 34 years ago. Nevertheless, it was intended to govern the prevention and control of infectious diseases, and in fact, it may serve as a legal basis for any preventive actions taken by the government. Therein, infectious disease includes any disease specified in Part II of the First Schedule of the Act. Despite not being one of the listed diseases, yet, this new disease, Coronavirus Disease 2019 (COVID-19), has been inserted into the list via the Prevention and Control of Infectious Diseases (Amendment of First Schedule) Order 2020.

Notably, under this 342 Act, the Minister of Health is empowered to declare by gazette any area in Malaysia which is believed to cause an outbreak/threat of any infectious disease. Apart from that, the Minister is also empowered to prescribe by regulations, any measures to be taken to control or prevent the spread of infectious disease within or from an infected local area. Such measures are not only enforceable on any individual person, but also on a class or category of persons, which may include organisations or corporations if the Minister is satisfied that there is any risk of virus transmission. Among the examples of the regulations that have been progressively designed for preventive measures are the Prevention and Control of Infectious Diseases (Declaration of Infected Local Areas) Order 2020 and the Prevention and Control of Infectious Diseases (Measures Within the Infected Local Areas) Regulations 2020, where the government strictly imposed the movement control order ("MCO") throughout Malaysia and later the restricted movement control order ("RMCO") on certain infected areas to prevent the spread of the virus.

At that particular period, there was a halting of economic activity, with the exception only of those categorised as essential services with strict conditions. Ideally, this measure is seen as the best way to prevent infection by avoiding exposure to the virus and thus preventing further spread. This was an initial step taken by the government, applicable to all in order to prevent the spread of the virus before gradually imposing other preventive measures for corporations to resume operation. As a result, any employers other than those in the essential service category who fail

[9] "COVID-19 Global Employer Guide", *Baker McKenzie*, Last Modified March 30, 2020, https://www.bakermckenzie.com/-/media/files/insight/publications/2020/04/baker-mckenzie_covid-19-global-employer-guide.pdf?la=en.

Table 7.1 *Source* The Malaysia Ministry of Health

Employers' responsibilities at workplaces:	Employers' responsibilities at accommodation area:
• Provide places for hand cleaning / hand sanitizer • Practice 1 meter social distance of work space / pantry • Avoid workers gathering at crowded area • Avoid too many workers at one time • Practice 1 meter physical distance while having conversation • Regularly conduct disinfection and defilement for common area	• Avoid crowded, confined and close conversation • Make sure that lounge/ television watching space is not crowded • Avoid group meal preparation • Make sure the cleanliness of accommodation area • Regularly carry out sanitation and cleaning • Make sure the arrangement of bed / sleeping place 1 meter from one to another

to implement the prescribed preventive measures, such as requiring or insisting on their employees' attendance at work, may face penalties under the Act (Table 7.1).

Further, in 2021, other subsidiary laws were issued, namely the Prevention and Control of Infectious Diseases (Measures Within the Infected Local Areas) (Movement Control) Regulations 2021, the Prevention and Control of Infectious Diseases (Measures Within the Infected Local Areas) (Conditional Movement Control) Regulations 2021, where movement to and from certain states is restricted subject to fulfilment of prescribed conditions. Through these regulations, the government may restrict the movement of people from one place to another, thus controlling the crowd and any risk of infection, including that at the workplace. Apart from that, there is also the Prevention and Control of Infectious Diseases (Compounding of Offences) (Amendment) Regulations 2021, where this regulation provides for compoundable offences for those who break the law and order. Presently, there are plenty of regulations and orders issued mainly for prescribing SOPs, including COVID-19 preventive measures at workplaces. For that purpose, the MOH elucidated the SOPs as tabulated in Table 7.1.[10]

More importantly, the 342 Act spells out that it is an offence for anyone who knows or has reason to believe that he is suffering from an infectious disease to expose other people to the risk of infection by his presence or conduct in any public place or any other place used in common by persons other than family members and household.

[10] Ministry of Health, "Langkah-Langkah Pencegahan Penularan COVID-19 di Tempat Kerja," Last Modified May 28, 2021, https://covid-19.moh.gov.my/semasa-kkm/2021/05/langkah-pencegahan-covid-19-di-tmpt-kerja.

In addition, the Act also provides that any person who disobeys any lawful order or breaches any rules or regulations made under this Act commits an offence. Currently, RM1,000.00 is the maximum fine under the Prevention and Control of Infectious Diseases Act that can be issued to individuals and organisations that flout COVID-19 SOPs.[11] Nonetheless, with the passage of time and technological advancement, the Act is said to be inadequate for controlling a pandemic in 2021, to meet with the more recent application of electronic detection devices and phone applications to prevent the spread of infectious diseases.

Together with the 342 Act, there are pieces of employment-related legislation concerning health and safety at workplaces. The enforcement of these laws as tools to prevent COVID-19 transmission at workplaces is seen to be relevant and beneficial. Among them is the Occupational Safety and Health Act 1994 ("OSHA"), which is the major law dealing with industrial health and safety. The law aims mainly to prevent and reduce the number of industrial accidents and occupational diseases in the workforce. Though common law has already recognised the obligation of an employer to ensure a safe working environment for workers, special safety laws need to be enforced to make it compulsory for employers to introduce certain measures relating to the safety of workers. The Act spells out the duties of employers to provide a workplace which, so far as is practicable, is without risk to health. This includes the risk of COVID-19 disease, which the responsibilities of an employer not only on his immediate subordinates/employees but may extend to any independent contractor and his employees who may be working on the employer's premises.[12]

For example, there are provisions in the OSHA which empower the Minister to make regulations for or with respect to the safety, health, and welfare of people at work in order to achieve the objectives of this Act.[13] This includes the power to prescribe any regulations pertaining to the health and safety of workers during a pandemic.[14] Another important aspect is the law's stipulation of who is to be held accountable for offences committed by corporations. They are directors, managers, secretaries, or other like officers of the body corporate who can be charged jointly in the same proceedings with the body corporate or severally, and they shall be deemed to be guilty of the offence.[15]

Besides, other relevant laws are the Employment Act 1955 ("EA") and the Employees' Social Security Act 1969, under which the latter generally provides benefits to workers who are unable to work temporarily or permanently as a result

[11] "Dr Noor Hisham: Amendment to Infectious Diseases Act Cannot Wait for Next Parliament Sitting, More COVID-19 Threats Looming," Malays Mail, December 14, 2021. https://www.malaymail.com/news/malaysia/2021/12/14/dr-noor-hisham-amendment-to-infectious-diseases-act-cannot-wait-for-next-pa/2028398.

[12] Maimunah Aminuddin, *Malaysian Industrial Relations & Employment Law* (Kuala Lumpur: McGraw-Hill Education (Malaysia) Sdn.Bhd, 2013), 92–93.

[13] S. 66 (1) of the OSHA 1994.

[14] Department of Occupational Safety and health, Ministry of Human Resources Malaysia, "Safe Work Procedures For COVID-19 Prevention at Work", https://www.dosh.gov.my/index.php/prosedur-kerja-selamat-pencegahan-covid-19-di-tempat-kerja/file.

[15] S. 52 (1) of the OSHA 1994.

of a work-related accident or illness, while the former provides for basic benefits including termination, rights to rest day, annual leave, and sick leave, including those affected by COVID-19. Above all, these statutes may have direct or indirect relation to employers' duties and responsibilities to carry out preventive measures against COVID-19 as imposed by the government.

Although these provisions are generally enacted to govern normal situations and not intended solely or specifically for COVID-19 disease, they are still relevant in the context of it with modifications. As early stated, in some aspects, the existing laws need to be amended for the passage of time and technological advancement to suit new changes and demands. By having all these statutes, it would justify the state's intervention to compulsorily impose certain preventive measures on the corporation in order to avoid the spread of COVID-19, hence requiring the corporation to impose them on their workers.

It is worth noting that the imposition of COVID-19 preventive measures by the government requires support and commitment from corporations in order for the national agenda in the fight against COVID-19 to be successful. Nonetheless, despite the efforts made, there are criticisms about the state's involvement in the corporations' management of the COVID-19 pandemic. It was argued that states typically adopt and enforce radical measures or harsh restrictions to prevent the spread of the infection.[16] Making certain preventive measures compulsory or making certain people in a corporation liable for breaching regulations or rules issued by the government on this matter is a strict approach. Among the significant contentions is that COVID-19 crisis management practices implemented in organisations should be based on leaders' approaches following the nature and kind of business as the effects of the pandemic are manifold for most organisations and not follow the standard and general rules issued by the government. While there is no 'one size fits all," corporations should have freedom in responding to the coronavirus crisis in order to minimise the impact on public health and to limit disruptions to economies and supply chains. Therefore, the key question here is whether such involvement by the state is justifiable.

Having highlighted the foregoing, this chapter would address the issue of the state's intervention in organisations to require COVID-19 prevention measures under public health law and criminal law, beginning with a philosophical discussion concerning the justifications of public health and criminal law in disease prevention and control, followed by a discussion of the approach in arguments about how corporations could be regulated to prevent the spread of disease. Following that, discourse on governments' imposition of requirements upon corporations to undertake preventive measures against COVID-19 transmission in the workplace becomes the next section of this chapter.

[16] Dalia Vasarienė and Lyra Jakulevičienė, "Freedom to Conduct Business During the COVID-19 Pandemic" Tilburg Law Review 26 no 1 (2021); 16–29, https://doi.org/10.5334/tilr.246.

Conceptual Framework Governing Criminal Law and Public Health

The discussion will take cognisance of the major strands of conceptual frameworks underpinning the legitimacy of public health and criminal law, such as legal liberalism, legal paternalism and legal moralism. This is important for showing the breadth of every public health and criminal justice method.

(i) Public health

The concept of public health is centred on promoting and protecting community health. The Institute of Medicine defines public health as 'what we, as a society, do collectively to assure the conditions for people to be healthy'.[17] According to Larry Gostin:

> Public health law is the study of the legal powers and duties of the state, in collaboration with its partners (e.g. health care, business, the community, the media, and academe), to ensure the conditions for people to be healthy (to identify, prevent, and ameliorate risks to health in the population), and of the limitations on the power of the state to constrain for the common good the autonomy, privacy, liberty, proprietary, and other legally protected interests of individuals. The prime objective of public health law is to pursue the highest possible level of physical and mental health in the population, consistent with the values of social justice.[18]

As a result, instead of focusing on individuals, public health prioritises populations. It demands government intervention to improve the health and well-being of individuals. It also boosts the legitimacy of public health measures such as legislation's promulgation and implementation. The WHO-endorsed Ottawa Charter for Health Promotion identifies five categories of population health actions: establishing health-promoting national agendas, encouraging health conditions, enhancing community responsiveness, expanding individuals' or societies' abilities, and reorienting health services.[19] Hence, public health realigns attitudes and approaches to health-related issues.

The public health premise has already been called into question since it may encroach on the rights of people who are affected. This issue typically arises in the context of coerced-based interventions such as forced screening, treatments, and quarantine in the interest of public health. While modern public health recognises mutual participation, as opposed to the forcible public health authority or 'police power' that was focused in the 20th and 21st centuries, the government retains the discretion to dictate the scope of power and the necessity for coercive interventions. As a result, depending simply on the public health reason for legalising coercive health interventions may be insufficient.

---

[17] Institute of Medicine, *The Future of Public Health* (Washington, D.C.: National Academy Press, 1988).19.

[18] Lawrence. O. Gostin, *Public Health Law: Power, Duty, Restraint*, 2nd ed. (Berkeley: University of California Press, 2008), 4.

[19] World Health Organization, *Ottawa Charter for Health Promotion* (Ottawa: World Health Organization & Canadian Public Health Association, 1986), 6–7.

After weighing alternative options and interests, it should be restricted to major health risks. Because of overlaps between the state's coercive jurisdiction and certain other concerns, including security and civil liberties, its necessity may have to be judged case by case using criminalisation principles.

(ii) Legal liberalism.

Legal liberalism emphasises the notion of autonomy. On the basis of autonomy, competent individuals have the freedom to act without intervention. The concept of autonomy promotes the idea that humans have free will and should be allowed to make independent decisions to the maximum extent possible. However, if the exercise of freedom of action causes harm to others, the state may limit it. This is the essence of John Mill's important 'harm principle,' which outlines a necessary pre-premise for criminalization.

Joel Feinberg expanded on Mills' premise; 'It is always a good reason in support of penal legislation that it would be effective in preventing (eliminating, reducing) harm to persons other than the actor (the one prohibited from acting), and there is no other means that is equally effective at no greater cost to other values'.[20] It is noteworthy that neither self-harm, harmlessness, nor morality are adequate justifications for the government to intervene, according to liberalism. A utilitarian harm-oriented technique necessitates the state presenting relevant evidence establishing a relationship between the incriminating behaviour and its adverse outcomes for everyone other than the actor. According to Feinberg, this includes the possibility of injury.[21]

Feinberg, on the other hand, restricts the application of the harm principle to 'wrongful harms,' which he defines as the 'thwarting, setting back, or defeating of an interest' (of another person)[22] that 'violates the other's rights.'[23] The elements of significance are those that allow an individual to appreciate or pursue his life.[24] This suggests that unlawful harm can be used as a basis for criminalization. It is impossible to justify as a criminal simply opposing the interests of others without trampling on their freedoms, or vice versa.

If harm and offence concepts are employed, the state will investigate criminalization issues through a consequentialist perspective. However, establishing the definitions of these words in the absence of sufficient exposition from their proponents is a fundamental difficulty with both ideas. According to some observers, the ambiguity of the word "harm" may lead to broader judgments

[20] Joel. Feinberg, *The Moral Limits of the Criminal Law: Harmless Wrongdoing*, vol. 4 (New York: Oxford University Press, 1988), xix.

[21] *The Moral Limits of the Criminal Law: Harm to Others*, vol. 1 (New York: Oxford University Press, 1984), 11.

[22] Ibid.33.

[23] Ibid.34.

[24] Andrew. P. Simester et al., *Simester and Sullivan's Criminal Law: Theory and Doctrine*, 5th ed. (Oxford and Portland: Hart Publishing, 2013), 646.

about its applicability.[25] As a result, it may be claimed that criminal penalties for preventing injury should be restricted to exceptional instances.

(iii) Legal paternalism.
Punitive legislation is permissible under legal paternalism when an actor's behaviour is harmful. Paternalism is defined as the belief that "it is always a good reason in support of a prohibition that it is probably necessary to prevent harm (physical, psychological, or economic) to the actor himself and that there is likely no other means that is equally effective at no greater cost to other values".[26] This viewpoint holds that the state has a legal justification for interfering with human liberty in order to safeguard a person's security, wellbeing, or other interests or ideals, irrespective of his preferences, beliefs, or aspirations. According to paternalism, control over a person's behaviour may extend to his act of putting himself in danger, including the chance of more catastrophic injuries in an accident that the unhelmeted rider willingly undertook.
The fundamental complaint levelled towards paternalism is that it undermines the liberal concept of autonomy. Although paternalist law does not harm people's lifestyles, it does restrict an individual's freedom to behave freely in accordance with his or her own desires and preferences, including taking self-regarding actions.[27] As a result, it becomes reasonable to conclude that before a government chooses to penalise acts owing to a paternalistic ground, they must provide a convincing justification for their interference as to why improving the actor's welfare and safety supersedes their liberty.

(iv) Legal moralism.
Legal moralism justifies the criminalisation of specific conduct by claiming that it is inherently immoral. It thinks that"it can be morally permissible to prohibit activity on the grounds that it is intrinsically immoral, even if the actor or others are not harmed or offended".[28] Unlike the principles of liberalism and paternalism, moralism does not impose any negative repercussions or violations of individual rights on the employment of criminal law.
Lord Patrick Devlin attempted to qualify the punishment of immorality by attaching it to strong social condemnation of a specific deed. Because moral norms are such an integral aspect of society's structural framework, Devlin argues that their transgression should be forbidden in order to preserve the social system. Allowing morally repugnant behaviour to be sanctioned, he says, will wreak havoc on the social fabric, the disintegration and anarchy of humanity.[29] It is vital to argue that the primary consequentialist-based concern of Devlin in justifying the criminal law's usage is the implications of the

---

[25] For example, Simester et al., *Simester and Sullivan's Criminal Law: Theory and Doctrine*, 650–51.

[26] Joel. Feinberg, *The Moral Limits of the Criminal Law: Harmless Wrongdoing*, vol. 4 (New York: Oxford University Press, 1988), 26–27.

[27] Simester et al., *Simester and Sullivan's Criminal Law: Theory and Doctrine,* 657–58.

[28] Feinberg, *The Moral Limits of the Criminal Law: Harmless Wrongdoing*, 4. xix–xx.

[29] Patrick. Devlin, *The Enforcement of Morals* (New York: Oxford University Press, 1959/1965), 9.

law on the sustenance of society rather than the consequences of behaviour.[30] Given the inconclusive basis of animosity for criminalization, Devlin's position is problematic. Furthermore, there appears to be insufficient data to support Devlin's consequentialist-based hypothesis that immorality contributes to societal breakdown.

Moralism, with the exception of Devlin's moralist assumption, requires no factual evidence due to its purely deontological nature. As a result, the adoption of criminal law that meets and advances citizens' fundamental moral viewpoints is expected to increase. Moralism, on the other hand, is insufficient on its own to justify the deployment of criminal law. The argument opposing moralism centres on the indeterminate ambit of morals as well as its incompatibility with the ideal of autonomy. As a result, rather than relying exclusively on moralism, justified violation through criminalization may necessitate additional persuasive explanations.

According to the philosophical rationale presented in this part, both public health and criminal law will play significant roles. We can articulate that the state's intervention in workplace safety through the application of public health and criminal law is the right and proper thing to do because 'public health' tells us that a disease outbreak warrants the state's intervention, and legal sociology assures us that criminalisation can accomplish this successfully. The next subsection will offer the perspective on the extent of the valid claim to domain over the subject of state intervention to require Malaysian organisations to implement COVID-19 prevention measures at work.

Can State Intervention Be Justified?

After considering the philosophical foundations of criminal law and public health approaches, the question is whether it is possible to resurrect the perspectives on whether the state's intervention in organisations to require COVID-19 prevention measures meets the requirements of criminal law and public health, as well as describe the appropriate areas of responding to the behaviour. In order to support this, Goldstein and Robert argue that ideas influence policy through a range of factors, including the principled or causal beliefs they contain, in order to create road maps that improve actors' clarity regarding goals or end-means links, as well as the embodiment of political institutions' ideologies.[31]

A value judgement on liberals' conviction that commercial entities, particularly companies, should be granted complete independence from government regulation in this urgent pandemic issue on the basis of their autonomy to manage their operations must be made. This argument for companies' ultimate independence is less

---

[30] Robert. J. MacCoun and Peter. Reuter, *Drug War Heresies: Learning from Other Vices, Times and Places* (Cambridge: Cambridge University Press, 2001), 67.

[31] Charles. R. Schuster, "Comments on MacCoun," in *Choice, Behavioural Economics and Addiction*, ed. N. Heather and R.E. Vuchinich (Oxford: Elsevier Ltd, 2003), 404.

convincing. Taking the alternative view to liberal principles appears reasonable. The failure to impose COVID-19 preventive measures in the workplace cannot potentially affect the director or officer in charge of corporate management only. Workplace activity that is not in accordance with preventive measures, such as working without social distance, may result in COVID-19 infection, posing a risk of harm to others, including other workers and their families.

Due to the abundance of evidence, there is little space for dispute in this case. COVID-19 is a potentially lethal infectious disease with significant mortality rates and the potential for long-term detrimental consequences for a broader population. By January 26, 2022, 31,930 deaths had been recorded among 2,844,969 COVID-19 cases in Malaysia, representing a 1.1 percent fatality rate.[32] Workplaces are one of the most common settings for COVID-19 outbreaks. A sero-survey on 1078 workers from 17 work sites in the Klang Valley and Perak undertaken by Noordin and others supports this conclusion. Ecotest, a lateral flow immunoassay, was used to test them for SARS-CoV-2-specific antibodies (LFIA). Between July and September of 2021, they assessed that 82.2% of employees had been exposed to COVID-19. Migrant workers had a 99.9% prevalence, while local workers had 12.1%.[33] There is a significant prevalence of COVID-19 among Malaysian migrants, as shown by the sero-prevalence data, which is in line with findings from other nations that host large numbers of migrant workers, such as Kuwait and Singapore.

Further, Malaysia's Deputy Minister for Human Resources, Awang Hashim, has reported that as of September 18, 2021, Pertubuhan Keselamatan Sosial (PERKESO or SOCSO) had paid approximately RM11.19 million in compensation to employees infected with COVID-19 at work. There were a total of 15,036 incidents, with 13,170 involving local workers and 1,866 involving foreign workers.[34]

In Malaysia, employers are required by law to provide a safe working environment for their employees as an implied requirement in their employment contracts. Additionally, it is mandated under OSHA. Section 15 of OSHA obliges the employers to provide a safe and healthy work environment for their employees. Some of the specific responsibilities that fall under this umbrella include a duty to create and maintain safe and risk-free plans, facilities, and systems of work and a duty to supply and maintain a safe, healthy, and adequate working environment for his employees, as far as is practical, which are provided by S. 15(2) of OSHA. Failure to comply with the OSHA obligation is punishable by a fine of up to RM50,000.00 or two years in prison, or both, if the employer is found guilty in court. In addition to being spelled out in OSHA, the duty to ensure a safe and healthy workplace is also found in Common

---

[32] Ministry of Health Malaysia. "COVID-19 Cases in Malaysia", January 27, 2022, accessed on 28 January 28, 20221. https://covidnow.moh.gov.my/cases.

[33] Noorliza Mohamad Nordin, Aziyati Omar, Ishmah Hana Isharudin, Raisah Idris, Intan Surianne Mat Sahat, Selvanesan Sengol, Zirwatul Adilah Aziz, Zhuo Zhi Lim, and Teck Onn Lim. "Sero-Prevalence of COVID-19 among workers in Malaysia." *medRxiv* (2022).

[34] Lester, Tan "Total of RM11.19 million Paid in Compensation to Malaysia Employees Infected with COVID-19 at the Workplace", September 27, 2021, accessed January 25, 2022. https://www.humanresourcesonline.net/total-of-rm11-19mn-paid-in-compensation-to-malaysia-employees-infected-with-covid-19-at-the-workplace.

Law. Workers and visitors alike have a right to a safe and healthy work environment, and employers have a responsibility to ensure that happens.

These general standards may constitute a responsibility on the part of the employer to take precaution to avoid COVID-19 infection at the workplace during an outbreak. Malaysians have a fundamental right to good health, which is protected by Malaysia's Federal Constitution. Specifically, the right to life and individual liberty is addressed in Article 5(1).[35] People's right to personal liberty has been limited to the right to control their own bodies. The right to life comprises "all those features that are an intrinsic part of life itself and those matters which contribute to shape the quality of life," which "includes the right to live in a relatively healthy and pollution-free environment." Since the right to life in article 5 includes the right to health, it is clear that they go synonymously.[36]

Individual and societal harms and risks may arise as a result of corporations' inability or neglect to implement COVID-19 workplace preventative measures. Workers' exposure to health and safety hazards is arguably not right with major ramifications for human accomplishment, perfectionist values, and quality of life. The value of concepts was taught by philosophers such as Aristotle and Plato. The resulting harms, threats of harm, and immorality may justify the state's engagement goals. This appears to be consistent with liberalism, paternalism, and moralism ideas. At the same time, because of the individual and collective health implications, it may fall under the scope of public health. Conversely, criminal justice and public health have legitimate claims to jurisdiction over corporations' failure or neglect to implement COVID-19 protective and preventive measures in their workplaces, and neither can be ignored.

Given its legitimate stance on medical, public health, and moral issues, it is argued that combined public health and criminal law principles should apply to the issue of the state's intervention to oblige the corporations' preventive measures against COVID-19 in their workplaces. Arguably, the state's intervention in the corporations for the pandemic prevention is a vital matter that is only partially explained. This is given its limitations, which include a narrow lens on the effects on COVID-19 protection and appropriate approaches. The associated philosophical viewpoints are

[35] Adopting proper COVID 19-reduction measures is also usually critical to ensuring individual internationally recognised right to good health. Article 25 of the Universal Declaration of Human Rights 1948 (UDHR) attests 'everyone has the right to a standard of living adequate for the health and wellbeing of himself and of his family, including [...] medical care and necessary social services'. Similarly, according to Article 12 of the International Covenant on Economic, Social and Cultural Rights 1996 (ICESCR), 'the right of everyone to the enjoyment of the highest attainable standard of physical and mental health'. The UN Committee on Economic, Social, and Cultural Rights (CESCR), which is in charge of monitoring nations' compliance with their obligations under the ICESCR, defines the scope of the right to health, including that 'the right to health must be understood as a right to the enjoyment of a variety of facilities, goods, services and conditions necessary for the realisation of the highest attainable standard of health' (paragraph 9). In other words, international legal instruments establish criteria that will justify the state's intervention to secure workers' safety and health in the face of COVID-19.

[36] Khairil Azmin Mokhtar. "Health and Human Rights within the Context of International Human Rights Laws and the Malaysian Constitution." *IIUM Law Journal* 29, no. 1 (2021): 123.

crucial in generating complementary public health and criminal law solutions, rather than either or both, to address the issue of state's intervention in corporations to protect workers' job security from COVID-19 hazards. Total medical participation and disease are reasons for state control and regulation of corporations based on the disease or public health model, as well as total punitive reactions based on the moral model, may be avoidable.

While voluntary methods of lowering virus threats in the workplace are promoted, corporations must also be subjected to clear regulations requiring their undertaking of COVID-19 preventive measures at workplaces. It is also argued that the corporations that fail or neglect to adhere to established COVID-19 infection prevention and control measures should not be criminalised at first, but rather provided with behavioural changing interventions based on medical and public health models. When proper COVID-19 protective and preventive initiatives are not complied, it is permissible for the government to further interfere in order to implement behavioural modification measures other than criminal sanctions, such as education programmes, to corporations that have not adhered to the regulations meant to ensure worker safety and health and protection from COVID-19 infection for the first time.

The interventions can be integrated with other modes and means of communicating scientific information and prudent risk mechanisms to control COVID-19 infection to directors and officers of corporations that are breaking the law, in order to change their perceptions of virus risk and inspire them to protect their employees from infection. António Guterres, the Secretary-General of the United Nations, issued a statement on March 28, 2020, calling for "urgently promote facts and science".[37] Educating corporate directors and officers about reputable sources of health information, raising support for public health regulations if necessary, and concentrating efforts on vulnerable workers are all critical steps that providers can take to combat misinformation.[38] These non-coercive means are more credible, more humane and less intrusive on corporations' autonomy than traditional criminal methods such as incarceration, fines, and property confiscation in dealing with violators' behaviour.

However, it could be legitimate to use criminal coercion against corporations that fail to participate in and commit to the government's behavioural change programmes, as well as to comply with the specified COVID-19 infection prevention and control procedures. This would become a dependable system for attaining workplace protection and prevention of communicable diseases, including COVID-19 for the purpose of satisfying the public health and safety targets. The prospect of regulatory liability and criminal penalties may also become an effective means of inducing voluntary commitment.

This means that criminal legislation is only employed as a last recourse when alternative non-restrictive strategies fail to accomplish both compelling individual and

[37] Edith M Lederer. "U.N. Chief Antonio Guterres: Misinformation About COVID-19 is the New Enemy," March 28, 2020, accessed March 29, 2020. https://time.com/5811939/un-chief-coronavirus-misinformation/.

[38] Valerie A Earnshaw, and Ingrid T. Katz. "Educate, Amplify, and Focus to Address COVID-19 Misinformation." *JAMA Health Forum*, 1, no. 4, (2020). e200460-e200460. 2.

communal aims. As a result, corporations that breach the state's approved COVID-19 infection prevention and control procedures must face the liability. This means that directors, CEOs, managers, and officers in charge of corporations could be also tried, convicted, and sentenced based on the doctrine of lifting the corporate veil. The trial, prosecution, and conviction could serve as a strong deterrence in the future to ensure corporations' preventive measures and protection from COVID-19 infection.

If criminal control is indeed necessary in dire cases, it must be implemented in precise accordance with a set of foundational concepts. Coercive measures must be utilised in facilities and procedures of an allowable quantity that is neither too little nor too large, and in a quality that is consistent with verifiable evidence. According to Ashworth and Horder, criminal strategies should be abandoned if they offer no preferred or worse outcomes than other ways.[39] They need to conform to due process and fair procedural criteria. The period of criminal pressure must cease when the prerequisites for first responsibility are no longer met, rather than being extended. Rather than punishing the corporations or directors, CEOs, managers, and officers in charge of corporations, law enforcement should endeavour to educate them and appeal to their disease-controlling and disease-prevention responsibilities.

Conclusion and Recommendations

After considering the previously presented grounds for public health interventions through policy and legal tools, principally, it shows that the Malaysian government's requirements for corporations to undertake preventive measures at the workplace, particularly on a compulsory basis, are not imposed arbitrarily. Instead, they are congruent with aspirations to have safe and healthy working environments, as enunciated in statutes such as the Prevention and Control of Infectious Diseases Act 1988 and the Occupational Safety and Health Act 1994, together with several government recovery plans (phase one to current phase).[40]

In order to facilitate the Decent Work Agenda as advocated by the International Labour Organisation (ILO), Malaysia has been taking active and progressive actions by establishing the Malaysia Decent Work Country Programme (MDWCP 2019–2025).[41] Through this, the aspects of the well-being and safety of workers have been emphasised. In order to implement a safe, healthy, and dynamic work culture as one of MDWCP 2019–2025 core strategies, the Department of Occupational Health and Safety ("OSH") under the Ministry of Human Resources plays a crucial role. Their

---

[39] Andrew Ashworth, and Jeremy. Horder. *Principles of Criminal Law*. 7th ed. (Oxford: Oxford University Press 2013). 31–35.

[40] See further in the Malaysian National Security Council's website at https://www.mkn.gov.my/web/ms/.

[41] International Labour Organisation, "Malaysia Decent Work Country Programme - (2019–2025)" https://www.ilo.org/wcmsp5/groups/public/---ed_mas/---program/documents/genericdocument/wcms_762076.pdf.

role is extremely relevant during pandemics, particularly in dealing with pandemic management and workers' ability to resume work.[42]

Furthermore, one of the primary objectives of OSH is to prevent occupational and physical risks as well as to promote workplace physical, psychological, and interpersonal well-being. This may involve averting the harmful consequences of the COVID-19 pandemic on workers' physical, mental, and emotional well-being.[43] In this regard, danger diagnosis and risk analysis must incorporate not only the physical well-being of the workers but also their mental and emotional aspects. On top of that, corporations' top priority should be the right to operate in clean, safe, and healthy conditions. Equally crucial, adequate risk control, as well as safety and health measures, must be specifically adapted to the demands of the workforce. For example, frontline workers may require more consideration than other workers when designing risk control measures since the risks of infection may be higher for them.

Based on the above-mentioned premises, it is reasonably echoed that state intervention in business entities' COVID-19 preventive mechanism in order to slow the transmission of the virus at workplaces is justifiable. Possibly, civil and criminal lawsuits can be taken against corporations that ignore the government's policy and notions on public health or expose their employees to any risks that may accelerate the spread of COVID-19.

It might be claimed that by reiterating important basic tenets underlying the state's interventions to protect public health, each public health and criminal law principle has a fair expectation of justification for the state's intervention in organisations in Malaysia to require their COVID-19 prevention measures. Hence, the discussion in this chapter contends that none of these methods can be dismissed but can be reconciled by rephrasing or altering their terrains in the context of the state's intervention to oblige the corporations to undertake measures to prevent the transmissible COVID-19 virus at the workplace. This is critical in order to keep the distinctions between the two as distinct as feasible.

Interventions based on medical and public health concepts must be included in the final strategy to encourage voluntary participation and behaviour modification. Criminal penalties may be justified in some circumstances, such as a company's unwillingness or lack of commitment to participate in and commit to the government's behaviour change programs, or the ineffectiveness of less stringent approaches. Nonetheless, every mentioned goal should be accompanied by appropriate modifications to applicable policies, laws, and guidelines, as well as a clear description of corporations' mandatory obligations with regard to the primary COVID-19 preventive measures at work.

[42] Silvia Fernández Martínez, "Occupational Safety and Health and Workplace Health Promotion: An Essential Area for a Recovery from COVID-19 Based on Decent Work," *E-Journal of International and Comparative Labour Studies,* 10, no. 2 (2021): 62 http://ejcls.adapt.it/index.php/ejcls_adapt/article/view/940.

[43] International Labour Organisation, "Workers must be Protected with a Safe and Healthy Work Environment," International Labour Organisation (ILO), April 28, 2021, https://reliefweb.int/sites/reliefweb.int/files/resources/367306eng.pdf.

References

1. "About 61% of New Mass Cluster Infections Occurred in Workplaces." *The Hankyoreh,* March 1, 2021. Accessed on November 2, 2021. http://www.hani.co.kr/arti/society/health/984971.html
2. Al-Kuwari, Mohamed Ghaith, Asma Ali Al-Nuaimi, Jazeel Abdulmajeed, Sandy Semaan, Hamad Eid Al-Romaihi, Mujeeb Chettiyam Kandy, and Selvakumar Swamy. "COVID-19 Infection Across Workplace Settings in Qatar: A Comparison of COVID-19 Positivity Rates of Screened Workers from March 1 Until July 31, 2020." *Journal of Occupational Medicine and Toxicology,* 16, no. 1 (2021): 1–9.
3. Aminuddin, Maimunah. *Malaysian Industrial Relations & Employment Law.* Kuala Lumpur: McGraw-Hill Education (Malaysia) Sdn.Bhd, 2013.
4. "ANNEX 25: COVID-19 Management Guidelines for Workplaces." October 8, 2021 https://covid-19.moh.gov.my/garis-panduan/garis-panduan-kkm/
5. Ashworth, Andrew., and Horder. Jeremy. *Principles of Criminal Law.* 7th ed. Oxford: Oxford University Press, 2013.
6. Clarkson, Christopher M.V., Heather M. Keating, and Sally R. Cunningham. *Clarkson and Keating Criminal Law: Text and Materials* Vol. 7, London: Sweet & Maxwell, 2010.
7. "COVID-19 Global Employer Guide", Baker McKenzie. March 30, 2020, https://www.bakermckenzie.com/-/media/files/insight/publications/2020/04/baker-mckenzie_covid-19-global-employer-guide.pdf?la=en.
8. Department of Occupational Safety and Health, Ministry of Human Resources Malaysia, "Safe Work Procedures For COVID-19 Prevention at Work." https://www.dosh.gov.my/index.php/prosedur-kerja-selamat-pencegahan-covid-19-di-tempat-kerja/file.
9. "Dr Noor Hisham: Amendment to Infectious Diseases Act Cannot Wait for Next Parliament Sitting, More COVID-19 Threats Looming." December 14, 2021, https://www.malaymail.com/news/malaysia/2021/12/14/dr-noor-hisham-amendment-to-infectious-diseases-act-cannot-wait-for-next-pa/2028398.
10. Edwards, Christina Hansen, Gianpaolo Scalia Tomba, and Birgitte Freiesleben de Blasio. "Influenza in Workplaces: Transmission, Workers' Adherence to Sick Leave Advice and European Sick Leave Recommendations." *The European Journal of Public Health* 26, no. 3 (2016): 478–485.
11. Feinberg, Joel. *The Moral Limits of the Criminal Law: Harm to Others.* Vol. 1, New York: Oxford University Press, 1984.
12. Goldstein, Judith and Robert O Keohane. "1. Ideas and Foreign Policy: An Analytical Framework" In Ideas and Foreign Policy: Beliefs, Institutions, and Political Change edited by Judith Goldstein and Robert O. Keohane, 3–30. Ithaca, NY: Cornell University Press, 2019. https://doi.org/10.7591/9781501724992-003
13. Gostin, Lawrence.O. *Public Health Law: Power, Duty, Restraint.* Second ed. Berkeley: University of California Press, 2008
14. International Labour Organisation, "Malaysia Decent Work Country Programme - (2019–2025)", https://www.ilo.org/wcmsp5/groups/public/---ed_mas/---program/documents/genericdocument/wcms_762076.pdf
15. International Labour Organisation, "Workers must be Protected with a Safe and Healthy Work Environment." April 28, 2021, https://reliefweb.int/sites/reliefweb.int/files/resources/367306eng.pdf.
16. Institute of Medicine. *The Future of Public Health.* Washington, D.C.: National Academy Press, 1988.
17. *International Covenant on Economic, Social and Cultural Rights,* Geneva, December 16, 1966, General Assembly Resolution 2200A (XXI). https://www.ohchr.org/Documents/ProfessionalInterest/cescr.pdf
18. International Network for Government Science Advice 23 > 2020 – Medical Workers With COVID-19 Eligible for Workplace Accident Insurance. Accessed

January 25, 2022. https://www.ingsa.org/covid-19-policy-tracker/asia/china/23-january-2020-medical-workers-with-covid-19-eligible-for-workplace-accident-insurance/
19. International Social Security Association "Can COVID-19 Be Considered an Occupational Disease?" 2020. Accessed November 17, 2021. https://ww1.issa.int/news/can-covid-19-be-considered-occupational-disease.
20. Isa, Yusramizza Binti Md. "*Harm Reduction in the Context of Drug Use in Malaysia, A Critical Analysis of its Justification and Its Compatibility with the Criminal Justice Approach.*" PhD Diss., University of Lancaster, 2015.
21. "Langkah-Langkah Pencegahan Penularan COVID-19 di Tempat Kerja." May 28, 2021, https://covid-19.moh.gov.my/semasa-kkm/2021/05/langkah-pencegahan-covid-19-di-tmpt-kerja.
22. Lo, Ying-Ru Jacqueline, and Chihoko Asada-Miyakawa. World Health Organization Representative Office for Malaysia, Brunei Darussalam and Singapore.
23. Lupton, Deborah. "Risk and Emotion: Towards an Alternative Theoretical Perspective." *Health, Risk & Society* 15, no. 8 (2013): 634-647.
24. MacCoun, R.obert J., and Reuter, Peter. *Drug War Heresies: Learning from Other Vices, Times and Places.* Cambridge: Cambridge University Press, 2001.
25. Martinez, Silvia Fernández. "Occupational Safety and Health and Workplace Health Promotion: An Essential Area for a Recovery from COVID-19 Based on Decent Work," *E-Journal of International and Comparative Labour Studies,* 10, no. 2 (2021): 62 http://ejcls.adapt.it/index.php/ejcls_adapt/article/view/940.
26. Miller Derek et al., "Overview of Legal Measures for Managing Workplace COVID-19 Infection Risk in Several Asia-Pacific Countries," *Safety and Health at Work,*12, no 4, (December 2021) https://doi.org/10.1016/j.shaw.2021.08.003.
27. Ministry of Health Malaysia. "COVID-19 Cases in Malaysia", January 27, 2022. Accessed on January 28, 20221. https://covidnow.moh.gov.my/cases
28. Mokhtar, Khairil Azmin. "Health and Human Rights within the Context of International Human Rights Laws and the Malaysian Constitution." *IIUM Law Journal* 29, no. 1 (2021): 103-127.
29. Noordin, Noorliza Mohamad, Aziyati Omar, Ishmah Hana Isharudin, Raisah Idris, Intan Surianne Mat Sahat, Selvanesan Sengol, Zirwatul Adilah Aziz, Zhuo zhi Lim, and Teck Onn Lim. "Sero-Prevalence of COVID-19 Among Workers in Malaysia." *medRxiv* (2022).
30. Peter, Devlin. *The Enforcement of Morals.* New York: Oxford University Press, 1959/1965.
31. Sandal, Abdulsamet, and Ali N. Yildiz. "COVID-19 as a Recognized Work-Related Disease: The Current Situation Worldwide." *Safety and Health at Work* 12, no. 1 (2021): 136-138.
32. Sasaki N., Kuroda R., Tsuno K., Kawakami N. Workplace Responses To COVID-19 Associated with Mental Health and Work Performance of Employees in Japan. *J. Occup. Health.* 2020; 62: e12134. doi: https://doi.org/10.1002/1348-9585.12134
33. Schuster, Charles R. "Comments on Maccoun." In *Choice, Behavioural Economics and Addiction*, ed. Nick Heather and Rudy E. Vuchinich. 402-06. Oxford: Elsevier Ltd, 2003.
34. Simester, Andrew P., John R. Spencer, G.R. Sullivan, and G.J. Virgo. *Simester and Sullivan's Criminal Law: Theory and Doctrine.* 5th ed. Oxford and Portland: Hart Publishing, 2013.
35. Tan, Lester, "Total of RM11.19mn Paid in Compensation to Malaysia Employees Infected with COVID-19 at the Workplace." September 27, 2021. Accessed January 25, 2022. https://www.humanresourcesonline.net/total-of-rm11-19mn-paid-in-compensation-to-malaysia-employees-infected-with-covid-19-at-the-workplace
36. *United Nations Committee on Economic, Social and Cultural Rights (CESCR) General Comment No. 14: The Right to the Highest Attainable Standard of Health (Art. 12 of the Covenant)*, Geneva, August 11, 2000, available from https://www.ohchr.org/Documents/Issues/Women/WRGS/Health/GC14.pdf.
37. United Nations Department of Global Communications. "UN Tackles 'Infodemic' of Misinformation and Cybercrime in COVID-19 Crisis." Accessed May 17, 2021. https://www.un.org/en/un-coronavirus-communications-team/un-tackling-%E2%80%98infodemic%E2%80%99-misinformation-and-cybercrime-covid-19
38. *Universal Declaration of Human Rights*, New York, December 10, 1948, General Assembly Resolution 217 A, available from https://www.un.org/sites/un2.un.org/files/udhr.pdf. University Press, 2013.

39. Vasarienė, Dalia, and Jakulevičienė, Lyra. "Freedom to Conduct Business During the COVID-19 Pandemic." *Tilburg Law Review* 26, no 1 (2021): 16–29, DOI: https://doi.org/10.5334/tilr.246.
40. Webster, Rebecca Katie, Regina Liu, Kristina Karimullina, Ian Hall, Richard Amlot, and Gideon James Rubin. "A Systematic Review of Infectious Illness Presenteeism: Prevalence, Reasons And Risk Factors." *BMC public health* 19, no. 1 (2019): 1–13.
41. World Health Organization and International Labour Organization. "Preventing and Mitigating COVID-19 at work", Policy Brief, May 19, 2021. Accessed September 27, 2021. https://apps.who.int/iris/rest/bitstreams/1347444/retrieve
42. World Health Organization. *Ottawa Charter for Health Promotion*. Ottawa: World Health Organization & Canadian Public Health Association, 1986.
43. "Workers Must be Protected With a Safe and Healthy Work Environment." April 28, 2021. Accessed September 5, 2021. https://www.who.int/malaysia/news/commentaries/detail/workers-must-be-protected-with-a-safe-and-healthy-work-environment
44. "Workplace Clusters are Key Source of COVID-19 Infections in Malaysia." *New Straits Times*, January 23, 2021, https://www.straitstimes.com/asia/se-asia/workplace-clusters-are-a-key-source-of-covid-19-infections-in-malaysia.

Chapter 8
The Effect of COVID-19 on the Capital Market

Shanti Geoffrey

Abstract This chapter provides an analysis of the effect of the COVID-19 pandemic on the capital market. It focuses on the efforts taken by the government to alleviate some of the challenges faced by public listed companies due to the pandemic and highlights some of the future trends that are beginning to emerge. In particular, participants in the capital market, both listed companies and investors have gravitated towards technology in addressing some of the difficulties posed by the movement control restrictions which were put into place in order to slow down the spread of the disease. A focus area for the government has been in responding to the challenges faced by small and medium sized businesses who have been particularly hard hit during this period. An analysis has also been carried out on the sectors which have been more severely impacted as a result of the pandemic. At the same time there have been certain businesses that have seen unprecedented growth, such as face mask and glove producers and this has been set out in this chapter. The period of financial upheaval oftentimes provides fertile ground in terms of opportunities and incentives for financial fraud. The writer explores this area given the financial pressures faced not only by companies but by individuals during the pandemic. Some examples of investment scams and financial fraud have been highlighted.

Introduction

As Malaysia prepares to transition from the pandemic[1] to an endemic[2] stage, it is timely to consider what these changes will spell for the Malaysian economy, and in particular, its capital market.

[1] A pandemic is generally understood to mean a disease that *spreads* across many countries and many continents around the world.

[2] The disease is relatively constant in a population with largely predictable patterns.

S. Geoffrey (✉)
Christopher & Lee Ong, Kuala Lumpur, Malaysia
e-mail: shantig2018@gmail.com

L. Krishnan and W. M. Chan (eds.), *The Impact of COVID-19 on Corporations and Corporate Law in Malaysia*, https://doi.org/10.1007/978-981-19-5519-8_8

With 94.6% of its adult population fully vaccinated as of October 25, 2021,[3] the reopening of businesses, schools and the relaxation of travel restrictions, both domestically as well as internationally, the sentiment of cautious optimism coupled with relief, is palpable. The situation now is in sharp contrast to that of a year ago when vaccines were still being tested, infection and death rates were on an upward trajectory and movement restrictions were de rigueur.

Unlike a financial crisis which often spreads to the real economy after a certain time delay, the COVID-19 pandemic has caused abrupt disruptions in a broad range of activities in countries around the world within a very short span of time. This in turn has affected national and global incomes, economic growth rates and resulted in socioeconomic impacts at a scale which have not been witnessed since World War 2. An estimate by the International Monetary Fund ("IMF") underscored this stark reality, stating that the global economy shrunk by an estimated 3.3% in 2020, the steepest peacetime economic contraction since the Great Depression of the 1930s.[4] Encouragingly, the global economy is projected to grow by 5.5% in 2021 and 4.9% in 2022.[5]

What had started out as a health crisis therefore, has permeated into and demonstrated its ill effects in lives, livelihoods and economies spanning the globe. Malaysia's own Gross Domestic Product ("GDP") growth contracted by 5.6% in 2020, in stark contrast to the 4.3% growth in 2019, leading the central bank to take measures to mitigate the impact of economic contraction and promote economic recovery. These included reducing the Overnight Policy Rate to its lowest level in Malaysian history and rolling out debt relief measures and funding programmes for Small and Medium-Sized Enterprises ("SMEs") to help affected borrowers and businesses to alleviate cash flow constraints and maintain credit flows to the economy.[6]

Efforts Taken to Mitigate the Impact of the Pandemic on Households and Businesses

The policy response by the government to mitigate the impact of COVID-19 on businesses and to promote economic recovery can be seen in a slew of measures that were introduced in early 2020. The Overnight Policy Rate ("OPR") was reduced by a cumulative 125 basis points from 3.00 % to 1.75% from January to July 2020. At 1.75%, the OPR is at its historical low. These reductions were designed to provide appropriate support to economic activities and to cushion the impact of the pandemic, both on businesses and households. Given the impact of movement restrictions on

[3] CovidNow. https://covidnow.moh.gov.my/.

[4] Securities Commission Capital Market Masterplan 3, page 34.

[5] World Economic Outlook by IMF (October 2021) https://www.imf.org/en/Publications/WEO/Issues/2021/10/12/world-economic-outlook-october-2021.

[6] Bank Negara Malaysia Annual Report 2020, Governor's message.

economic activity, the OPR reductions were intended to ease debt servicing burdens and thus cash constraints for households, SMEs, and corporates. The lower interest rates also reduced the cost of financing and lent support to new credit expansion and fund-raising activity.[7] As at September 2021, OPR rates were maintained at 1.75%.[8]

A blanket loan moratorium which was first introduced in 2020 provided much needed relief to individuals and SMEs. The moratorium was applicable on all loan and financing repayments (except for credit card balances) for a period of six months with effect from April 1, 2020. A subsequent moratorium was again introduced in July 2021. Effective on July 7, 2021 it was made available to all individuals regardless of whether they are in the B40, M40, and T20 groups,[9] microenterprises, and affected SMEs.

COVID-19 and the Capital Market

Capital markets around the world were roiled by the effects of the pandemic and the Malaysian market was no exception. Proactive initiatives by the government were aimed at alleviating the economic and regulatory burden faced by various market segments and intermediaries as a result of several movement control orders in 2020 and 2021.

Margin Trading

The weaker investor sentiment facing the stock market resulted in falling share prices and consequently an increased likelihood of margin calls. As an example, the FBM KLCI index stood at 1602 points on January 2, 2020, sliding to 1372 points on April 29, 2020. Under Bursa Malaysia's trading rules, brokers are required to automatically liquidate clients' margin accounts if the equity in those accounts falls below 130% of the outstanding balance. In March 2020, the SC announced that brokers may, at their discretion, decide not to make margin calls or impose haircuts on any collateral and securities purchased and carried in margin accounts. They were also empowered to exercise their discretion as to whether to impose force selling measures on clients.

This measure which came into effect on March 26, 2020 and which was initially allowed up to September 30, 2020 had a dual purpose, which was to mitigate the force selling pressure on the market as well as to enable margin clients to offer other types of collateral to protect their investments. This flexibility was subsequently extended to June 30, 2021. However, brokers were required to comply with relevant requirements on capital adequacy and shareholders' funds.

---

[7] Bank Negara Malaysia, Annual Report (Kuala Lumpur: Bank Negara Malaysia, 2020) 8.

[8] theedgemarkets.com September 9, 2021.

[9] Bottom 40%, middle 40% and top 20% respectively.

Access to Capital

As economies across the globe ease into a period of recovery, there is a clear need to ensure efficient access to capital so as to power growth by companies. The capital market provides a critical link between companies who require capital and investors who provide the necessary funds.

For corporations in general, continued access to capital markets is critical to weather the effects of the pandemic by reducing the dependence on bank lending. Capital markets can therefore complement and reduce the dependence on bank lending on the road to recovery. South East Asia witnessed a rise in new initial public offerings ("IPO's") in the first half of 2021 and the projections are that this trend will continue into the second half of the year. In Malaysia there were 13 new IPO's in the first half of the year, raising some RM395 million with an IPO market capitalisation of RM1.5 billion on Bursa Malaysia. This involved a 102% rise in funds raised compared to the first half of 2020 where only 7 IPO's were listed with RM196 in proceeds and a market capitalisation of RM0.85 billion. The steps introduced by the regulators to alleviate some of the costs involved in listing exercises is a step in the right direction in reducing the burden that issuers face at this time.

During the pandemic, some measures were introduced by the government in order to ease the burden of financial compliance by listed issuers and facilitate fundraising in a timely and cost effective manner. This is consistent with the policy approach taken in other jurisdictions around the world. For example, the Financial Conduct Authority ("FCA") in the United Kingdom expanded its capacity to review prospectuses and highlighted existing possibilities for using shorter form prospectuses. In Italy, temporary measures have been put in place to waive the supermajority requirement for equity issuance by listed companies. In China, the China Securities Regulatory Commission ("CSRC") has removed the minimum requirement for profitability and leverage and relaxed the pricing framework required to do secondary equity offerings, aiming to facilitate capital access to listed companies.[10]The European Commission's EU Capital Markets Recovery Package, which is part of the broader Capital Markets Union initiative, allows for a temporary short-form prospectus for secondary equity issuances during 18 months. The standardised short-form prospectus of a maximum of 30 pages is estimated to cost half that of a regular prospectus and would be available for issuers that have been listed for at least 18 months on a regulated or an SME Growth market.[11]

In Malaysia, the authorities have introduced a raft of measures to alleviate the burden faced by public listed companies ("PLC's") due to the pandemic. In 2020, the Securities Commission Malaysia ("SC") announced a waiver of listing related fees for 12 months, which was applicable up to 26 February 2021 for companies seeking listing on LEAP or ACE Markets as well as those with a market capitalisation of

---

[10] Organisation for Economic Co-operation and Development, "The Future of Corporate Governance in Capital Markets Following the COVID-19 crisis," https://www.oecd.org/corporate/the-future-of-corporate-governance-in-capital-markets-following-the-covid-19-crisis-efb2013c-en.htm.

[11] Ibid at Chap. 3, paragraph 3.2.4.

less than RM500 million on the Main Market.[12] PLCs were also granted a rebate of 50% of their annual listing fees for the year 2020. In terms of new issuances, PLCs were also allowed to seek a general mandate from their shareholders in a general meeting to issue new securities up to 20% of the total number of issued shares (excluding treasury shares). The increased limit from 10 to 20% was allowed until December 31, 2021. Relaxations were also introduced for rights issues with eligible listed issuers being allowed to seek shareholder approval via general meeting to issue new securities up to 50% of their total number of issued shares (excluding treasury shares) or units to their existing securities holders on a pro-rata basis, up to December 31, 2021. According to the SC, a total of 389 companies benefited from the various listing fee waivers while 47 companies announced fundraising exercises under the increased or new general mandates.

On March 19, 2021, the SC and Bursa Malaysia provided further details on the additional relief measures under the Government's PEMERKASA Strategic Programme.

These measures, which include a 12-month waiver and rebate on listing-related fees, will reduce the fundraising cost for companies and provide further financial relief to listed issuers. Details of these measures include–

- A 12-month waiver on listing-related fees for IPOs effective March 17, 2021, which include a 100% waiver on processing fee, including prospectus registration fee for companies seeking to list on ACE and LEAP Market, as well as those with less than RM500 million market capitalisation on Bursa Malaysia's Main Market.
- A 100% waiver on initial fees and annual listing fee for companies with less than RM500 million market capitalisation
- A 50% waiver on initial fee and annual listing fee for companies of RM500 million market capitalisation and above.
- A 50% rebate of annual listing fees for the year 2021 for listed issuers that meet the following criteria:
  - Market capitalisation below RM500 million as of December 31, 2020.
  - Report financial losses as measured by group loss after tax in their quarterly report for a quarter ended on any date between February 1, to April 30, 2021 notwithstanding the date of submission of the same.
- A waiver on processing, perusal and listing fees on regularisation proposals received by December 31, 2021 from listed issuers that are in financial distress, among others.[13]

[12] Securities Commission Malaysia, Annual Report (Kuala Lumpur: Securities Commission Malaysia, 2020), p.32.

[13] Companies that have been classified as a PN17/GN3 company, cash companies as set out in para 8.03 of the Main Market Listing Requirements and ACE Market Listing Requirements and companies with an inadequate level of operations as set out in para 8.03A of the Main Market Listing Requirements and ACE Market Listing Requirements.

Insolvency Protection

An important measure introduced by the government has been directed at supporting companies which are otherwise viable but who have been impacted by the disruptions caused by the pandemic.

Section 466(1)(a) of the Companies Act 2016 ("CA 2016") provides that a company is considered to be unable to pay its debts if it is indebted for a sum exceeding an amount prescribed and neglects to pay the sum stipulated in the notice of demand within 21 days of being served with the said notice. Under the Prescription of Amount of Indebtedness of Company published on January 26, 2017 ("2017 Threshold Order"), this amount was fixed at RM10,000.

The threshold for insolvency of companies was first increased in April 2020[14] from a sum of RM10,000 to RM50,000, coupled with an extension of the timeline of 21 days as prescribed under S. 466(1)(a) of the CA 2016 to six months. This however was applicable only for notices of demand served between April 23, 2020 and December 31, 2020.

On April 1, 2021, following from the Prescription of Amount of Indebtedness of a Company[15] the amount of indebtedness for purposes of the term 'inability to pay debts' under S. 466(1)(a) of the CA 2016 has been permanently increased to RM50,000. This Prescription Order remains in effect at the time of writing.[16]

The policy response of providing relief for companies in financial distress has similarly been adopted in the capital market. Under Bursa Malaysia's Listing Requirements, ordinarily, a listed issuer is required to take certain steps to regularise its financial condition if certain criteria as set out in Practice Note 17 is triggered.[17] These criteria include thresholds involving shareholder equity, winding up of the listed issuer's subsidiary, appointment of receivers and managers, concerns relating to the going concern status and a default in payment by a listed issuer. In this respect, Bursa Malaysia in April 2020 provided temporary relief to listed issuers who had triggered the following criteria, namely:

- where the shareholders' equity of the listed issuer on a consolidated basis is 25% or less of the share capital (excluding treasury shares) of the listed issuer and such shareholders' equity is less than RM40 million;
- the auditors have highlighted a material uncertainty related to going concern or expressed a qualification on the listed issuer's ability to continue as a going concern in the listed issuer's latest audited financial statements and the shareholders' equity of the listed issuer on a consolidated basis is 50% or less of share capital (excluding treasury shares) of the listed issuer; and
- a default in payment by a listed issuer, its major subsidiary or major associated company, as announced by a listed issuer pursuant to paragraph 9.19A of

[14] Companies (Exemption) (No. 2) Order 2020 ("Exemption Order") gazetted on April 22, 2020.

[15] Gazette Notification No. 21841.

[16] As at October 30, 2021.

[17] See paragraph 8.04 of Main Market Listing Requirements of Bursa Malaysia.

the Listing Requirements and the listed issuer is unable to provide a solvency declaration to the Exchange.

As a result of this announcement, listed issuers that triggered the Suspended Criteria from April 17, 2020 to June 30, 2021 were not classified as a PN17 Listed Issuer. They were exempted from complying with the obligations relating to regularisation of their financial affairs[18] for a period of 12 months from the date of triggering the specified criteria and were only required to make an immediate announcement when the specified criteria were triggered and the relief provided. Similar temporary relief from Guidance Note 3 (GN3) classification under the ACE Market Listing Requirements was also granted by Bursa Malaysia for companies listed on the ACE Market. As at December 31, 2020, 13 companies were reported to have benefited from the relief measures.

Adaptation of Corporate Governance Policies—Leveraging on Technology in Holding Company Meetings.

A sustainable corporate sector is key to enabling the growth that is needed for economies to recover from the pandemic. To this extent, corporate governance practices have required some short term adaptations in order for companies to be able to comply with their regulatory requirements.

The movement control order imposed by the government in 2020 gave rise to the growing use of virtual meetings by companies to fulfil their regulatory requirements. While this was initially seen to be a novel route in enabling large numbers of shareholders to participate in and exercise their voting rights, this mode of convening meetings quickly gained traction as Malaysia entered into further lockdowns in 2021.

On April 18, 2020, the SC issued a Guidance and set of Frequently Asked Questions (FAQs) on the Conduct of General Meetings for Listed Issuers. This Guidance addressed common questions on the conduct of fully virtual general meetings and meetings of unitholders. Since then, the guidance has been revised several times with the latest revision issued on July 16, 2021.[19]

As at December 31, 2020, a total of 1017 general meetings were held virtually, 824 of which were AGM's and 192 were EGM's, with one-unit holder meeting. Interestingly, a survey conducted by the SC[20] indicated that 74% of the respondent shareholders would like the option of attending virtual meetings in the future,[21] demonstrating the changing attitudes among shareholders and the willingness to embrace the benefits brought about by digitisation. When broken down to age groups,

[18] Under paragraph 8.04 and PN17 of the Main Market Listing Requirements.

[19] https://www.sc.com.my/api/documentms/download.ashx?id=c5fbbbcd-3ab0-40ce-a22b-e8bb1d1fe0a8.

[20] Ibid at p.31.

[21] Securities Commission Malaysia, Annual Report (Kuala Lumpur: Securities Commission of Malaysia, 2020), p.30.

the study[22] indicated that 82% of the respondents who were below the age of 30 were keen to have the option to participate in remote meetings while only 43% of those aged 71 and above were interested in this option. An interesting conclusion of this survey is that this number grew to 71% among baby boomers (those aged 51–60), suggesting that the more digitally savvy investors were open to alternative modes of meetings.

The SC's guidelines are consistent with S. 327 of the Companies Act 2016 ("CA 2016") which provides that a company may, subject to its constitution, convene a meeting of members at more than one venue using any technology or method that enables its members to participate and exercise their rights to speak and vote at the meeting. The CA 2016 however requires that the main venue of the meeting shall be in Malaysia and the chairperson shall be present at the main venue of the meeting.

In addition to its guidance, the SC has included a useful set of FAQ's dealing with issues such as infrastructure, raising of questions and the voting process. Listed issuers are also encouraged to continue leveraging on technology to conduct their general meetings beyond the movement control order which includes conducting fully virtual or hybrid general meetings.

Achieving a fine balance between efficiency and effectiveness is often a challenge in business and this is acutely evident in the case of virtual meetings. Complaints such as poor connection, broadcasting interruptions, unanswered questions, insufficient time being devoted to issues raised from the floor and unreliable vote counting mechanisms can arise in virtual settings. Bearing this in mind, the SC, in its latest release of the Code on Corporate Governance[23] has provided guidance to companies that seek to leverage on technology in convening virtual meetings.

Among the changes introduced in the Code are that the Chairman of the board should ensure that general meetings support meaningful engagement between the board, senior management and shareholders. The engagement should be interactive and include robust discussion on among others, the company's financial and non-financial performance as well as the company's long-term strategies. The Code also recommends that shareholders be provided with sufficient opportunity to pose questions during the general meeting and that all questions should receive a meaningful response.

Practice 13.5 of the Code in particular, provides that the board must ensure that the conduct of a virtual general meeting (fully virtual or hybrid) supports meaningful engagement between the board, senior management and shareholders. This includes having in place the required infrastructure and tools to support a smooth broadcast of the general meeting and interactive participation by shareholders. Questions posed by shareholders should be made visible to all meeting participants during the meeting itself. Its guidance to this practice further elucidates the point by providing that the board and the Chairman should ensure that the conduct of virtual general meetings

[22] The study involved 29 listed issuers, which conducted fully virtual general meetings during the first movement control order and conditional movement control order period (April 18, to June 2020). A total of 309 individual shareholders responded to the survey.

[23] Effective April 28, 2021.

supports meaningful engagement between the board, senior management and shareholders. It also recommends that measures are taken to ensure a seamless experience for shareholders, with those participating remotely feeling as much as possible like they are in a physical meeting. The Code also eschews a one-way monologue by the board, a practice that can occur in a remote setting. Instead, it underscores the importance of providing the opportunity for shareholders to have real-time interaction with the board and senior management and for the latter to respond to any questions or remarks posed.[24]

The tone from the regulator is one that clearly supports the use of technology. In terms of electronic voting, the Code spells out some of its benefits which include more accurate and transparent voting results, shorter turnaround time for declaration of results, making voting more accessible even for the disabled, reducing administrative cost and paperwork and removing the need for physical ballot papers.

Takeovers

A healthy capital market is able to facilitate various types of corporate activity and for this reason, the SC's measures in the area of take-over activities were designed to introduce flexibilities in complying with the relevant regulatory requirements. A hybrid method of serving take-over notices and documentations was introduced. This involved electronic publication on dedicated pages through either the SC or Bursa Malaysia websites. At the same time, the offeror was required to send a physical Summary Notification to all offeree shareholders to inform them of the offer and the availability of the relevant notices and documents on the relevant websites. Shareholders were also allowed to accept an offer either electronically or by the conventional method of responding via post.

In the case of compulsory acquisitions under S. 222(1)(B) of the Capital Markets and Services Act 2007 ("CMSA 2007"), flexibilities pertaining to the copy of a statutory declaration that was required to accompany the notice of compulsory acquisition were announced in April 2020. This flexibility was subsequently uplifted in October 2021. With this upliftment, an offeror must revert to providing a copy of a statutory declaration to accompany the notice of compulsory acquisition, confirming that the conditions for the giving of the notice are satisfied.[25]

[24] Malaysian Code on Corporate Governance, April 28, 2021.

[25] Securities Commission Malaysia, "Update On Flexibilities in Complying With Take-Over Offer Requirements under Capital Markets And Services Act 2007 and Rules On Take-Overs, Mergers And Compulsory Acquisitions, October 4, 2021. https://www.sc.com.my/covid-19.

Regulated Short Selling

The onset of the COVID-19 pandemic had led to a sell down that depressed stock values, resulting in regulators around the world imposing short selling restrictions in their respective stock markets. Korea, for example, had a short selling ban of 14 months which was lifted on May 4, 2021.[26] Italy, Belgium, France and Austria were among European countries that introduced temporary short selling bans in 2020.

In Malaysia, the temporary suspension on short selling began on 24 March 2020 and was initially scheduled to end on 30 April 2020. It was subsequently extended to June 30, 2020 and then to December 31, 2020.[27] It was introduced by the SC and Bursa Malaysia, as part of a raft of measures designed to address some of the adverse effects of increased volatility resulting from the COVID-19 pandemic. Activities which were suspended were Intraday Short Selling ("IDSS") and Regulated Short Selling ("RSS"), as well as intraday short selling by Proprietary Day Traders. The suspension did not apply to Permitted Short Selling ("PSS") which is necessary for market makers to execute in order to provide the liquidity in the trading of exchange traded funds.

A further extension of the suspension of intraday short selling and intraday short selling by Proprietary Day Traders ("PDT Short Sale") to December 31, 2021 was announced by the SC on August 26, 2021.[28] This suspension does not however apply to RSS which has been allowed since January 1, 2021.

We note that in imposing the suspension of RSS in 2020, the authorities emphasised that the measure was temporary and regarded as a short-term step to provide stability and confidence in the Malaysian capital market.[29] Given the importance of RSS in providing liquidity in the market by allowing investors to take either a long or short position in stocks, it would suggest that the lifting of the ban is consistent with this need. Bans on short selling in fact have been decried by some authors who suggest that they are often accompanied by an increase in bid-ask spreads, particularly for smaller companies. The suggestion is also that bans on short selling fly in the face of informational efficiency of security markets, as short sellers have the ability to bring negative information to a market.[30] The continued ban on IDSS and PDT short sales have also led to observations that the price discovery process, will increasingly get muted.[31] It is interesting to note the UK's Financial Conduct Authority's statement on this issue in March 2020:

> Some European countries have introduced short selling bans . . . The FCA has not introduced such a ban. Most European National Competent Authorities have not introduced such bans.

---

[26] Ng Zhu Hann. "Is Shortselling a Fair Game", *The Star*, October 9, 2021.

[27] SC media release dated June 26, 2020.

[28] SC media release dated August 26, 2021.

[29] SC media release dated April 28, 2020. https://www.sc.com.my/resources/media/media-release/sc-and-bursa-extend-temporary-short-selling-suspension-amid-covid-19-volatility.

[30] Luca Enriques, and Marco Pagano, "Emergency Measures for Equity Trading: The Case Against Short-Selling Bans and Stock Exchange Shutdowns." http://ssrn.com/abstract_id=03598151.

[31] Jagdev Singh Sidhu. "Short Sightedness in Short Selling Ban", *The Star*, February 27, 2021.

Nor has the United States or any other major financial market . . . [T]here is no evidence that short selling has been the driver of recent market falls.[32]

The Pervasive Effect of the Pandemic on Companies

While the effects of the pandemic have been felt throughout the economy, some sectors in the capital market have been more acutely affected than others. Others have been able to ride the storm as a result of the high demand for their products or services. With a sharp increase in demand for protective gear amid the pandemic, companies producing items such as gloves and masks registered extraordinary profits. Top Glove, a rubber glove and face mask maker had their shares scaling to record highs in 2020,[33] with a profit of RM1.79 billion (up 384% vs. FY2019).[34]

On the other hand, companies in the airline and hospitality industry have faced significant pressures in light of the travel restrictions which were in force since early 2020. According to the Malaysian Association of Hotels, average hotel occupancy rates for 2020 stood at 32%. This compares with pre-pandemic times of around 64.2% in 2019 and 60.7% in 2018.[35]

In the airline sector, the Malaysian High Court had, on February 19, 2021, granted leave pursuant to the provision of S. 366(1) of the CA 2016 to AirAsia X Berhad, a Malaysian based long-haul low-cost airline, a sister company of AirAsia, to convene meetings of certain classes of AirAsia X's creditors. The meetings were intended to consider and approve a scheme of compromise or arrangements to be proposed by AirAsia X Bhd. The terms of the proposed Scheme are that the company's total estimated debts and liabilities of RM64.15bil will be reduced and will instead see the Scheme Creditors sharing a general pool of RM200mil, amounting to a haircut of 99.7%.[36]

More recently, it was reported that AirAsia X Bhd is proposing to pay 0.5% of debt owed to each of its creditors and to terminate all existing contracts so that it can restructure some RM33.65 billion (US$8.1 billion) of liabilities. The Malaysian low-cost long-haul airline reported that it had set a date of November 12, 2021 for creditor meetings to vote on the restructuring proposal. To gain approval for its proposal, Air Asia X Bhd needs agreement from creditors holding at least 75% of the total debt value in each of three classes of creditors.[37]

---

[32] Financial Conduct Authority, "Statement on UK Markets," March 23, 2020.

[33] RM26.60 on July 28, 2020. See also "Top Glove Share Price Rises New Record," *The Edge*, https://www.theedgemarkets.com/article/top-glove-share-price-rises-new-record-high-rm2660.

[34] Top Glove Corporation Bhd. Annual Report 2020 at p. 40.

[35] Zunaira Saieed, "Hotel Industry's Defining Moments", *The Star*, July 24, 2021.

[36] Airasia X Bhd v BOC Aviation Ltd & Ors [2021] MLJU 189.

[37] "AirAsia X Proposes Paying 0.5% of US$8.1b Debt Owed to Creditors", *The Star*, October 18, 2021.

The lifting of the travel bans effective October 11, 2021 have led to forecasts of a recovery in certain sectors. One research unit was of the view that the transportation sector stands to benefit the most from the lifting of the interstate bans. Other stocks that are anticipated to recover include those in the banking, energy, plantation, airlines, hotel, airports, casino, real estate investment trusts, brewery and media sectors.[38]

Apart from the obvious 'winners' and 'losers', there have been other consequences arising from movement restrictions that have influenced the global supply chain. The movement restrictions have resulted in an increased demand for digital devices such as laptops and smart phones which require semiconductor chips. At the same time, factory closures have resulted in supply constraints.[39] And while the shortage of semiconductor chips have resulted in lost sales for car makers throughout 2021, the global shortage of these chips have in turn resulted in a rally in the share prices of major outsourced semiconductor assembly and test ("OSAT") companies chip makers, including Malaysian listed companies such as Inari Amertron Bhd, Unisem (M) Bhd and Malaysian Pacific Industries Bhd ("MPI"), as well as automated test equipment ("ATE") manufacturers such as ViTrox Corp Bhd and Greatech Technology Bhd which saw their market capitalisations grow significantly over the last 12 months.[40]

SME's

The pandemic has demonstrated the vulnerabilities of micro, small and medium sized enterprises ("MSME") in accessing capital and this should be a significant priority for the government. It is clear that the ability of markets to respond to the changes brought about by the pandemic will require the right policy responses by governments coupled with resilience, adaptability and dynamism by the private sector. In addressing what some of these pressure points are, some market segments are clearly in need of focused attention by governments, both in terms of providing resources as well as adopting policies that will provide a clear trajectory of recovery and consistent growth. With a contribution of some 39% of GDP and almost 50% of total employment, SME's are a critical pillar of economic growth. However, this segment of the economy has been disproportionately affected by the pandemic with lower profit margins and narrower cash buffers. Malaysia suffered a total of RM40.7 billion losses in 2020 from the MSME sector as a result of a nationwide strict lockdown order imposed by the government to tackle the COVID-19 issue. The MSME

[38] Thomas, Huong. "All eyes on recovery stocks", The Star October 12, 2021.

[39] "Stock Investors Fret About Supply Chain Woes," *Starbiz*, October 12, 2021.

[40] "Tech Mania Amid Global Chip Shortage," *The Edge Weekly*, February 1, 2021.

sector's GDP contribution suffered more than 7% year-on-year decline to RM512.8 billion in 2020 against RM553.5 billion in 2019.[41]

Bank Negara Malaysia's ("BNM") proactive approach in assisting this segment was evident through its increase in allocation of financing assistance under the BNM's Fund for SMEs (BNM's Fund) from RM9.1 billion to RM23.1 billion. These facilities, which are channelled through the financial institutions, are designed to render immediate cash relief to adversely affected SMEs, support recovery of hard-hit economic sectors and enhance innovative capacity of high-tech SMEs. This Fund complements the much larger provision of SME financing by the financial institutions, which disbursed a total of RM256.8 billion in loans/ financing to SMEs in 2020.[42]

This market segment has also been a focus area for the SC. In its Capital Market Masterplan 3, the regulator notes that the conventional equity and bond markets mainly cater to listed companies, which contribute to only an estimated 15% of GDP, resulting in a shortage of access to capital within the wider economy. At the same time, mid-tier companies[43] ("MTC's") and MSME's make up roughly 60% of the economy. MTC's are gaining the government's attention as a market segment that is currently heavily reliant on banks and to some extent, private equity, for funding. In April 2020, the SC lifted fundraising limits on Equity Crowdfunding ("ECF") platforms and allowed ECF and peer-to-peer financing ("P2P") platforms to operationalise secondary trading. The amendments effected to the SC's Guidelines on Recognized Markets remove the yearly limit of maximum fundraising of RM3 million and increase the maximum amount that an issuer may raise from ECF platforms from RM5 million to RM10 million during their lifetime.[44]

From April until September 30, 2020, the government co-investment fund MyCIF, administered by the SC, also increased its funding matching ratio from 1:4 to 1:2 for eligible ECF and P2P campaigns, to provide additional liquidity into the alternative fundraising space.

This is a segment of companies that the SC views as a key development area with needs ranging from access to financing, corporate governance and professional development.[45] It is important therefore to consider how to improve the ability of this market segment to access capital more efficiently and hence achieve a more inclusive capital market.

---

[41] MSME sector suffered RM40.7b losses in 2020, Entrepreneur Development and Cooperatives Minister Datuk Seri Dr Wan Junaidi Tuanku Jaafar quoted in Malaysian Reserve, July 29, 2021.

[42] Bank Negara Malaysia, Annual Report (Kuala Lumpur: Bank Negara Malaysia, 2020), 30.

[43] Defined by the Malaysian Trade Development Corporation (MATRADE) as manufacturing sector enterprises with an annual revenue of RM50 million to RM500 million and services sector enterprises with an annual revenue of RM20 million to RM200 million. See Adeline Paul Raj, 'Mid-tier Companies' Funding Increasingly in Focus," *The Edge Weekly,* October 4, 2021.

[44] Paragraph 13.19 Guidelines on Recognized Markets.

[45] Adeline Paul Raj, "Mid-tier Companies' Funding Needs Increasingly in Focus". *The Edge,* October 4, 2021.

Digitisation

While brick and mortar based retail businesses have been severely impacted by the closure of shops, digital based models have flourished during the pandemic due to the acceleration in the adoption of technology, both by companies and individuals. Many expect these changes to be long lasting with increased funding for digital initiatives. As in other sectors, individuals have moved rapidly towards the use of online channels in the capital market with the regulator noting the increase in the opening of online accounts during the pandemic and urging industry to accelerate their digitisation transformations and offer more online products and services to investors.[46]

In terms of distribution of capital market products, the introduction of the regulatory framework for e-Services Platforms within the Guidelines on Recognised Markets permit platforms such as e-payment platforms, e-commerce platforms and e-wallets to partner with Capital Markets and Services licence ("CMSL") holders to distribute capital market products, thus providing additional investment channels for investors.

CMSL holders can now tap the captive customer base of these digital platforms and provide a more seamless and convenient investment experience. Investments made via e-Services Platforms are executed on a pass-through basis to the partner CMSL holder. This allows both the platform and the CMSL holder to build and maintain relationships with investors while ensuring that the investors' monies and assets are properly safeguarded. In 2020, the SC had also approved three additional digital investment management ("DIM") companies. The services offered by the new DIM companies provide more value-added options for investors such as spare change investing and differentiated investment strategies. By end December 2020, DIM had acquired 199,224 clients and RM466.20 million in total assets under management ("AUM"). This is a promising increase when compared to the figures at the end of 2019 which involved 23,803 clients and RM74.7 million in total AUM.

Recognising the need for fundraising for early-stage entrepreneurs with innovative business proposals, the SC introduced its Guidelines on Digital Assets on October 28, 2020. The digital token or initial exchange offering ("IEO") is a form of alternative fundraising where an issuer offers digital tokens using block chain technology to raise funds for their business projects. The SC intends to leverage the expertise of platform operators to review applications for the issuance of digital tokens for fundraising. Under this framework, all offerings of digital tokens in Malaysia are to be carried out only through an IEO platform operator registered with the SC. IEO platform operators will assess an issuer's proposal and the disclosures in the whitepaper, which is akin to a prospectus and gauge the issuer's ability to comply with the requirements of the Guidelines on Digital Assets, the Guidelines on Prevention of Money Laundering and Terrorism Financing for Capital Market Intermediaries and the Guidelines on

[46] Securities Commission Malaysia, "SC Announces Series of Capital Market Measures To Support Businesses," April 16, 2020.

Implementation of Targeted Financial Sanctions Relating to Proliferation Financing for Capital Market Intermediaries.[47]

Financial Fraud

Oftentimes, periods of financial upheaval and economic recession provide fertile ground for the proliferation of financial fraud. For example, following the 2008 global financial crisis, a majority of the participants of one survey[48] experienced an observable increase in the number of frauds, and 80% said they believe fraud levels increase in times of economic distress. According to the Fraud Triangle,[49] there are three reasons why fraud by an individual or company can occur—pressure or incentive, opportunity and rationalization. In the case of a pandemic, companies may be faced with severe financial pressures, resulting in a need to falsify financial earnings. The opportunity to falsify financial documentation can intensify as companies reallocate their resources to operational matters whilst reducing the focus on compliance and other internal controls. The constraints brought about by movement restrictions and remote working arrangements may also provide increased opportunities for fraud to be perpetuated as auditors face challenges in carrying out the audit verification process. This can be a particularly acute issue in terms of financial audits where there is limited access to clients' books and records.[50]

In other instances, companies themselves may be the victims of fraud perpetrated by their employees. These could be caused by supply chain disruptions during the pandemic that have led to companies seeking new vendors, without carrying out adequate vetting. Employees intending to commit fraud may collude with such suppliers by duplicating invoices or falsifying other documentation. Employees may also misappropriate confidential company data such as customer lists, pricing calculations or intellectual property.[51] In other instances, ongoing investigations by companies may have been halted due to the lack of resources or a shift in priorities during the pandemic.

In this respect, it is worthwhile to heed a cautionary tale of the US from two decades ago. The reallocation of resources from policing white collar crime to counter terrorism following the 9–11 attacks provides an interesting perspective. According to one study, the shift in the Federal Bureau of Investigation's ("FBI") resources

[47] Securities Commission Malaysia, Annual Report (Kuala Lumpur: Securities Commission Malaysia, 2020) 80.

[48] "Coronavirus Pandemic is a Perfect Storm for Fraud," Association of Certified Fraud Examiners, March 31, 2020 https://www.acfe.com/press-release.aspx?id=4295010491.

[49] https://corporatefinanceinstitute.com/resources/knowledge/accounting/fraud-triangle/.

[50] Securities Commission's AOB Emphasises the Need for High Quality Audit in Light of COVID-19, SC Press release April 7, 2020.

[51] "COVID-19 Operating in the 'New Normal'—A Backdoor to Increased Fraud Risk?" Deloitte. https://www2.deloitte.com/ch/en/pages/financial-advisory/articles/covid-19-operating-in-the-new-normal-fraud-risk.html.

following the attacks resulted in 1800 agents pursuing terrorism related offences. These resulted in fewer referrals for prosecution of white collar offences. However, the analysis indicated an increase in such breaches including a 40% increase in the rate of wire fraud in some areas. Meanwhile, banks were sounding alarms. The study found a 22% increase in the rate of Suspicious Activity Reports (SARs) filed by financial institutions, which cover such crimes as checking fraud, commercial loan fraud and self-dealing. The conclusion of the study was that spikes in white-collar crime likely occurred because criminals in those areas realised that they faced less FBI scrutiny and could get away with breaking the law.[52] Given that the world is slowly easing out of lockdowns, it would be useful to consider how best to address some of these possible outcomes particularly as it is said that a typical fraud case lasts some 14 months before detection.[53]

The pandemic has also seen a rise in reports of investment scams around the world. In New Zealand, for example, the Financial Markets Authority ("FMA") noted an increase in complaints about scams in the first half of 2021 and subsequently issued more public warnings about them compared to both 2020 and 2019. From January to June 2021, the FMA received 158 complaints about investment scams and fraud, an increase of 79% compared to the 88 complaints received during the same period in 2020, when the pandemic began, and up 49% on the 106 complaints in the first half of 2019.

Scams included pump and dump schemes and so-called "safe haven" assets, including cryptocurrencies or precious metals such as gold, silver or platinum and products supposedly effective against COVID-19, such as vaccines, medications and protective gear or equipment. Other scams included using social media platforms to identify and make contact with possible victims and the use of imposter websites – using the names, logos, addresses, certifications and other details of legitimate businesses, to fool investors that the website and its managers are part of, or associated with, the legitimate business.[54]

In the US, the Securities Exchange Commission ("SEC") has singled out pump and dump schemes as an area for investors to be aware of. The typology in this case, which is prompted by the pandemic, involves manipulators spreading false information about the products and services of publicly traded companies. This is often carried out using the internet, where claims are made that the products or services of such public listed companies can prevent, detect or cure the coronavirus. Often these false rumours cause the prices of such stocks to increase, following which the promoters and persons acting in collusion with them quickly dump the shares before the hype ends. When the stock price falls, the remaining investors lose

---

[52] Jay itzgerald. "Why White-Collar Crime Spiked in America After 9/11". https://hbswk.hbs.edu/item/white-collar-crime-enforcement.

[53] "Report to the Nations, 2020, Global Study on Occupational Fraud and Abuse," (Association of Certified Fraud Examiners). https://acfepublic.s3-us-west-2.amazonaws.com/2020-Report-to-the-Nations.pdf.

[54] "COVID-19 Related Scams," September 13, 2021, (Financial Markets Authority). https://www.fma.govt.nz/investors/scams/covid-19-related-scams.

their money. Smaller capitalised stocks are said to be particularly vulnerable to these schemes.

It is critical therefore for investors to be adequately equipped with the right tools when investing in the stock market. The SC has also noted an increase in illegal investment schemes. For the nine month period to September 2021, the SC has received over 2,000 queries and complaints about illegal investment schemes, which is more than double the total number reported in 2020.[55]

According to the SC, modes of illegal schemes include the promotion of non-existent investment schemes promising high returns with little or no risk within a short span of time. For example, "Invest RM200 and get RM10,000 within 24 h". Surveys conducted by the SC indicate that a sizeable number of survey respondents have an unrealistic expectation of returns as high as 24% to more than 31% per annum. Such unrealistic expectation of returns makes them susceptible to scams, which thrive on the promise of high returns, with little or no risk involved.[56]

Other illegal investment schemes include products which are marketed via social media platforms such as Facebook, WhatsApp and Telegram, requests for money to be deposited into a personal bank account and getting victims to part with more money in the pretext of income tax payment and miscellaneous fees. Other typologies include investments which are disguised as "Shariah compliant" to attract investors and the use of fake certificates, invoices and payment receipts from authorities such as the SC, CCM, BNM and the Inland Revenue Board of Malaysia ("LHDN"). Scams also include the use of clone firms where firms pose as legitimate entities by using names, logos, credentials, websites and other details of legitimate entities to promote bogus investment schemes.[57]

Moving Forward

With more than 90% of the adult population or 66.6% of the total population vaccinated as at October 13, 2021,[58] the capital market is priming itself for the road to recovery. While it is difficult to predict with any degree of certainty as to what the path to recovery will involve, the indicators on a macro perspective are encouraging. BNM and the Department of Statistics Malaysia ("DOSM") have announced that Malaysia's GDP expanded by 16.1% year-on- year ("YoY") in the second quarter of 2021 (Q2 2021). This indicates a continued recovery trajectory following a smaller decline of 0.5% in the preceding quarter (Q1 2021), and a decline of 3.4% during

[55] "Virtual Investsmart® Fest: SC Aims to Enhance Investment Literacy," Securities Commission Malaysia, October 8, 2021.

[56] Securities Commission Malaysia, Annual Report (Kuala Lumpur: Securities Commission Malaysia, 2020), 63.

[57] "Beware of Scams During COVID-19 Crisis", Securities Commission Malaysia. https://www.sc.com.my/covid-19/scam.

[58] https://covidnow.moh.gov.my/vaccinations/.

the fourth quarter of 2020 (Q4 2020). Based on a six-month perspective, GDP rose by 7.1%, relative to a contraction of 8.4% during the same period in 2020.[59] This positive trend is also evident in other metrics such as the Industrial Production Index which recorded an expansion of 8.2% from January to August 2021 when compared with the same period of the previous year.[60]

Yet there is still some suggestion that the road to recovery may not be smooth. While vaccines have been proven effective at mitigating some of the health risks involved, issues such as the spread of the Delta and other new variants continue to have an implication on the rate of recovery.

At the same time, the question arises as to what further measures can be put into place to alleviate the effects of pandemic on household debt. In 2020, Malaysia reported an additional 12.5% of households with incomes of less than RM2,500. 20% of those in the middle income or B40 group earning between RM4850 and RM10,959 have moved to the lower income B40 group. Those in the T20 income group were also affected where 12.8% have shifted to the M40 group.[61]

Around the world governments have formulated large-scale rescue packages to ensure the survival of their economies. Regulators have introduced various measures which are focused on market segments that are most in need of support. The road ahead may be rocky and the resilience and adaptability of the markets and their constituents will signal the measure of success in achieving and sustaining a recovery.

Conclusion

As we segue into the phase of recovery, resilience and adaptability are imperatives which will augur well for the capital market. Asia is poised for growth and Malaysia can be a part of this story if both the public and private sector do not lose sight of the opportunities that can be key to its successful recovery. The government needs to consistently formulate policies that promote rather than hinder the growth of the capital market while businesses have to adapt effectively to achieve gains in productivity, especially through the use of technology and knowledge. At the same time, key institutions are being looked upon to display the highest standards of governance and integrity as this is part of the branding that will impact Malaysia's competitiveness in world markets.

---

[59] Official portal of Ministry of Finance Malaysia, https://www.mof.gov.my/en/news/press-release/malaysia-s-2q-2021-gdp-grows-by-16-1-economy-expected-to-continue-on-recovery-path.

[60] The Statistics Department, quoted in The Star, October 13, 2021.

[61] Anthony Dass. Chief Economist and Head of AmBank Research. "Urgency to Address Rising Cost of Living", The Star, October 11, 2021.

References

1. Association of Certified Fraud Examiners. See ACFE Press Release 'Coronavirus pandemic is a perfect storm for Fraud', March 31, 2020 https://www.acfe.com/press-release.aspx?id=4295010491.
2. Bank Negara Malaysia Annual Report 2020, Governor's message.
3. "Beware of scams during COVID-19 crisis", SC website at https://www.sc.com.my/covid-19/scam.
4. https://covidnow.moh.gov.my/vaccinations/.
5. Cover Story: Tech mania amid global chip shortage, the Edge Weekly, February 1, 2021.
6. CovidNow. https://covidnow.moh.gov.my/.
7. COVID-19 Operating in the 'new normal' – A backdoor to increased fraud risk? https://www2.deloitte.com/ch/en/pages/financial-advisory/articles/covid-19-operating-in-the-new-normal-fraud-risk.html.
8. COVID-19 related scams, 13 September 2021, Financial Markets Authority https://www.fma.govt.nz/investors/scams/covid-19-related-scams.
9. Dass Anthony. Chief Economist and Head of AmBank Research. "Urgency to address rising cost of living", The Star, October 11, 2021.
10. Department of Statistics Malaysia, quoted in *The Star*, October 13, 2021.
11. Fitzgerald, Jay. "Why White-Collar Crime Spiked in America After 9/11". https://hbswk.hbs.edu/item/white-collar-crime-enforcement.
12. Huong, Thomas. "All Eyes on Recovery Stocks", *The Star,* October 12, 2021.
13. https://corporatefinanceinstitute.com/resources/knowledge/accounting/fraud-triangle/.
14. Jagdev Singh Sidhu. "Short sightedness in short selling ban", The Star, February 27 2021.
15. Luca Enriques University of Oxford, EBI and ECGI, and Marco Pagano 2020, University of Naples Federico II, CSEF, EIEF, CEPR and ECGI, Emergency Measures for Equity Trading: The Case Against Short-Selling Bans and Stock Exchange Shutdowns, http://ssrn.com/abstract_id=03598151.
16. Media release by the SC, Virtual Investsmart® Fest: SC Aims To Enhance Investment Literacy, 8 October 2021.
17. Ng Zhu Hann. "Is shortselling a fair game", The Star, October 9, 2021.
18. Official portal of Ministry of Finance Malaysia, https://www.mof.gov.my/en/news/press-release/malaysia-s-2q-2021-gdp-grows-by-16-1-economy-expected-to-continue-on-recovery-path.
19. Paul Raj, Adeline. "Mid tier companies' funding needs increasingly in focus". The Edge, October 4 2021.
20. "Report to the Nations, 2020 Global study on Occupational Fraud and Abuse," Association of Certified Fraud Examiners. https://acfepublic.s3-us-west-2.amazonaws.com/2020-Report-to-the-Nations.pdf.
21. Saieed, Zunaira. "Hotel industry's defining moments," *The Star*, July 24, 2021.
22. Securities Commission Malaysia. Annual Report (Kuala Lumpur: Securities Commission, 2020).
23. Securities Commission Malaysia, Capital Market Masterplan 3.
24. Securities Commission Malaysia. https://www.sc.com.my/resources/media/media-release/sc-and-bursa-extend-temporary-short-selling-suspension-amid-covid-19-volatility. April 28, 2020.
25. Securities Commission Malaysia, "Intraday Short Selling Suspension Extended to End of 2021t," Media Release, August 26, 2021.
26. Securities Commission Malaysia's AOB Emphasises the Need for High Quality Audit in Light of COVID-19, SC Press release, April 7, 2020.
27. Securities Commission Malaysia, "SC and Bursa Malaysia Extend Short Selling Suspension Until December 31, 2020," Media Release, June 26, 2020.
28. Securities Commission Malaysia. "SC Announces Series Of Capital Market Measures To Support Businesses," April 2020.

29. "Stock Investors Fret About Supply Chain Woes," *Starbiz*, October 12, 2021.
30. Theedgemarkets.com September 9, 2021.
31. "The Future of Corporate Governance in Capital Markets Following the COVID-19 Crisis," The Organisation for Economic Co-operation and Development. https://www.oecd.org/corporate/the-future-of-corporate-governance-in-capital-markets-following-the-covid-19-crisis-efb2013c-en.htm.
32. Top Glove Corporation Bhd. Annual Report 2020.
33. World Economic Outlook by IMF (October 2021) https://www.imf.org/en/Publications/WEO/Issues/2021/10/12/world-economic-outlook-october-2021.
34. www.sc.com.my/api/documentms/download.ashx?id=c5fbbbcd-3ab0-40ce-a22b-e8bb1d1fe0a8.

Chapter 9
Impact of COVID-19 on Corporations in Malaysia from a Corporate Restructuring and Insolvency Law Perspective

Hasani Mohd Ali

Abstract The COVID-19 pandemic has caused economic stagnancy that triggered many companies to suffer from financial distress and close down. The pandemic also sparks the practicality of the present laws on corporate restructuring. This chapter outlines the Malaysian government's intervention through fiscal injection and statutes amendments. Further, it addresses the existing laws governing directors' duties at a critical time within the insolvency zone. Besides, the discussion focuses on the applicability of restructuring measures available under the Malaysian Companies Act 2016. Methodologically, the chapter draws on the current updates for Malaysia on the issue through reliable secondary sources, employs doctrinal analysis to the relevant statutory provisions, and, whenever relevant, compares them with the UK and Australian positions. In the end, the discussion finds that Malaysia has adequate laws to cater to the restructuring needs of the impacted companies during the pandemic. Not to mention some changes were hastily introduced. The situation benefits from statutory rescue mechanisms, apart from the informal ones. The courts are mindful of protecting creditors yet are willing to get the ailing companies through the predicament. In addition, the law has many options to keep up with the demanding situations. Unfortunately, the restructuring mechanisms in place are too secured-creditors oriented. Hence, it should set out more rescue-friendly measures for stakeholders' broader interests, especially the entrepreneurship community, unsecured creditors and employees. The finding also reveals weaknesses in fraudulent trading provisions and lack of risk management as best practices in corporate governance.

Introduction

COVID-19 pandemic caused extensive travel bans and restrictions, including workplace closures and complete or partial lockdown to prevent the spread of the coronavirus. The COVID-19 norms (also known as the new normal) emerges with standard

H. Mohd Ali (✉)
Universiti Kebangsaan Malaysia, Bangi, Malaysia
e-mail: hmohdali@ukm.edu.my

L. Krishnan and W. M. Chan (eds.), *The Impact of COVID-19 on Corporations and Corporate Law in Malaysia*, https://doi.org/10.1007/978-981-19-5519-8_9

operating procedures that promote social distancing while encouraging online interactions and remote working. At the same time, the pandemic has brought about economic stagnancy to the nation and worldwide generally. Consequently, as the economy's main drivers, some corporations struggle with losses and experience difficulties in meeting their debt obligations. Many face the threat of winding up and must be closed down. The likely social impacts include mass layoffs and impediments of services and products to customers and suppliers.

Thus, to a certain extent, the pandemic brings the nation unnecessarily from general impoverishment of economy and emotional health among communities' members following the loss of confidence in commercial, financial, banking, and political systems.[1] To reduce the impact of the pandemic, the Malaysian government employed various methods such as enacting legislation, introducing changes in the Central Bank of Malaysia's policies, and introducing fiscal stimulus packages.

This chapter will highlight the impacts of COVID-19 on the economy and corporations generally. The movement control orders have brought many companies to the brink of insolvency. The principal analysis is on the law relating to insolvency and corporate restructuring in Malaysia. Therefore, it is interesting to analyse how the applicability of law relating to corporate restructuring interacts with economic policies' dynamism to minimise the COVID-19 impact. What are the likely deficiencies that the law and practice reveal in responding to the crisis?

The Economic Impact of COVID-19 and Official Policy Reactions

The Malaysian government has implemented preventive measures to curb the spread of COVID-19 through Movement Control Orders ("MCO") based on the current country's pandemic situation from time to time. Based on the estimation, Malaysia has suffered billions of Ringgit losses due to the implementation of the MCO. As reported, the country's economy lost RM2.4bil every day during the first MCO from March 18, 2020 till May 2020.[2] The government expected the country to lose RM600 million daily due to the Conditional MCO from May 4, 2020 till June 9, 2020 ("MCO 2.0").[3] The parliamentary ministerial statement of the Minister of the Entrepreneur Development and Cooperatives stated that 37,415 businesses closed following the

[1] Coincidently Malaysia has suffered from political instability during the relevant period. For the implications of business closed-downs, see Alice Belcher, *Corporate Rescue: A Conceptual Approach to Insolvency Law* (London: Sweet & Maxwell, 1997). http://library.dundee.ac.uk/F/?func=direct&local_base=DUN01&doc_number=000430231.

[2] Jo Timbuong, "Our Economy Loses RM2.4bil Everyday MCO is Active, Says PM," *The Star*, April 25, 2020, accessed November 22, 2021. https://www.thestar.com.my/news/nation/2020/04/25/our-economy-loses-rm24bil-every-day-mco-is-active-says-pm.

[3] "Finance Minister: MCO 2.0 Less Impact to the Economy," *Malaysian Development Investment Authority*, January 19, 2021, accessed November 22, 2021. https://www.mida.gov.my/mida-news/finance-minister-mco-2-0-less-impact-to-the-economy/.

MCO 3.0 implementation beginning May 2021. The figures were from an impact study of MCO 3.0 conducted between June 15, and 28, 2021. The statement also said that 26,007 were micro-enterprises and 2,738 were small and medium enterprises ("SME").[4]

The COVID-19 pandemic negatively impacted most sectors of the economy. The worst-hit sector is in the tourism industry, including aviation and hospitality. Besides, industrial and chemicals, energy, mining, utilities and construction are also severely affected. However, service-driven businesses, which could adapt more pragmatically by shifting to home-working models, are managing better. In general, sectors such as technology, pharmaceuticals, and retail parts, primarily through online transactions, have benefitted from the lockdowns.[5]

The companies worst affected by the pandemics are mainly unprepared by the onslaught of the COVID-19 impact. The fall in demand and disrupted business operations brought losses and financial distress. In addition, it has caused companies to face disruptions in fulfilling their wage commitment and debt repayment.[6] The policymakers introduced several strategies to mitigate the impact. First, fiscal and specific legislative changes were introduced to assist companies and individuals encumbered with losses and difficulty repaying their loans. The following are the stimulus packages introduced since the outbreak of COVID-19[7]:

1. PRIHATIN & PENJANA Economic Stimulus Package in February 2020, worth USD 4.8 billion.[8] In addition, Bank Negara Malaysia ("BNM") allocated a RM 2 billion relief facility deployed explicitly in working capital for SME.[9]
2. PEMERKASA (Strategic Programme to Empower the People and Economy) stimulus package amounting to RM20 billion launched on March 17, 2020.[10]
3. PEMULIH (People's well-being and Economic Recovery) was launched on June 28, 2021. This stimulus package is worth RM150 billion, with a fiscal injection of RM10 billion.
4. The Budget 2022, announced in the parliament by the Malaysian Finance Minister on October 29, 2021, provided the additional RM40 billion worth

---

[4] Nuradzimmah Daim and Arfa Yunus, "37,415 SMEs Closed During MCO 3.0," *New Straits Times*, September 29, 2021, accessed November 22, 2021. https://www.nst.com.my/news/nation/2021/09/731825/37415-msmes-closed-during-mco-30.

[5] See Ben Collins (ed), "2021 Corporate Restructuring Report," *SS&C Intralinks® & Acuris*, January 8, 2021, accessed November 22, 2021. https://www.intralinks.com/insights/publication/2021-corporate-restructuring-report.

[6] Collins. "2021 Corporate Restructuring Report".

[7] See Prime Minister of Malaysia Official Website. https://www.pmo.gov.my/.

[8] "Measures to Address COVID-19 Impact," *Bank Negara Malaysia*, accessed November 22, 2021. https://www.bnm.gov.my/covid19.

[9] "Measures to Address COVID-19 Impact," *Bank Negara Malaysia*.

[10] See Adib Povera, and Hana Naz Harun, "PM Unveils RM20 Billion Pemerkasa Assistance Package," *NSTTV*, March 17, 2020, accessed December 29, 2021. https://www.nst.com.my/news/nation/2021/03/674643/pm-unveils-rm20-billion-pemerkasa-assistance-package-nsttv.

of financing package for small to big businesses under the SemarakNiaga initiative.[11]

Salient Legislative and Policy Changes

Through the Temporary Measures for Reducing the Impact of Coronavirus Disease 2019 (COVID-19) Act 2020 ("COVID-19 Act"), the legislature has introduced many provisions that may help companies and individuals in distress. Some of the measures conferred by the COVID-19 Act include S. 23—No taking possession of goods according to S. 16 Hire Purchase Act 1967 (default payment) from April 1, 2020 to September 30, 2020. Further, S. 26—No legal action against defaulting consumers under S. 24v Consumer Protection Act 1999; and S. 30—No action to recover the rent due under S. 5(1) Distress Act 1951. Similar treatments are present in the provisions under Limitation Act 1953, Public Authorities Protection Act 1948, and Housing Development Act 1966. In addition, S. 7 of the COVID-19 Act recognises construction contracts adversely affected by the COVID-19 pandemic, and thus this provision reduces the impact against companies in the construction business.

Furthermore, S. 20 of COVID-19 Act 2020 increases the amount of indebtedness under the Insolvency Act 1967—from RM50,000 to RM100,000 (personal insolvency)—as a prerequisite for a creditor to present a bankruptcy petition against an individual. Regarding a company, a creditor may petition to wind up a company if it cannot pay its debts. Section 466 of the Companies Act 2016 ("CA 2016") prescribes three presumptions when a company is unable to pay its debts. One of the presumptions in para (a), i.e., the company fails to pay, secure or compound a sum exceeding the amount prescribed by the Minister within 21 days from demand. The creditor has six months from the expiry date of the notice to file a creditor's petition against the debtor company.

On April 21, 2020, the Minister issued "A Direction of the Minister under Paragraph 466(1)(a)". The purpose is to increase the indebtedness threshold from RM10,000 to RM50,000 as a temporary measure from April 23, 2020 to December 31, 2020. It is also noteworthy that the Minister made the Companies (Exemption) (No. 2) Order 2020 to extend the timeframe given to a debtor company to pay, secure or compound the debt from 21 days to six months. According to Gerard Tang and Tan Hei Zel, the order was ultra vires and flawed.[12] Section 615 of the CA 2016 allows the Minister to exempt a person, corporation or class of corporations from the provisions

---

[11] Izzul Ikram, "SME Association Commends Budget 2022 for Being Pro-Growth and Supportive of SMEs," *The Edge Markets*, October 21, 2021, accessed November 22, 2021. https://www.theedgemarkets.com/article/sme-association-commends-budget-2022-being-progrowth-and-supportive-smes.

[12] Gerard Tang, and Hei Zel Tan, "The Companies Exemption Order on Winding Up – Ingenious or Illegal?" *The Malaysian Lawyer*, May 28, 2020, accessed December 30, 2021. https://themalaysianlawyer.com/2020/05/28/companies-exemption-order-ingenious-illegal/#:~:text=The%20Companies%20%28Exemption%29%20%28No.%202%29%20Order%202020%20%28%E2%80%9C,to%20a%20statutory%20demand%20up%20to%20six%20months.

of the Act. However, the order exempted all companies; hence, it was arguably ultra vires since no express wording authorised the Minister to grant a blanket exemption. The writers also argued that the order was flawed. While intending to extend the 21 days under S. 466(1)(a), the order made no mention of a similar extension of the limitation period under S. 466(2) for creditors to file a winding-up petition. Section 466(2) requires creditors to file a winding-up petition within 6 months from the expiry of the 21 days in S. 466(1)(a). The failure of the order to similarly vary the limitation period in S. 466(2) gave rise to uncertainties that concerned creditors' rights. As a result, the order was subject to dispute as manifested in cases.[13]

Later, the Companies Commission of Malaysia ("CCM") permanently raised the indebtedness threshold for companies from RM10,000 to RM50,000 effective April 1, 2021 to reduce the risk of winding-up faced by companies coping with cash flow problems.

Insolvency and Winding-Up Proceeding

Section 464 of the CA 2016 lists the persons who may apply for a winding-up proceeding of the company. The circumstances are listed in S. 466, one of which is its inability to pay its debts. Thus, even a solvent company may be subject to being wound up. A winding-up order will cause liquidation that may bring the company to its end.[14] However, until the liquidation begins, the company may turn back to the path of profitability through a rescue mechanism by working out a turnaround plan to evade winding up. Rescue mechanisms can be formal and informal (see below).

The insolvency statutorily occurs when a company falls under any of the situations prescribed by S. 466 of the CA 2016. Conceptually, insolvency is determinable according to cash flow and balance sheet tests. The cash flow test of insolvency implies that a company is deemed unable to pay its debts "if it is proved to the satisfaction of the court that the company is unable to pay its debts (as they fall due)". However, S. 466(1) does not include the usual phrase "as they fall due" after the word debts. Instead, it presumes the status of inability to pay debts when a company fails to pay its debts after the expiration of 21 days after the creditor serves a notice of demand to the debtor company. The wordings of S. 466(1) nonetheless clearly shows that the description relates to the cash flow insolvency test, also known as the commercial test of insolvency.

The balance sheet test refers to when its liability exceeds its assets, which according to S. 466(1)(c) of the CA 2016, includes contingent and prospective liabilities of the company. In addition, S. 466(1)(b) relates to the ground of insolvency following a judgment debt.

[13] See *Re Sabah Development Bank Bhd* [2021] MLJU 1375; and *Geoforce East Sdn Bhd v Melati Evergreen Sdn Bhd* [2021] MLJU 549.

[14] For an excellent review of the concept of insolvency, see Professor Roy Goode, *Principles of Corporate Insolvency Law* (London: Sweet & Maxwell, 1990).

The statistics show that the number of winding up cases among Malaysian companies declined in 2020 and 2021. The number is surprising as the timeframe referred to the period when the COVID-19 outbreak struck, and many companies faced financial hardship. The decrease in the number of petitions could be a consequence of the automatic moratorium coupled with the increased threshold for inability to pay debts initially introduced in 2020. As CCM expected earlier, about 1,500 companies would benefit from increasing the debt threshold within the six months after April 1, 2021 (when CCM permanently increased it).[15]

Further, there are creditors, too, who may find it not worthwhile to petition for the winding-up of their debtors, mainly if both creditor and debtor belong to the same business chain affected by the economic stagnancy during this COVID-19 pandemic. Nevertheless, some unpaid creditors may consider filing a creditors' petition to get payment through the distributed assets of the company in liquidation. Nonetheless, the winding up of the company is not always the best option available to the creditors. They are subject to the ranking of claims under S. 527 of the CA 2016. Therefore, they may find it not expedient to petition if they are unsecured creditors or subject to other senior claims. The company's assets might not even be sufficient to pay the "senior claims", thus leaving the unsecured general creditors unpaid, especially when the worsening economic situation and the overall value of property plunge—worst when the value is determinable through fire-sales. For example, in the Airasia case,[16] most creditors may find it more advantageous to put a restructuring effort instead of pursuing winding-up proceedings. The restructuring exercise may proceed, even though its return may be lower than the original debt owed. Nevertheless, the amount is considerably better than the fire-sale estimate of the assets left after a winding up.[17]

The Threat of Insolvency and The Shifting of Directors' Duty

Case law development: Insolvency and the winding-up proceedings of a company carry two different connotations. A technically insolvent company can remain in business while the process of winding up has not begun. During such a time, the directors especially are prone to personal liability to pay the company's debts by allowing the company to continue trading when the company is on "the brink" or

[15] See "Increase to the Value of Indebtedness From RM10,000 To RM50,000 Until December 31, 2020," *Companies Commission of Malaysia*, accessed November 22, 2021. https://www.ssm.com.my/Documents/FAQ%20SECTION%20466%20INCREASE%20TO%20THE%20VALUE%20OF%20INDEBTEDNESS%20FROM%20RM10,000%20TO%20RM50,000%20(6.4.20).pdf.

[16] See *Airasia X Bhd v BOC Aviation Ltd & Ors* [2021] 10 MLJ 942.

[17] See Ben Collins (ed), "2021 Corporate Restructuring Report," *SS&C Intralinks® & Acuris*, January 8, 2021, accessed November 22, 2021. https://www.intralinks.com/insights/publication/2021-corporate-restructuring-report.

"the verge" of insolvency.[18] Such a critical time is where the zone of insolvency lies. When a company is within this zone, there is a recognition that directors' duty is shifting towards considering creditors' interests. At such a time, they should not consider the interests of shareholders, even worse, their interests as directors. One of the most challenging directors' duties decisions faced by boards of distressed companies relates to drawing down on unutilised revolving credit facilities to support much-needed liquidity when there is uncertainty about a borrower's ability to avert insolvency.[19]

Case law describes this time zone in many ways, such as in *Nicholson v Permakraft (NZ) Ltd*.[20] Cooke J explained that the director's duty to count the interests of creditors arises if the company is "insolvent, or near insolvent, or of doubtful solvency, or if a contemplated payment or other course of action would jeopardise its solvency." Hence, the shift of directors' duty to creditors may arise even when the company is not within the insolvency zone. Further, the English Court of Appeal in *BTI 2014 LLC v Sequana S.A.*[21] also departed from the need to refer to the insolvency zone and upheld that the directors' duty to creditors arises "when the directors know or should have known that the company is, or is likely to become, insolvent."

If the business is still viable, the company may opt for restructuring. In doing so, the creditors' interests are eminent. When the company proposes a restructuring plan, it should assess the restructuring impact on the credit profile and commence suitable arrangements with significant customers. In addition, with the ambiguity surrounding the length of COVID-19 or MCO causing business disturbances, if companies are the creditors, they should sensibly assess counterparty risk and take relief measures to protect accounts receivables. On the other hand, the companies within the same production chain should seek to safeguard sustainable but troubled companies, provide a genuine potential of gain, and boost their shared interests, which would be a healthier alternative than winding up the distressed company.[22]

During this critical time, the emerging legal principle suggests that the directors' act or omission may lead to liability as a director's duty includes taking action or intervening when required. The creditors may impeach the passive directors. The director's inaction can amount to a breach of fiduciary duty to the company, as

---

[18] See the case law development which recognised the shifting of directors' duty to take into account creditors' interests in *Grove v Flavel* (1986) 11 ACLR 161; *Brady v Brady* [1989] AC 755; *Winkworth v Edward Baron Development Ltd* [1986] 1 WLR 1512; [1987] 1 All ER 114, and *Ring v Sutton* (1980) 5 ACLR 546.

[19] Paul Bagon, and James Whelan, "COVID-19: The Suspension of Wrongful Trading Provisions and a Moratorium for Businesses in Restructuring—What is the Likely Impact on Your Business?" *Reynolds Porter Chamberlain LLP*, March 31, 2020, accessed December 30, 2021. https://www.rpc.co.uk/perspectives/restructuring-and-insolvency/covid19-the-suspension-of-wrongful-trading-provisions/.

[20] (1985) 3 ACLC 453 at 459.

[21] [2019] EWCA Civ 112.

[22] See Ben Collins (ed), "2021 Corporate Restructuring Report," *SS&C Intralinks® & Acuris*, January 8, 2021, accessed November 22, 2021. https://www.intralinks.com/insights/publication/2021-corporate-restructuring-report.

highlighted in the Privy Council's decision in *Byers and others v Chen Ningning (British Virgin Islands)*.[23] This Privy Council's decision has persuasively extended farther the directors' fiduciary duties at the times when insolvency is an issue. The directors' failure to act in the interest of creditors may attract personal liability. In this case, the liquidators of Pioneer Freight Futures Ltd ("PFF") brought a claim against Ms Chen, a company director, for breach of fiduciary duties. The Privy Council held that the respondent had breached her fiduciary duties for her failure as a director in intervening and preventing the loan repayment to Zenato Investments Ltd when PFF was insolvent. Such repayments amounted to undue preference and thus were in breach as she failed to exercise her powers for purposes that would further the creditors' interests.

The Malaysian judgments have already extended the directors' duty when their company is insolvent. For example, in *CIMB Bank Berhad v Jaring Communications Sdn Bhd*,[24] the director had made advances of money and loans using the company's money when the company was already insolvent. The court stated that the director had violated the statutory duties and fiduciary duties by doing so. Further, in *Dan-Bunkering (Singapore) Pte Ltd v The Owners of The Ship or Vessel' Pdz Mewah' (IMO No.: 9064009) of Port Klang & Anor*,[25] the court held that the director had breached his fiduciary duty when they sold a vessel at an undervalue whilst the company was already insolvent. As such, the transaction was unlawful since it denied the creditors of their rights. Likewise, in *Ng Pak Cheong v Global Insurance Co Sdn Bhd*,[26] the directors transferred property when the company was likely to become insolvent. The court found that the directors had disguised the true accounts of the company and thereby had misled creditors.

The above cases show the court may sanction directors when the directors' mala fide is present. Most cases suggest the directors had acted in their interests. Nonetheless, it is too far to argue that the directors may breach their fiduciary duties for failure to institute a restructuring plan as part of taking necessary steps to minimise loss to creditors. Unfortunately, such a dilemma is rife among corporations impacted by COVID-19. In corollary, some commentators point out that opting for a rescue mechanism can improve their possibilities of evading liability associated with their conflict of interest during such a time.[27] The formal restructuring would ensure creditor protection against jeopardising assets and letting the court supervise the process.[28] Still, the rescue mechanism can only start if the directors honestly believe that the business or part of it is still viable and not hopelessly insolvent.

---

[23] [2021] UKPC 4.

[24] [2016] MLJU 920.

[25] [2020] MLJU 1574.

[26] [1995] 1 MLJ 64.

[27] See e.g., Stacey Steele, "Directors' Duties to Prevent Insolvent Trading in a Crisis: Responses to COVID-19 in Australia and Lessons from Germany," *International Insolvency Review* 30(S1):S89-S110. https://doi.org/10.1002/iir.1424.

[28] Shih Lee, and Lynn Huey, "Case Update: The Interim Judicial Manager to Protect Assets in Jeopardy," *themalaysianlawyer.com,* October 26, 2020, accessed November 22, 2021. https://themalaysianlawyer.com/2020/10/26/singapore-interim-judicial-manager/.

Statutory provisions: A statement of directors' duty enshrined under S. 213 of the CA 2016 provides that a director of a company shall at all times exercise his powers for a proper purpose, in good faith and the best interest of the company. He must also exercise reasonable care, skill and diligence with the knowledge, skill and experience, which one may reasonably expect of a director having the same responsibilities and any additional knowledge, skill and experience he possesses. While the company is in the insolvency zone, the directors' decisions are fraught with peril. They need to delicately balance between the survival of the company and the creditors' interests. The directors' option is either to cease trading or to restructure. Ceasing trading may save them from insolvent trading liability.

In Malaysia, the directors can be liable for fraudulent trading through civil liability under S. 540(1) and S. 540(2) of the CA 2016.[29] In contrast, the criminal liability is under S. 539(3) or S. 540(5). Sections 539(3) and 540(1) require the element of knowledge of the delinquent director or officer in question. Such a similar requirement also presents in the fraudulent trading laws under S. 380 of the New Zealand Companies Act 1993; S. 339 and S. 341 of the Companies Act (Cap 50) (Singapore); S. 303 and S. 305 of the Corporations Act 2001 (Australia), and under S. 213 of the UK Insolvency Act 1986. The intent to defraud creditors in this way needs a heavy burden of proof since it must be proven that directors knowingly continued to trade with no intention of paying their debts. In *Dato' Gan Ah Tee & Anor (in their capacity as liquidators of Par-Advance Sdn Bhd (in liquidation)) v Kuan Leo Choon & Ors*,[30] the court adopted a lower degree of proof. The applicable standard of proof is the civil standard, which is one of the balances of probabilities based on the phrase "if…it appears" in S. 304(1) of the Companies Act 1965[31] (which is the equivalent to S. 540(1) of the CA 2016). In Malaysia, the significance of the provisions received growing judicial approval through the increased cases of fraudulent trading provisions recently.[32]

Many jurisdictions address the need to hasten a duty to the directors in such a situation by enacting specific provisions that protect creditors by disallowing the company from continuing trading to the detriment of the creditors whilst insolvency is at issue. The provisions are the Australian insolvent trading under S. 588G of the Corporations Act 2001; the UK's fraudulent and wrongful trading under S. 213 and S. 214 of the Insolvency Act 1986, respectively; and New Zealand's reckless trading under S. 339 of the Companies Act 1993. Usually, even where fraudulent trading is suspected, an application is made concerning an allegation of "wrongful trading" (or "insolvent trading") where the burden of proof is relatively lower.

---

[29] See S. 539(3), 540(1) and (2) of the CA 2016.

[30] [2012] 2 AMCR 829; [2012] 10 MLJ 706.

[31] The Companies Act 1965 was repealed when the CA 2016 came into force on January 31, 2017.

[32] For most recent cases, see *Tetuan Sulaiman & Taye v Wong Poh Kun & Anor* [2020] 10 CLJ 121, *Mega Trinity Sdn Bhd v Chin Thau Vui & Ors* [2021] MLJU 1193, *Lee Teck Meng v Prem Kumar A/L Ganasaratnam & Ors* [2021] MLJU 394, *Ananda Kumar A/L Krishnan v LS Fishery Sdn Bhd & Ors* [2021] MLJU 343, *Jalex Sdn. Bhd. v City Properties Sdn. Bhd. & Ors* [2020] MLJU 329[2020] 10 MLJ 100.

However, the COVID-19 impact may require more leniency to directors. For example, several businesses that would otherwise be viable have found themselves in financial difficulty in the UK due to the COVID-19 pandemic. As a result, the UK legislature introduced an amendment to the existing wrongful trading provisions[33] to provide that company directors and other responsible officeholders are "not responsible for any worsening of the company's financial position that occurs during the period November 26, 2020 to April 30, 2021". The government argued that these measures are due to the economic uncertainty caused by the COVID-19 pandemic, citing the impediment in trading conditions following lockdowns and trading restrictions that have been imposed on companies to control the spread of the virus.[34] Consequently, the measures aimed to reduce the unwarranted corporate insolvency filings and let viable companies trade through the COVID-19 crisis and recover once normal trading activities resume.

In this regard, Malaysia has not availed itself of the broader concept of insolvent trading, such as under Australian insolvent trading law and the UK wrongful trading law with the relatively lower burden of proof.[35] Interestingly, referring to the Malaysian Limited Liability Partnership Act 2012, S. 21 provides a similar UK wrongful trading provision in that a partner may incur personal liability for receiving distribution when he knows or ought to know that insolvent liquidation is unavoidable within two years.[36] A broader provision is arguably applicable and worth considering for Malaysia once the economic recovery resumes as part of checks and balances that help directors fulfil their duties properly.

Apart from actions based on fraudulent trading provisions, the liquidator also can institute actions to set aside certain transactions amounting to preferences to particular creditors, floating charges created within six months before winding up, or transactions at undervalue.[37]

Insights Into Corporate Manoeuvre During The Uncertain Times

Corporate governance presents a framework of control mechanisms that helps the company accomplish its goals while averting undesirable conflicts. The Malaysian Code on Corporate Governance ("MCCG") was introduced in 2000 and has been

[33] The UK Corporate Insolvency and Governance Act 2020 (Coronavirus) (Suspension of Liability for Wrongful Trading and Extension of the Relevant Period) Regulations 2020.

[34] UK Parliament, "COVID-19: Suspension of Wrongful Trading Liability Provisions," accessed December 30, 2021. https://lordslibrary.parliament.uk/covid-19-suspension-of-wrongful-trading-liability-provisions/.

[35] See e.g. Stacey Steele, Ian Ramsay and Miranda Webster, "Insolvency Law Reform in Australia and Singapore: Directors' Liability for Insolvent Trading and Wrongful Trading," *International Insolvency Review* 28, no 3 (2019). https://doi.org/10.1002/iir.1349.

[36] See S. 214 of the UK Insolvency Act 1986.

[37] See S. 528, 529 and 530 of the CA 2016 respectively.

reviewed and updated latest in 2021. Among others, corporate governance outlines the rules and procedures for decision-making, internal control and risk management.

If the company has adopted an effective monitoring risk mechanism as the corporate governance code recommends,[38] the company may shift to risk management more promptly. Risks represent a multidimensional perspective, in which the company should always be attentive to them, such as impacts on business operations due to disturbances to the supply chain and elevated workforce non-appearance, which may hinder an organisation's capability to provide products and services to its customers. Some commentators point to the failure of the risk management system that corporate governance cultivates to practice.[39] At the same time, the pandemic triggered an unprecedented crisis that not many companies could anticipate and cope with the risks. Together with effective audit, risk management is one of the critical principles of good corporate governance. The system should ensure a sound framework for internal controls and risk management to identify, analyse, evaluate, manage, and monitor significant financial and non-financial risks.[40]

Proper risk management and internal control are essential features of a company's governance, management and operations. Risk management aims at identifying threats and opportunities, while internal control helps deal with threats and takes advantage of opportunities. Proper risk management and internal control support companies in arriving at informed decisions about the degree of risk they are ready to take and executing the required controls to achieve their objectives. Positive companies incorporate effective governance structures and processes with performance-focused risk management and internal control at every company level and all activities.[41]

At the pandemic's peak, not many businesses can effectively put up long-term plans or financial decisions.[42] Government assistance might manage to hold up businesses for a while. The COVID-19 crisis may go beyond the assumed timeline, while its financial impact persists and is uncertain. During this time, companies should review their financial status. For example, if the company cannot repay its debts, it may review any force majeure provisions. The force majeure clause can only be referred to and relied upon where it is set out in a contract.[43] A contracting party who seeks to rely on the COVID-19 outbreak as a force majeure event should first establish whether the contract has a force majeure clause and whether the clause is broad enough to include the COVID-19 outbreak. A notice stating the force majeure clause

---

38 See the Malaysian Code on Corporate Governance 2021 ("MCCG 2021").

39 Charlie Maclean-Bristol, "COVID-19—A Massive Failure of Risk Management?" *BC Training Ltd,* June 12, 2020, accessed November 22, 2021. https://www.b-c-training.com/bulletin/COVID-19-a-massive-failure-of-risk-management.

40 See Principle B, MCCG 2021.

41 Principle B, MCCG 2021.

42 See Ben Collins (ed), "2021 Corporate Restructuring Report," *SS&C Intralinks® & Acuris,* January 8, 2021, accessed November 22, 2021. https://www.intralinks.com/insights/publication/2021-corporate-restructuring-report.

43 See *Muhammad Radhiedeen Bin Abdul Khalid v Saujana Triangle Sdn Bhd* [2017] MLJU 950.

must be given to the other contracting party.[44] Parties may recourse to the contract's frustration doctrine without a force majeure clause. A contract is frustrated as S. 57(2) of the Contracts Act 1950 states, "[a] contract to do an act which, after the contract is made, becomes impossible, or by reason of some event which the promisor could not prevent, unlawful, becomes void when the act becomes impossible or unlawful."

The distressed company can also initiate internal restructuring, negotiation with lenders for possible "haircut", or rescheduling of debts based on the operational volume of the business. The arrangements may include restructuring/rescheduling existing facilities, allowing short-term cash line facilities to address urgent trade lines needs or even providing additional assets to secure existing financing to maintain the security cover ratio expected by bank creditors.[45]

The company may initiate discussions with creditors or financiers to avail itself of any corporate rescue mechanism or financial relief measures proposed by the relevant financial institutions. First, however, it must take crucial measures to boost its resilience and prepare itself for revival at the earliest possible.[46] Further, since the pandemic and its effects continue, the economic condition could worsen once government assistance ends. Thus, the options for the management are to restructure to survive or face a winding-up petition.

The best advice by the experts is to begin restructuring at the earliest possible.[47] The restructuring will provide more room for manoeuvre and reduce risk. In addition, the management may consider new ways of working through restructuring processes. Unfortunately, few companies can afford to appoint independent advisors to restructure their businesses. The more formal option for restructuring requires court's intervention, which is costly and time-consuming. Therefore, many companies opt for the informal route of restructuring instead. According to Belcher, it refers to "the restructuring of the terms of a company's debt contracts to remedy or avoid default achieved by private negotiations with its creditor outside formal bankruptcy or insolvency proceedings." Such an informal workout covers arrangements to obtain financial investments or rescheduling or restructuring debts. The company's leading

[44] See example of the applicability of the clause in Syafiqah Salim, "Smelting Says Force Majeure Will Be Lifted From December 20 as COVID-19 Situation Improves," *theedgemarkets.com,* December 17, 2021, accessed December 30, 2021. https://www.theedgemarkets.com/article/malaysia-smelting-says-force-majeure-will-be-lifted-dec-20-covid19-situation-improves.

[45] Adrian Hong, "Stay the Course: Restructuring Towards Recovery," *KPMG,* accessed November 22, 2021. https://home.kpmg/my/en/home/insights/2021/02/stay-the-course-restructuring-towards-recovery.html.

[46] See Ben Collins (ed), "2021 Corporate Restructuring Report", *SS&C Intralinks® & Acuris*, January 8, 2021, accessed November 22, 2021. https://www.intralinks.com/insights/publication/2021-corporate-restructuring-report.

[47] Khoo Siew Kiat, "COVID-19 and Banks, Road to Recovery," *Deloitte*, June 23, 2021, accessed November 22, 2021. https://www2.deloitte.com/my/en/pages/about-deloitte/articles/covid-19-banks-road-to-recovery-pr.html.

banks usually would take the lead in the workout, but at times it also involves significant shareholders, bondholders, clients, and suppliers, who are directly interested to see the company's continued existence.[48]

An informal route for rescue suggests that the measure is cheap and less bureaucratic. Accordingly, the company can keep its low profile and avoid bad publicity.[49] However, the disadvantages include that the process may result from in-house thoughts that lack independent professional input. Further, a disgruntled creditor may disrupt the whole scheme. He may have the means to enforce his claims through foreclosure or forfeiture of properties and appoint a receiver.[50] In addition, an unsecured creditor can initiate a petition for a company's winding up. At the same time, some creditors prefer to stick to strict legal rights rather than resort to negotiation at the time of crisis.[51] Therefore, the distressed company typically needs a moratorium to provide a breathing space to work out alternative arrangements with their creditors. Hence, the restructuring measures backed by the court's sanctions are necessary for the debtor company. The distressed company might have no option but revert to a moratorium and opt for the formal route.

A moratorium period may apply to companies amid debt restructuring or scheme of arrangement. For example, corporate rescue mechanisms (see below) may provide companies with an opportunity to put forward a debt restructuring scheme to their creditors at an initial stage of financial difficulty. The provision of a moratorium period in the meantime would allow the company to concentrate its resources on the completion of its planned scheme, considerably reducing additional cash flow complications.[52] In the meantime, the moratorium also reduces the risk of creditors' actions that jeopardise the restructuring.

Besides debt restructuring, the companies may consider suitable defensive strategies, i.e., efforts to reduce costs and focus on underlying assets. The companies may be cautious of aiming for growth during this time, such as through mergers and

[48] See Alice Belcher, *Corporate Rescue: A Conceptual Approach to Insolvency Law* (London: Sweet & Maxwell, 1997). http://library.dundee.ac.uk/F/?func=direct&local_base=DUN01&doc_number=000430231. See also Ruzita Azmi, and Adila Abd Razak, "Corporate Workout: The Corporate Debt Restructuring Committee Revisited," *International Corporate Rescue* 8, No. 5 (2011).

[49] Alice Belcher, *Corporate Rescue: A Conceptual Approach to Insolvency Law* (London: Sweet & Maxwell, 1997). http://library.dundee.ac.uk/F/?func=direct&local_base=DUN01&doc_number=000430231.

[50] For example, under the UK Administration, an administrator is independent and does not necessarily represent the interest of secured creditors. See John Armour, and Riz Mokal, "Reforming the Governance of Corporate Rescue: The Enterprise Act 2002 (2004)," *ESRC Centre for Business Research Working Paper* No. 288. https://ssrn.com/abstract=567306 or http://dx.doi.org/10.2139/ssrn.567306.

[51] See Sarah Paterson, "Bargaining in Financial Restructuring: Market Norms, Legal Rights and Regulatory Standards," *Journal of Corporate Law Studies* 14, no 2 (2014): 333–365. https://doi.org/10.5235/14735970.14.2.333.

[52] See Ben Collins (ed), "2021 Corporate Restructuring Report," *SS&C Intralinks® & Acuris*, January 8, 2021, accessed November 22, 2021. https://www.intralinks.com/insights/publication/2021-corporate-restructuring-report.

acquisitions. Among the appropriate strategies include divestments and withdrawals from minor business areas. Insolvency practitioners who are expert third-party advisors may contribute to restructuring. In such an environment, restructuring advisers' expertise and experience working with businesses in similar positions will likely prove instrumental.[53]

While a moratorium may be in place, anticipating the restructuring process to complete, various creditors may apply to challenge or set aside such a moratorium. Thus, a scheme of arrangement proposal must have a real prospect of viability and is not an abusive process to delay the inevitable. The courts have often found the applicants applying moratorium or restraining orders to delay the legal process when no actual restructuring or rehabilitation efforts exist.[54] In the meantime, the risks of asset depletion are imminent during this period.[55]

The following discussion will highlight the main features of the rescue mechanisms under the CA 2016.

Malaysian Corporate Restructuring Mechanisms

On March 1, 2018, the Companies Commission of Malaysia ("CCM") enforced Division 8 Part III of the CA 2016 as part of the insolvency framework to aid the rehabilitation of companies in financial difficulties through Corporate Voluntary Arrangement ("CVA") or Judicial Management ("JM") procedures. As a result, Malaysia has three options of corporate restructuring mechanisms: the enhanced scheme of the arrangement ("SOA"), CVA and JM. In addition, CCM had also introduced and enforced on the same date the Companies (Corporate Rescue Mechanism) Rules 2018 and Practice Directive No. 4/2018 for such companies to complete the corporate rescue mechanism process. Besides, CCM released Guidelines for Corporate Rescue Mechanism Under Division 8 Part III CA 2016, according to S. 20C of the Companies Commission of Malaysia Act 2001, to inform the general requirements relating to CVA and JM.[56]

(i) Corporate Voluntary Arrangement ("CVA").
The company's directors may initiate CVA by presenting the proposal to its creditors. A CVA is a mechanism wherein the company may put forward a debt restructuring scheme to its unsecured creditors.[57]

The proposal would involve the appointment of an independent nominee (an insolvency practitioner) nominated by the creditors. The nominee will consider

[53] Collins, "2021 Corporate Restructuring Report."

[54] See *Sri Hartamas Development Sdn Bhd v MBf Finance Bhd* [1992] 1 MLJ 313.

[55] See above on directors' duty within an insolvency zone.

[56] See Companies Commission of Malaysia, "Guidelines for Corporate Rescue Mechanism under Division 8 Part III of the Companies Act 2016," accessed November 22, 2021. https://www.ssm.com.my/Pages/Legal_Framework/Document/Guidelines%20for%20CVA%20JM.pdf.

[57] S. 396(1) of the CA 2016.

and advise on the proposed CVA. In addition, the nominee must make a statement to the directors on whether the proposed CVA has a fair likelihood of being approved by the court. Further, he must also ensure the company will likely have adequate funds to carry on its business during the proposed moratorium.[58]

The directors may apply to the court based on the supportive statement by the nominee.[59] Under CVA, the court's involvement is only to serve as a filing platform for the required documents. The filing of the relevant court papers will activate a 28-day moratorium automatically,[60] throughout which the company is protected against any legal proceedings by the unsecured creditors. Additionally, the company cannot be subject to a winding-up and JM during this time. Besides, no shareholders can transfer any shares of the company.[61]

Within these 28 days, the nominee will summon a meeting of the company and a meeting of the creditors.[62] Making the CVA effective requires the approval of a simple majority of the shareholders and at least 75% of the creditors holding the total value of the company's debts present and voting at the meeting either in person or by proxy.[63] After that, it will be effective and binding on all creditors.[64] Nevertheless, the moratorium can extend to a maximum of 60 days extension at its expiry.[65] The extension is subject to the conditions stipulated in paragraph 3 of the Eighth Schedule to the CA 2016.

The main advantage of CVA is that it allows the company's management to continue in control during the process with the supervision of an insolvency practitioner.[66] At the same time, an independent insolvency practitioner will supervise the proposal's implementation to protect the creditors' interests.[67] As a result, CVA involves minimal court intervention.

However, it does not apply to public companies, licensed institutions or operators of a designated payment system regulated by Bank Negara Malaysia or a company subject to the Capital Markets and Services Act 2007.[68] It also

[58] S. 397(2) of the CA 2016 and paragraph 1 of the Seventh Schedule to the CA 2016.

[59] S. 396(2) of the CA 2016.

[60] S. 398(1) of the CA 2016.

[61] Paragraph 17 of the Eight Schedule to the CA 2016.

[62] S. 399(1) of the CA 2016.

[63] S. 400(2) and (3) of the CA 2016.

[64] A company which has created a charge over its property is not eligible to apply for CVA, See paragraph 1(d) of the Eighth Schedule to the CA 2016.

[65] Paragraph 3 of the Eighth Schedule to the CA 2016.

[66] Paragraph 1 of the Eighth Schedule to the CA 2016.

[67] See S. 397(2)(c), 399(2), 400(2) and 401(4) of the CA 2016.

[68] S. 395 of the CA 2016.

does not preclude a secured creditor from enforcing its security interests over the companies' properties.[69]

The CVA may provide relief to viable but distressed companies if the proposal provides a real return prospect and maximises creditors' interests. Thus, CVA serves as an alternative to winding up the distressed company.

(ii) Judicial Management ("JM").

JM is a mechanism where the Judicial Manager, a qualified insolvency practitioner,[70] undertakes the company's recovery or restructuring efforts. This procedure occurs when the company or its creditor applies to the court to appoint an independent and qualified Judicial Manager to take over its running. The condition is that the company is unable to pay its debts, and there is a reasonable probability of rehabilitating the company or preserving all or a fraction of its business as a going concern.[71] In this regard, the return for the creditors (mainly the secured ones) would be better than the anticipated return under a winding up. Therefore, the court will decide to place the company under a JM if there is a reasonable probability that the business could be salvaged. Thus, the interests of creditors are better protected than in a winding up.[72]

The Judicial Manager's mission is to prepare a restructuring plan for the company, and a temporary moratorium for six months will follow.[73] A JM order shall continue in force for six months from the order's date unless the company discharges the Judicial Manager. On the application of the Judicial Manager, the court may increase such a period for another six months on terms imposed by it.[74]

JM order covers a moratorium that any receiver or receiver and manager shall vacate its office. Further, the company cannot pass a resolution for winding up. Petition to wind up the company cannot be presented while the JM is in force. Also, creating a company's charge, share transfer, and membership change require leave of court. Finally, any enforcement of security interest over the company's property and any other legal proceedings against the company or its property cannot be taken except with the leave of court.[75]

The appointment of the Judicial Manager can convince creditors that professionals now supervise the company with related skill-sets to aid it in resolving

[69] Under the Seventh Schedule, a nominee may withdraw his consent to act if the information provided under paragraph 2 is inaccurate relating to that the property of the company is under charge. See paragraph 5(c) of the Seventh Schedule to the CA 2016.

[70] S. 407 of the CA 2016; see S. 417(2) of the CA 2016 for disqualification.

[71] S. 404 of the CA 2016.

[72] S. 405(1)(a), (b) and (c) of the CA 2016. See *Loh Teck Wah v Fintree Capital Sdn Bhd* [2021] MLJU 995, and *Spacious Glory Sdn Bhd v Coconut Three Sdn Bhd* [2020] MLJU 1827 where the court strictly interpreted the requirements.

[73] See S. 405(1)(b) of the CA 2016.

[74] S. 406 of the CA 2016.

[75] S. 411 of the CA 2016.

its financial issues. Since most companies have never had COVID-19-impact related experiences, they will need expert assistance to guide them through the rough patch. The appointment of a Judicial Manager does not mean the existing shareholders have lost control of the company. Instead, it is a temporary measure taken to facilitate the revival of the company.[76]

The Judicial Manager must convene a creditors' meeting within 60 days, or a period allowed by the court to approve the restructuring proposal.[77] The creditors must approve the restructuring plan whose claims the Judicial Manager has accepted by having at least 75% of the overall value of the company's debts present and voting at the meeting either in person or by proxy. The creditors may approve the proposal with modifications.[78] Unlike the SOA, it is noteworthy that the JM does not require any class of creditors' meeting approval. The restructuring plan obliges all creditors upon approval.[79] There is a duty required on the Judicial Manager to run the company's affairs following the proposal approved by the creditors.[80] There is no requirement of a class of creditors to approve the proposal. Therefore, the procedure inclines towards the secured creditors with a substantial stake of the company's liability.

In practice, JM is more prevalent than CVA. JM suits most ailing applicants, public companies and companies with encumbered assets. JM offers a more extended moratorium timeframe during the JM order, substantially longer than the CVA's 28-day moratorium period. A Judicial Manager has certain powers to deal with charged property, in contrast with the nominee appointed under CVA. Contrasting a CVA proposal, a JM proposal only requires approval by the creditors holding at least 75% of the overall value of the company's debts present and voting at the meeting. There is no condition for the approval of a simple majority of shareholders as required under CVA. Besides, the JM proposal shown at the creditors' meeting can be subject to the necessary modifications as may be reviewed among the creditors, with the Judicial Manager's consent.

This court-supervised rescue mechanism does not apply to licensed institutions or operators of a designated payment system regulated by Bank Negara Malaysia, a company subject to the Capital Markets and Services Act 2007[81] and a company that has gone into liquidation.[82] The reality of JM shows nonetheless that the number of approved proposals is significantly smaller than the number of applications made. For example, since its inception in March

[76] Mark Lim, and Eddie Chuah, "Malaysia: Survival of Companies Impacted by the COVID-19 Outbreak," *Baker McKenzie*, March 24, 2020, accessed November 22, 2021. https://www.bakermckenzie.com/en/insight/publications/2020/03/survival-of-companies-impacted-by-covid19.

[77] S. 406 and 420(1) of the CA 2016.

[78] S. 421(2) of the CA 2016.

[79] S. 421(3) of the CA 2016.

[80] S. 414(3) of the CA 2016.

[81] S. 403 of the CA 2016.

[82] S. 405(6) of the CA 2016.

2018, Lee Shih stated that as of July 26, 2021, 20 companies have applied for JM. Out of those, ten companies were placed in JM, but two of those JM Orders were subsequently set aside. Eight companies had their JM applications dismissed. Meanwhile, one of the applications was withdrawn, and the other was still pending as of July 26, 2021.[83]

(iii) Scheme of Arrangement ("SOA").

Through its director, shareholder, creditor, or even Judicial Manager, a company under financial hardship may consider applying to the court to sanction an SOA, i.e., a compromise or arrangement between the company and its creditors.[84] SOA was previously available under S. 176 of CA 1965. Then it was the only formal route or mechanism to restructure or reorganise companies' debts and financial obligations. However, the main disadvantage of this mechanism is that it requires full supervision by the court. Currently, S. 366 of the CA 2016 provides SOA with slight modifications.

The company can petition the court to order a meeting of creditors. The meeting considers an SOA between a company and its creditors or a class of creditors. The court may endorse the SOA if it obtains the agreement of 75% of the creditors' total value or class of creditors or members in attendance and voting either in person or by proxy at the meeting. Upon approval by the court, the terms of the SOA will bind all creditors or the relevant class of creditors (as the case may be).[85]

While the company proposes a compromise or arrangement, the company usually also applies a restraining order to prevent proceedings against the company.[86] The court may grant the restraining order that is taking effect between a company and its creditors or any class of creditors. The company needs the court's approval to dispose of property to protect creditors against asset dissipation. Such disposition includes property acquisition by the company other than those in the ordinary course of business.[87] In addition, the moratorium is for not more than three months. However, the court may increase this period for not more than nine months (inclusive of the initial three months), provided that the company fulfil certain conditions.[88]

It is noteworthy that though the process can be time-consuming as it requires an order for the court-convened meeting and the SOA's approval afterwards, this mechanism is available to all types of companies. Further, an SOA is more versatile as it covers not only the rescheduling of debts. It can also include

[83] See Shih Lee, "Judicial Management Trends After Three Years: Part 1," *THEMALAYSIAN-LAWYER.COM*, July 28, 2021, accessed November 22, 2021. https://themalaysianlawyer.com/2021/07/28/judicial-management-malaysia-trends-part-1/.

[84] S. 366(1) of the CA 2016.

[85] S. 366(2) of the CA 2016.

[86] S. 368(1) of the CA 2016.

[87] S. 368(4) of the CA 2016.

[88] S. 368(2) of the CA 2016.

issuing straight debt financial instruments, issuing quasi-equity financial instruments to creditors to mitigate repayment pressures, and injecting additional equity by existing shareholders or new potential investors.[89]

For Malaysia, corporate rescue mechanisms are generally available to cater to most restructuring needs involving companies of various types, sizes, and industries. The JM provides the most dynamic mechanism, based on the timeframe and the power and function of the judicial manager. However, the mechanism could be broader and more flexible if more stakeholders get fair access to the procedures. For example, classes of creditors may participate in a restructuring decision under the SOA. However, under the JM, the 75% majority of the creditors in value decide on the proposal. In addition, the initiation of the procedures is also primarily creditors oriented. For example, a secured creditor may object to a proposal under the CVA.

A more flexible and pragmatic procedure for a corporate restructuring analogous to the UK administration may be worth considering as the additional option. From September 15, 2003, the UK Enterprise Act 2002 allows the out of court appointment apart from the court appointment of an administrator. The Enterprise Act 2002 became part of UK administration law under Schedule B1 of the UK Insolvency Act 1986. Through this 2002 Act, the directors or shareholders of a company have a swifter and cheaper route of getting their company under administration without a court hearing. However, the law expects the directors to be responsible and proactive in going for rescue early. The primary governance mechanism still lies in the creditors' meeting, to which the administrator must refer his proposals. However, unsecured creditors may vote in the meeting but only require a meeting if this group is genuinely interested in the outcome. For example, if the company is so hopelessly insolvent that there will be zero left for the unsecured, the administrator may realise the secured creditors' assets. The scheme seeks to serve what is best to do to the group likely to be most affected.[90]

The UK legislature has also introduced a new stand-alone moratorium procedure as part of the Corporate Insolvency and Governance Act 2020 to assist companies' restructuring and rescue process. The moratorium is a director-led process in which directors remain in control of their business's day-to-day running, with an insolvency practitioner acting in the role as a "monitor" overseeing the company's affairs. The aim is to protect from creditor pressure whilst formulating a rescue plan without bearing high professional costs. The moratorium aims to rescue the company as a going concern rather than selling the business and its assets. In addition, the process provides requisite breathing space for businesses after the lockdown. The moratorium provides 20 business

[89] Mark Lim, and Eddie Chuah, "Malaysia: Survival of Companies Impacted by the COVID-19 Outbreak," *Baker McKenzie*, March 24, 2020, accessed November 22, 2021. https://www.bakermckenzie.com/en/insight/publications/2020/03/survival-of-companies-impacted-by-covid19.

[90] See John Armour, and Riz Mokal, "Reforming the Governance of Corporate Rescue: The Enterprise Act 2002 (2004)," *ESRC Centre for Business Research Working Paper* No. 288. https://ssrn.com/abstract=567306 or http://dx.doi.org/10.2139/ssrn.567306.

days of protection from creditor action. Directors can extend it for 20 business days by filing the relevant papers in court without creditor consent or up to 12 months with the pre-moratorium creditor's consent or court approval. To allow the moratorium to proceed and continue, the monitor must believe that the company's rescue is achievable.[91]

COVID-19 and Judicial Attitude on the Debtors' Obligation to Pay and Restructuring

Court cases that concerned COVID-19 and the insolvency situation at the time of writing are relatively limited. Most of the cases do not enter the courtrooms, despite the increase of restructuring exercises applying corporate rescue mechanisms. In the meantime, it is not yet time to know whether those mechanisms serve their purposes well. Nevertheless, some of the judgments may indicate the favourable courts' attitude in dealing with the debtor companies' plight during COVID-19.

As highlighted, the policymaker attempts to mitigate the severity of debt-ridden companies' problems through immediate constructive policies. The attempts succeeded to a certain extent as statistics revealed a decline in companies' winding-up cases. At the same time, the adverse impact of COVID-19 on the obligations of the debtor company receives expected adequate consideration within the courtroom. In addition, the court is mindful of interpreting the relevant creditors' protective provisions, mainly to avoid any abuse that causes injustice. In the case of *Re Sabah Development Bank Bhd*,[92] the petitioner bank presented a winding-up petition against the respondent company because three judgments in default ("JID") against the respondent company remained unsatisfied. The respondent, among others, argued that the company was still financially healthy. Celestina Stuel Galid J, in her judgment, asserted that the respondent failed to rebut the presumption that the respondent was not "commercially insolvent". Interestingly, the judgment referred to Mohd Nazlan Ghazali J who reiterated the legal position in *Karisma Synergy Sdn Bhd v Gates PCM Construction (M) Sdn Bhd*[93] at para 57 and 58 as follows:

> The solvency or otherwise of the respondent is in this context of little relevance. Once the debt is shown not to be bona fide disputed on substantial grounds, and the presumption of insolvency unrebutted, even if the respondent could show that it was solvent, its refusal to pay up would still entitle the petitioner to pursue the winding up of the respondent.
>
> It is settled law that the issue on the inability to pay a debt is to be considered in the commercial context, which is the neglect to pay current demands regardless of whether the debtor has assets which, if realised, would permit it to discharge its liabilities. The test of commercial insolvency means that the respondent company is not able to meet current debts

[91] See Corporate Insolvency and Governance Bill, accessed January 13, 2022. https://publications.parliament.uk/pa/bills/cbill/58-01/0128/20128.pdf.

[92] [2021] MLJU 1375.

[93] [2019] 1 CLJ 122.

when they fall due (see *System Communication Engineering Sdn Bhd v. Zabidin Sdn Bhd* [1999] 1 LNS 79; [1999] 1 AMR 1187).

In *Geoforce East Sdn Bhd v Melati Evergreen Sdn Bhd*,[94] the petitioner had obtained an adjudication order under an adjudication proceeding commenced against the respondent under the Construction Industry Payment and Adjudication Act 2012 (CIPAA). The court rejected the respondent's plea to benefit from the Companies (Exemption) (No.2) Order 2020 (see the relevant discussion above) because the case was out of the applicable timeline. The respondent, however, argued that it deserved equal protection. Nadzarin Wok Nordin JC firmly rejected such arguments after being satisfied that the respondent has not averred the respondent's solvency. On the contrary, the petitioner proved that the respondent was insolvent and unable to pay its debts. Therefore, the respondent was unable to rebut the presumption that it was a 'commercially solvent' company in that a company must prove its ability to pay its debts as per the judgment of the Supreme Court in *Sri Hartamas Development Sdn Bhd v MBf Finance Bhd*.[95]

Nevertheless, the judgments allowed the company to restructure its debts with the restraining order (under S. 366(2) and 368(1) of the CA 2016). In addition, the restraining order will enable the company and its creditors a breathing time and space to focus and formalise the terms of the proposed scheme for approval by the requisite 75% majority of the creditors in value and attendance. Subsequently, the plan approved by the creditors is to be sanctioned by the court.

In *Sentoria Bina Sdn Bhd v Impak Kejora Sdn Bhd & Ors*,[96] some creditors under the purported scheme of arrangement of S. 366 challenged the debtor's application of a restraining order according to S. 368(1). Several scheme creditors sought to amend the amount due to them by the applicant. Additionally, they questioned whether the scheme was speculative. However, the court was satisfied that the scheme was more beneficial than liquidation. Further, most creditors' support of the scheme reinforced the submission that an intelligent and reasonable man would approve the scheme. Anand Ponnudurai JC referred to Hayne J's reasoning, which was adopted by Nallini Pathmanathan J (as she then was) in the case of *Transmile Group Bhd & Anor*,[97] that it is not up to the court to decide on the commercial viability of a scheme.

The court followed the statutory requirements before sanctioning the proposed scheme of arrangement and the restraining order under S. 366 and 368(1) of the CA 2016. Anand Ponnudurai JC stated that when the meeting attained the requisite approval of 75% majority, the scheme would bind the creditors, including those who had opposed the scheme. According to S. 366(5), the order's office copy lodged with the Registrar of Companies will indicate compliance with the requirement. Reference was made to the judgment of Ong Chee Kwan JC, in *Re Top Builders Capital Bhd & Ors*[98] that the principal reason for the provision was to prevent

[94] [2021] MLJU 549.
[95] [1992] 1 MLJ 313.
[96] [2021] MLJU 1184.
[97] [2012] 9 CLJ 1071.
[98] [2021] 10 MLJ 327.

dissenting and disgruntled creditors from frustrating a scheme accepted by creditors holding 75% of the value of the debts present and voting at the meeting. To require a 100% acceptance of a scheme was impracticable (see para 109).

In *Pilecon Engineering Bhd & Ors v Malaysian Trustees Bhd & Ors*,[99] the parties agreed upon a consent judgment in 2019 following a scheme of arrangement. The plaintiff sought an order by the court to allow the parties to amend or vary the 2019 consent judgment or grant an extension of time for the plaintiff to comply with the judgment or grant the plaintiff relief from forfeiture. The plaintiff argued, among others, that COVID-19 had impacted its businesses in the construction industry. In that case, the court was wary in allowing the plaintiff's attempt to use the pandemic to support its contention. The plaintiff had breached its payment obligations multiple times in previous consent judgments and settlement arrangements between the parties. The breaches had occurred even before the COVID-19 pandemic hit Malaysia.

Adlin Abdul Majid JC held to give the 2019 consent judgment its full effect as agreed upon by the parties and reiterated that the court is *functus officio* and does not have the power to amend or vary the judgment.

Airasia X Bhd v BOC Aviation Ltd & Ors[100] is a landmark judgment revealing how COVID-19 has impacted Airasia X Bhd (AAX), despite being a solid company before the outbreak.[101] In that case, the pandemic has caused the unexpected earnings loss that AAX could not commit under the lease and other commitments.

AAX proposed an SOA to restructure its obligations with its creditors under S. 366(1) of the CA 2016. However, some creditors obtained leave of the court to intervene. The main issue, apart from questioning whether the proposed debt restructuring was bona fide, was whether the constituent of the class was a matter that the court ought to determine at the convening stage.

Ong Chee Kwan JC stated that AAX was not hopelessly insolvent as the proposed scheme would make the company debt-free with a fresh capital injection to meet its operation. Further, the court refused to assess AAX's financial status, emphasising that it had no role or expertise to make such a commercial assessment.

On the question of classes' constituencies, the court held that AAX did not need to show all the documents to support their selection in each class of creditors at the convening stage. Therefore, the application by way of Originating Summon filed by AAX was not an abuse of process and was bona fide. There was also no material non-disclosure in the application. The court stressed that the principal jurisdiction question for the court was identifying the classes and ensuring the constituents of each class at the convening stage. Tables 9.1 and 9.2 show the number of winding up petitions from 2017 to 2021, and the features of the various restructuring mechanisms.

---

[99] [2021] MLJU 1167.

[100] [2021] 10 MLJ 942.

[101] AAX was a renowned regional provider of long-haul air transportation services linking Malaysia with various destinations.

Table 9.1 Winding up petitions from 2017 to 2021

Year	Number of petitions
2017	2070
2018	2583
2019	3044
2020	1627
2021	1598 (JAN–SEPTEMBER)

Source Malaysian Department of Insolvency[102]

Table 9.2 Features of restructuring mechanisms

Restructuring mechanism	Insolvency practitioner's involvement	Moratorium period	Existing management's power	Creditors' approval
Scheme of arrangement	No	3 months + 6 months	Yes	75% in value of all classes
Judicial management	Yes (Judicial Manager)	6 months + 6 months	No	75% of the total value of creditors
Corporate voluntary arrangement	Yes (Nominee)	28 days (proposal) + 60 days	Yes	75% of the total value of creditors

Source Companies Act 2016

Conclusion

The preceding discussion shows that the Malaysian corporate restructuring law may appropriately deal with the COVID-19 impacts upon ailing companies. Insolvency may be impending in certain circumstances, but the company may not necessarily be wound up. COVID-19 is impermanent, and the businesses impacted may still be viable. The paramount consideration revolves around the economic and social welfare of the employees. Besides, for companies that have in place corporate responsibility, the strategic contribution of the companies should continue to serve the surrounding community.

The Malaysian law dealing with the COVID-19 situation is relatively adequate to cater to the companies' needs. However, even though the government's pragmatic intervention becomes apparent, it is not entirely coherent. For example, the hasty COVID-19 Act initially caused an anomaly as seen in the Companies (Exemption) (No. 2) Order 2020 to extend the timeframe given to a debtor company to pay, secure or compound the debt from 21 days to six months.

---

[102] "Liquidation Statistics 2021," *Malaysian Department of Insolvency*, accessed November 22, 2021. http://www.mdi.gov.my/index.php/legislation/liquidation/1824-liquidation-statistic-april-2021.

Further, though the courts generally revealed a favourable attitude in assisting the corporate predicament in restructuring debts, it is vital to uphold the creditors' interests besides other stakeholders in many situations. Consequently, much of the restructuring efforts may emphasise protecting creditors. Therefore, the rescue regime in Malaysia is predominantly a secured creditors-centric model in which creditor interests persist to maintain influence.[103]

The JM is the most robust mechanism available for companies to restructure. However, in the wake of COVID-19, the JM is not accessible to distressed companies as it should be. Apart from the high rejection rate, most JM applications did not relate the distresses with the COVID-19 situation. Therefore, a more flexible rescue-friendly mechanism, available even to unsecured creditors to apply, analogous to the UK Administration model, may be worth considering. Nevertheless, the next challenging question is whether its feature of out-of-court appointment is suitable and applicable for Malaysia. Are our corporate players ready for such a vibrant rescue mechanism? In the meantime, there are weaknesses in CVA and SOA. The CVA mechanism does not manifest itself as a mechanism of choice during the pandemic. This trend is most likely attributable to its shorter timeframe. While the SOA may not be attractive to some creditors since the existing board of directors remain in control over the company's affairs.

If the businesses collapse, employees might lose their jobs, bringing about social impact. Suppliers, along with other unsecured creditors, who have their very debts to claim may find the assets subject to the risk of dissipation. Malaysia's fraudulent trading provisions still require intent to defraud, unlike Australia's or UK's insolvent or wrongful trading laws.[104] A more flexible regime to govern insolvent trading may be welcome during pandemic times as most financial problems are due to the externally driven factors triggered by COVID-19. However, there is still a need to have a check and balance mechanism to monitor the director's behaviour to be more responsible, especially once the crisis ends. The creditors, notably the unsecured ones, are vulnerable to the possibilities of losing through asset depletion following directors' conflict of interests.

The time has come for Malaysia to reconsider the plight of unsecured reluctant creditors, most likely employees, and the suppliers in the production chain with no funds available to meet their claims if insolvent liquidation is unavoidable. Furthermore, the SOA and JM emphasise the secured creditors' approval in practice. Alternatively, the UK administration procedure may serve as a model for the study in

[103] A comparison can be made for future research with the position of the debtor in possession available under Chapter 11. See Ian F Fletcher, "UK Corporate Rescue: Recent Developments – Changes to Administrative Receivership, Administration, and Company Voluntary Arrangements – The Insolvency Act 2000, The White Paper 2001, and the Enterprise Act 2002," *European Business Organization Law Review* (EBOR) 5, no.1, (2004): 119 – 151. https://doi.org/10.1017/S1566752904001193

[104] Kumar Kanagasingam, and Michele Yee Phui Hwa, "Suspension of Wrongful Trading Provision — Is Malaysia. Missing Out?" *LHAG Update*, April 30, 2020, accessed November 22, 2021. https://www.lh-ag.com/wp-content/uploads/2020/04/Suspension-of-Wrongful-Trading-Provision-LHAG-update-20200430.pdf.

which the administrator's appointment, unlike typically under a receivership, is not to represent secured creditors only.[105]

The corporate players also need to be more vigilant in internalising the corporate governance framework that includes risk management and the practical function of the committee. For example, such a committee may need to monitor the risks surrounding the company's indebtedness and to suggest a solution to resolve the issues at the earliest possible.

The above suggestions may complement the corporate restructuring law by addressing vulnerable parties among the unsecured creditors, mainly SMEs and micro-entrepreneurs. Moreover, at the same time, some operate their business on other platforms, including conventional partnerships and sole proprietors, which means corporate restructuring schemes are unavailable. On top of that, they have fewer means to fund a formal rescue exercise and engage professionals in doing so. These businesses also may be less likely to implement an effective internal control and risk management system in place.

References

1. Bank Negara Malaysia. "Measures to Address COVID-19 Impact." Accessed November 22, 2021. https://www.bnm.gov.my/covid19.
2. Bagon, Paul, and James Whelan. "COVID-19: The Suspension of Wrongful Trading Provisions and a Moratorium for Businesses in Restructuring – What is the Likely Impact on Your Business?" *Reynolds Porter Chamberlain LLP*, March 31, 2020. Accessed December 30, 2021. https://www.rpc.co.uk/perspectives/restructuring-and-insolvency/covid19-the-suspension-of-wrongful-trading-provisions/.
3. Belcher, Alice. *Corporate Rescue: A Conceptual Approach to Insolvency Law.* London: Sweet & Maxwell, 1997. http://library.dundee.ac.uk/F/?func=direct&local_base=DUN01&doc_number=000430231.
4. Collins, Ben (ed). "2021 Corporate Restructuring Report." *SS&C Intralinks® & Acuris*, January 8, 2021. Accessed November 22, 2021. https://www.intralinks.com/insights/publication/2021-corporate-restructuring-report.
5. Companies Commission of Malaysia. "Increase to the Value of Indebtedness From RM10,000 To RM50,000 Until 31 December 2020." Accessed November 22, 2021. https://www.ssm.com.my/Documents/FAQ%20SECTION%20466%20INCREASE%20TO%20THE%20VALUE%20OF%20INDEBTEDNESS%20FROM%20RM10,000%20TO%20RM50,000%20(6.4.20).pdf.
6. Daim, Nuradzimmah, and Arfa Yunus. "37,415 SMEs Closed During MCO 3.0." *New Straits Times*, September 29, 2021. Accessed November 22, 2021. https://www.nst.com.my/news/nation/2021/09/731825/37415-msmes-closed-during-mco-30.
7. "Finance Minister: MCO 2.0 Less Impact to the Economy." *Malaysian Development Investment Authority*, January 19, 2021. Accessed November 22, 2021. https://www.mida.gov.my/mida-news/finance-minister-mco-2-0-less-impact-to-the-economy/.

[105] UK Administration is more rescue oriented and favours unsecured creditors e.g., tax claims should come after creditors are paid. However, further discussion on this issue is outside the ambit of this chapter. See John Armour, and Riz Mokal, "Reforming the Governance of Corporate Rescue: The Enterprise Act 2002 (2004)," *ESRC Centre for Business Research Working Paper No. 288*. https://ssrn.com/abstract=567306 or http://dx.doi.org/10.2139/ssrn.567306.

8. Goode, Roy. *Principles of Corporate Insolvency Law.* London: Sweet & Maxwell, 1990.
9. Ikram, Izzul. "SME Association Commends Budget 2022 For Being Pro-Growth and Supportive of SMEs." *The Edge Markets*, October 21, 2021. Accessed November 22, 2021. https://www.theedgemarkets.com/article/sme-association-commends-budget-2022-being-progrowth-and-supportive-smes.
10. Lee, Shih, and Lynn Huey. "Case Update: The Interim Judicial Manager to Protect Assets in Jeopardy." *themalaysianlawyer.com*, October 26, 2020. Accessed November 22, 2021. https://themalaysianlawyer.com/2020/10/26/singapore-interim-judicial-manager/.
11. "Liquidation Statistics 2021." *Malaysian Department of Insolvency.* Accessed November 22, 2021. http://www.mdi.gov.my/index.php/legislation/liquidation/1824-liquidation-statistic-april-2021.
12. "Measures to Address COVID-19 Impact." *Prime Minister of Malaysia Official Website.* https://www.pmo.gov.my/ .
13. Povera, Adib, and Hana Naz Harun. "PM Unveils RM20 Billion Pemerkasa Assistance Package." *NSTTV*, March 17, 2020. Accessed December 29, 2021. https://www.nst.com.my/news/nation/2021/03/674643/pm-unveils-rm20-billion-pemerkasa-assistance-package-nsttv.
14. Steele, Stacey. "Directors' Duties to Prevent Insolvent Trading in a Crisis: Responses to COVID-19 in Australia and Lessons from Germany." *International Insolvency Review* 30(S1): S89-S110. https://doi.org/10.1002/iir.1424.
15. Tang, Gerald, and Hei Zel Tan. "The Companies Exemption Order on Winding Up – Ingenious or Illegal?" *The Malaysian Lawyer*, May 28, 2020. Accessed December 30, 2021. https://themalaysianlawyer.com/2020/05/28/companies-exemption-order-ingenious-illegal/#:~:text=The%20Companies%20%28Exemption%29%20%28No.%202%29%20Order%202020%20%28%E2%80%9C,to%20a%20statutory%20demand%20up%20to%20six%20months.
16. Timbuong, Jo. "Our Economy Loses RM2.4bil Everyday MCO is Active, Says PM." *The Star*, April 25, 2020. Accessed November 22, 2021. https://www.thestar.com.my/news/nation/2020/04/25/our-economy-loses-rm24bil-every-day-mco-is-active-says-pm.

Chapter 10
The Way Forward

Wai Meng Chan

Abstract This concluding chapter will revisit the challenges faced by companies during the COVID-19 pandemic, as revealed in the earlier chapters of this book. Instead of anchoring the company law framework on the shareholder theory, it would be more appropriate to also consider the interest of other stakeholders. A company is part of a community. Its actions have an impact on those connected to it, and vice versa. Thus, support from all stakeholders is necessary for its sustainability. In return, the company should uphold others in the chain during both good and bad times. The significance of corporate social responsibility in the sustainability of a company can no longer be denied. The Companies Act 2016 must be reviewed to close the gaps. On a brighter note, the COVID-19 pandemic has also shown the way forward. It has quickened the process of implementing good practices and leveraging information and communication technology ("ICT") in matters of keeping records, communication and meetings.

Introduction

The Companies Act 2016 ("CA 2016") came into effect on January 31, 2017 setting out a new legal framework to replace the Companies Act 1965. The new framework was supposed to facilitate the development of a conducive and dynamic business and regulatory environment for Malaysia which was in line with international standards. As it was to meet the current needs of the business community, it took into account, among others, the advances made in information and communication technology ("ICT").

In early 2020, Malaysia was hit by the COVID-19 pandemic. New standard operating procedures ("SOPs') were implemented and lockdowns were imposed to curb the spread of the deadly virus. The lives of the people were disrupted. What was the norm before the pandemic no longer apply. Instead, a new set of norms were introduced, and everyone must adapt to the new norms. The pandemic has also caused

W. M. Chan (✉)
University of Malaya, Kuala Lumpur, Malaysia
e-mail: chanwm@um.edu.my

L. Krishnan and W. M. Chan (eds.), *The Impact of COVID-19 on Corporations and Corporate Law in Malaysia*, https://doi.org/10.1007/978-981-19-5519-8_10

upheaval to the business community. The domino effect was felt by all, and many companies were put to test. The efficacy of the CA 2016 was also put to test.

In the earlier chapters of this book, we examined some of the impacts of the pandemic on companies and company law in Malaysia, and whether the provisions in the CA 2016 are sufficiently supple to meet the needs of companies to comply with the statutory requirements. Some of the problems were highlighted; interim measures initiated by the authorities to resolve or mitigate the problems were also discussed.

Many countries have since declared the COVID-19 an endemic and live with it. Malaysia is also cautiously moving towards this direction. However, the problems revealed during the pandemic cannot be swept under the carpet. They must still be addressed. Malaysia and the business community must be prepared to face the aftermath of the pandemic. For example, there are stories abound of the shortage of food and goods due to disruption in the supply chain. We hear stories of McDonald having to ration the sale of its fries, and KFC running low on fried chicken.[1]

The issues faced by companies during the COVID-19 pandemic which were raised in the various chapters in this book, may also be encountered by companies hit by the after-effects of other forms of disasters. For example, the massive and deadly flooding suffered in the Klang Valley in December 2021 shocked the nation. Not only were people flooded out of their homes, businesses in low lying areas also suffered unimaginable damage. It was ground zero for many, and they had to either restart or wind down. The resilient will survive.

Thus, though the pandemic might be over soon, the challenges are still lingering and must be tackled head on, if necessary. This concluding chapter will revisit the challenges faced by companies during the pandemic, as revealed in the various chapters of this book. We have seen that directors manage the companies. They owe a fiduciary duty towards the company. Similarly, the auditors being an independent party, are also imposed with duties to verify the company's financial health. Compliance with the requirements of the CA 2016 is important, and many found it a challenge to comply with the timeframe imposed to hold meetings and lodge documents with the Companies Commission of Malaysia ("CCM").

It is the foundation of company law that a company enjoys a separate legal entity from its members and officers. It is imposed with liability, including criminal liability. Companies have to comply with the new SOPs, failing which, it is imputed with liability. The pandemic has caused upheaval to the finances of companies. They may have to source for more capital to see them through the difficult period. Some may have to go through corporate restructuring and the unfortunate ones, proceed to winding up. The rescue mechanism and insolvency provisions under the CA 2016 were also examined in the previous chapter.

These areas will be revisited again in this concluding chapter, highlighting the weaknesses of anchoring the company law framework on the shareholder theory which imposes on companies the obligation to maximise profits for its shareholders.

[1] Keertan Ayamany, "After McDonald's 'Fry-tening' Shortage, KFC Malaysia Also Confirms Some Items Taken Off Menu". *The Malay Mail*. January 28, 2022.

The company has stakeholders other than shareholders. The pandemic has shown that the interests of other stakeholders are important, and that directors should consider their interests too. The significance of corporate social responsibility ("CSR") in the sustainability of a company can no longer be denied. Analysts, investors and financiers are including non-financial variables in the equation to evaluate a company. To facilitate this, companies provide information on their policies pertaining to environmental, social and governance. Such formal reporting known as environmental, social and governance ("ESG") is gaining popularity. Indeed, despite the emphasis placed on shareholder theory, the CA 2016 encourages companies to report their ESG in the business review attached to the directors' report in the financial statements.[2]

Directors' Duties

The general powers to manage a company is given to the board of directors ("Board").[3] The Board is to do so subject to the CA 2016 and the company's constitution. The Board consists of persons who have been appointed as directors of the company and whose terms are still continuing. Nevertheless, S. 2 of the CA 2016 has also defined directors to include *de facto* director and shadow director. Thus, though they are not members of the Board, they are imputed with the statutory duties and obligations imposed on a director under the Act. They cannot claim they are not directors of the company and thus not liable if they breach the duties of a director.

A director owes duties which can be generally categorised as fiduciary duty and duty of skill and care, to the company. On this note, it must be stressed that the director's duty of skill and care is different from his fiduciary duty. If he acts loyally but incompetently, he is not in breach of his fiduciary duty but may be in breach of his duty of care and skill.[4]

Directors' Fiduciary Duty

A director has fiduciary duty to the company as an entity.[5] Usually, the interests of the company as an entity overlap with that of its members, and thus members would not protest if an act is for the good of the company. However, where an act benefits the company as an entity but not some of the members, the directors cannot sacrifice

---

[2] The contents of the directors' report are prescribed in the Fifth Schedule of the CA 2016. According to Part II of the Fifth Schedule, the directors' report may contain a business review to provide an understanding of the development, performance or position of the company's business. It may include information about the company's policies on environmental matters, the company's employees, and social and community issues, and the effectiveness of those policies.

[3] S. 211 of the CA 2016.

[4] *Bristol* and *West Building Society v. Mothew* [1997] 2 WLR 436.

[5] See Siew Cheang Loh, *Corporate Powers Accountability* (Petaling Jaya: LexisNexis, 2018), 347.

the interest of the company in favour of that group of members. Needless to say, the directors must always act within their limits.[6]

S. 213(1) of the CA 2016 requires the directors of a company at all times, to exercise their powers in accordance with the Act, for a proper purpose and in good faith in the best interest of the company. Contrast this to S. 172 of the UK Companies Act 2006, which provides that a director has a duty to promote the success of the company for the benefits of members as a whole, and in doing so have regard to inter alia, the company's stakeholders such as employees, suppliers, customers, community and others. The UK provision recognises the paramount interest of the members as a whole, yet the interests of the other stakeholders cannot be ignored.

The Malaysian Act does not expressly recognise the interests of stakeholders, other than the members. Indeed, as we have seen in Chap. 2, when the CA 2016 was being drafted, the guiding principle was the shareholder theory. It was consciously decided that the social obligations of the company should not be incorporated in the Act.[7] Similarly, the regulation of the relationship between a company and its creditors and employees was also not included in the Act.

Nonetheless, we have seen that case law requires directors to take into consideration the interests of creditors when the company is insolvent or on the verge of insolvency.[8] There are also provisions in the CA 2016[9] which are aligned to this common law principle. However, employees do not have the same luck though they are considered as one of the most valuable assets in a business. The Act does not require the company and its directors to consider the interests of the employees when making decisions. This is not an oversight but an intentional outcome, for it was viewed that the relationship between a company and its employees was already sufficiently dealt with by other laws.[10] However, this may not be necessary. For example, the Employment Act 1955 applies only to categories of employees as stated in the First Schedule of the Act, and thus employees who are not covered may find themselves unprotected. In addition, the court had held that directors who made provisions for employees would have breached their duties towards the company as the *ex gratia* payments would not benefit the company.[11] The directors would have to first seek the approval of members before they were to do so.[12]

[6] *Re BSB Holdings Ltd (No 2)* [1996] 1 BCLC 155, at 222.

[7] Paragraph 4.4 of the Consultative Document No 5 issued by the Corporate Law Reform Committee on "*Clarifying and Reformulating the Directors' Role and Duties*".

[8] *Kinsela & Anor v Russell Kinsela Pty Ltd (In Liq* (1986) 4 ACLC 215 and *Colin Gwyer & Associates Ltd & Anor v London Wharf (Limehouse) Ltd & Ors* [2003] 2 BCLC 153.

[9] For example, S. 528, 529, 539 and 540 of the CA 2016.

[10] Some of the Acts of Parliament that deal with the employer-employee relationships are the Employment Act 1955, Industrial Relations Act 1967, Workmen's Compensation Act 1952, Occupational Safety and Health Act 1994, and Employees' Social Security Act 1969.

[11] *Parke v Daily News Ltd* [1962] 2 All ER 929.

[12] In *Bristol and West Building Society v Mothew (t/a Sapley & Co)* [1998] 1 Ch 1, the court held that a fiduciary may not act for the benefit of a third person without the informed consent of his principal. This view was endorsed by the Malaysian Federal Court in the case of *The Board of*

Another issue that was drawn out during the pandemic COVID-19 is that directors who authorised contributions to society could be held liable for breaching their fiduciary duties if such charitable acts were not done in the best interest of the company, if the company would not gain from those acts, but instead reduce the profits of the company for distribution to its shareholders. It is unfortunate indeed that the CA 2016, unlike its predecessor the Companies Act 1965, does not contain a provision empowering the company to make donations for patriotic or for charitable purposes. This gives rise to the issue whether directors may authorise donations without being called out for abusing their powers.

Director's Duty of Skill and Care

In order to arrest the spread of the COVID-19, the Malaysian Government imposed Movement Control Orders ("MCOs"). Businesses in non-essential services could not operate. Companies' contractual obligations were severely impacted and their finances were in tatters. Boards of directors were put to test.

The Department of Statistics conducted a survey on the impact of the COVID-19 pandemic on businesses,[13] and found that the three main issues facing businesses were salary payment, rental payment and no customers. Hence, the two main assistance required by businesses were tax reductions and financial assistance. In this connection, the government announced a bucket of assistance and it was crucial that directors took advantage of the assistance available to tide the companies over during this challenging time. Failure to do so could be seen as a breach of their duty of skill and care.

In Malaysia, the director's duty of skill and care is coded in S. 213(2) of the CA 2016. The provision combines an objective test expected of a director having the same responsibilities and a subjective test which adds on any special knowledge and skill of that particular director. The objective test would require a director to upskill himself to the level of another director having the same responsibilities. This would apply too during the pandemic when the directors were tasked to bring the company out of the crisis with minimum scar. Some businesses had to revamp to fit in with the new norm. Some had to venture into new businesses to stay afloat.

Where the company has an objects clause in its constitution, the director will have to ensure that the new business model or venture is within the objects clause,[14] failing which he may be held in breach of his fiduciary duties.[15] Further, the director

Trustees of the Sabah Foundation & Co v Datuk Syed Kechik bin Syed Mohamed & Anor [2008] 5 MLJ 461.

[13] "Summary of Findings: Special Survey Effects of COVID-19 on Economy and Companies/Business Firms (Round 1)," Department of Statistics Malaysia, accessed January 10, 2022. https://www.dosm.gov.my/v1/uploads/files/covid-19/Infographic.pdf.

[14] S. 35(2) of the CA 2016 provides that the company is restricted from carrying on any business or activity which is outside its objects clause.

[15] S. 213(1) of the CA 2016.

would also be required by S. 213(2) to have the skill and knowledge which may be reasonably expected of a director having the same responsibilities. If he does not and is not familiar with the new business model or venture, he must upskill himself.

Auditors

Every company, unless exempted, must have its annual accounts audited by an independent person. The auditor presents his opinion whether the accounts give a true and fair view of the company's affairs. Thus, he would have to view documents relevant to sampled transactions. The CA 2016 also requires companies to circulate the audited accounts to its members within a certain time frame.

However, these were hampered during the MCO. Despite the important role played by an auditor, the profession was not declared as essential services during the MCO period.[16] Further, even if the audit profession was held as an essential service, the auditor could not carry out the audit work as in pre-pandemic, especially if the client company was not carrying on business in the essential services sector. The client might not be able to attend to the auditor's queries or supply the documents required[17] as the office was closed. Thus, many auditors and client companies faced challenges in fulfilling their duties during the pandemic.

This unfortunate situation showcased the importance for companies to digitalise their financial records and store them in the cloud. Similarly, auditors have to adopt a digitalised audit process. Digitalising the records and processes will also mean going paperless, a step towards saving the environment. Be it as it may, the audit quality should not be compromised. Nevertheless, the pandemic has laid bare the importance of ICT, and the importance of upskill to meet the new demands and address the issues arising such as privacy and security.

Meetings and Shareholder Activism

The importance of ICT also came to the fore in matters connected to meetings. Due to the restrictions on movement, physical meetings could not be held. Instead, virtual meetings were the call of the day. Though the CA 2016 provides for this eventuality, it is subject to the company's constitution.[18] Thus, companies which have clauses in the

[16] Malaysian Institute of Accountants, "Circular to Members No. MF22/2021. Further Updates on the Operation of Firms During Total Lockdown."

[17] S. 266(12) of the CA 2016 provides that auditors have a right of access at all reasonable times to the accounting records and other records, and obtain from any officer of the company, such information and explanations as they require.

[18] S. 327 of the CA 2016.

constitution restricting virtual meetings would find it challenging, if not impossible, to carry on their meetings during the MCO.

The CA 2016 also contains provisions on the service of notice of a meeting. It allows notice to be given in hard copy, electronic form or hybrid. Where the notice is given in electronic form, it shall be transmitted to the electronic address provided by the member or by publishing on a website, unless otherwise provided by the company's constitution.[19] Thus, again the CA 2016 provides for use of technology.

Company meetings are an important agenda for activist shareholders, for they use the platform to pose questions to management on the company's financial and non-financial performance. Thus, they use their shareholders' rights to attend meetings, pose questions and speak at the members' meetings, with the aim to influence company policy and practice. It is noteworthy that shareholder activism remained active during the pandemic. At the annual general meeting of Malayan Banking Bhd in 2021, the Chairman and the Board made an effort to deal with the questions posed by the members. The meeting was for more than 5 hours, from 10am to 3.40pm on May 6, 2021.[20]

Compliance of Regulatory Requirements

We have seen that the CA 2016 has timelines for annual events such as annual general meetings for public companies, and circulation of audited financial statements to company members. The Act also prescribes timelines for the lodgement of documents to the CCM. It is noteworthy that the CCM has given guidance on the conduct of virtual meetings, granted moratorium for the lodgement of documents as well as assured extension of time for circulation of financial statements and annual general meeting. upon receipt of application from the company.

Nevertheless, the pandemic has revealed certain weaknesses and it is assuring that the CCM is taking steps to rectify some of them. For example, the CA 2016 does not empower the CCM to grant blanket automatic extension of time. Hence, the CCM has proposed to insert a new provision in the CA 2016 to the effect that the CCM may extend the time for lodgement of documents as well as to any action required by the Act, without any application from the company on certain circumstances which is just and in the interest of the public.

Further, the CCM should also escalate the process to fully digitalise the portal for lodgement of documents. Currently some documents still require physical lodgement to the CCM. In addition, it is submitted that it is timely for the regulator to review the list of documents which are to be submitted to the CCM. Some may be duplication and do not have any added value. For example, most of the information

[19] S. 319(2) of the CA 2016.

[20] Refer to Malayan Banking Bhd's minutes of meeting at its website https://www.maybank.com/iwov-resources/corporate_new/document/my/en/pdf/agm-egm/2020/Minutes-of-AGM-2021.pdf.

in the Annual Return is either lodged with the CCM as and when there is a change,[21] or in the company's financial statements and directors' report.[22] The lodgement of documents should not only be hassle free but the contents should be streamlined to avoid duplication.

Liability for Non-compliance with Measures to Curb the Spread of COVID-19

In Malaysia, public health interventions such as policies and legal tools were introduced to reduce the risk of transmission of COVID-19 in the workplace. Some of the statutes which were employed to enforce the measures are the Prevention and Control of Infectious Diseases 1988 and the Occupational Safety and Health Act 1994. Fines are imposed on employers for non-compliance. Chapter 7 discussed the issue of whether the state's involvement in the employers' management of COVID-19 was justifiable. It was argued that voluntary methods should first be employed to convince corporations to adhere to the measures introduced to prevent COVID-19 infection. If this fails, then the government may proceed to the next course of action and implement behavioural modification measures such as educating directors and officers. Criminal legislation should be employed only as a last recourse.

This debate would not have arisen if companies had co-opted the importance of sustainability, and less obsessed in maximising profits at the expense of other stakeholders. Curbing the spread of COVID-19 should be on the top of the agenda, without any prompting from the regulatory. The quicker the virus was contained, the better it would be for the company, community and nation.

Effects on Capital Markets

The MCOs have brought many companies to the brink of insolvency. Even companies with strong financial standing before the onslaught of COVID-19 were affected. In order to tide them over, some of the companies had to source for new funding. Funding could come in the form of borrowings or from the capital market. In order to keep borrowings cheap, the Overnight Policy Rate was gradually reduced from 3.00% at the start of the pandemic to 1.75% in July 2020. This reduced the cost of financing and provided support to new credit expansion and fund-raising activity.[23]

[21] For example, when the company changes its registered office, S. 46(3) of the CA 2016 requires the company to notify the CCM within 14 days; changes in the shareholder (S. 51); and changes in directors, managers and secretaries (S. 57 of the CA 2016).

[22] For example, the nature of its business and place of business; and the total amount of its indebtedness.

[23] Bank Negara Malaysia. *Annual Report 2020*, 8.

In addition, blanket loan repayment moratoriums were introduced in April 2020 and July 2021 to provide relief to borrowers.

With regards to the capital market, it is noteworthy that measures were introduced to support both the primary and secondary markets. Regulators not only relaxed rules but also reduced the costs of listing exercises. These measures effectively increased the number of Initial Public Offerings from seven in the first half of 2020 to 13 in the same period in 2021. For the secondary capital markets, discretion was given to stockbrokers whether to make margin calls due to the depressing share prices. Short selling rules were also revised. Similarly, the criteria leading to the suspension of the share listing as prescribed in Practice Note 17 were relaxed. All these measures were calculated to support the secondary capital market, and thus the nation's economy.

Corporate Restructuring

Notwithstanding the aforementioned measures to help companies survive the financial crisis resulting from the MCOs, some companies continued to suffer and became insolvent. The directors who continued to carry on the business were taking a risk for they might be found guilty of wrongful trading under S. 539 of the CA 2016. In addition, the shadow of the possibility being wound up remained in the scene. Against this backdrop, the regulators stepped up their act to protect businesses from being wound up. One of them was the revision of the definition of inability to pay debts in S. 466(1)(a). This provision provides that a company is deemed to be unable to pay its debts if the company fails to satisfy a notice of demand to pay a sum exceeding the amount prescribed by the Minister within 21 days after the service of the demand. The original amount prescribed was RM10,000 and the onslaught of COVID-19 saw it revised upwards to RM50,000. In addition, the timeframe to make payment was extended to six months. Though the validity of this extension of time is questionable, it cannot be doubted that the revised amount gave a lifeline to many companies.

As highlighted in Chap. 9, so long as the company is not wound up, a company may turn around its fortune through a rescue mechanism. In this connection, the company can avail itself to the financial relief measures introduced by the government and financial institutions. The company may also initiate discussions with its creditors to reschedule or restructure its debts. The CA 2016 has three options of corporate restructuring mechanisms: the enhanced scheme of the arrangement ("SOA"), Corporate Voluntary Arrangement ("CVA") and Judicial Management ("JM"). Chapter 9 highlighted the strengths and weaknesses of each of the aforementioned statutory arrangements which appeared to be skewed towards secured creditors. The author suggests that it is timely to consider the plight of unsecured creditors, such as employees and suppliers. The model of the UK administration procedure under the Enterprises Act 2002 may serve as a model, for the administrator is to represent both secured and unsecured creditors. Due consideration should be given to the company's stakeholders, and that the company's corporate responsibility and strategic contribution to continue serving its surrounding community should not be forsaken.

Corporate Social Responsibility

The pandemic COVID-19 has laid bare the importance of not only the adoption of ICT in the management of the businesses but also the stakeholder theory in the good governance of a company. It is worthy to note that the acknowledgment of the company's stakeholders other than shareholders, is gaining momentum. For example, the Malaysian Code of Corporate Governance 2021 which was issued on April 28, 2021 during the midst of the pandemic, gives emphasis to stakeholders' theory. Principle A1 says that the board of directors is collectively responsible for the long-term success of a company and the delivery of sustainable value to its stakeholders." It recognises that the interest of the members is important, but must be balanced with the needs of other stakeholders such as creditors, employees, society and the communities in which the company conducts its business.

In addition, the pandemic has also shown the relevance of corporate social responsibility, i.e. a company has a responsibility towards society and not just to make profit for its shareholders. Corporate social responsibility can be divided into four aspects namely, economic responsibility, ethical responsibility, environmental responsibility, and philanthropic responsibility.

The economic responsibility of companies is to produce goods and services that society needs and to profit on them. It recognises both shareholders' interest that their investment in the company would give them returns, as well as that it is important for the survival of a company to meet the needs of society. Thus, during the pandemic, the duty of skill and care of those in control of companies are put to test. They should be versatile to adapt to the changes to meet the needs of society and bring the company out of the doldrums so that the shareholders would not lose their investment. However, we have seen that they might be restricted by the company's constitution to carry on a new line of business.

When carrying on its business, the company must give due consideration to its ethical responsibility, i.e. to operate in a fair and ethical manner. It must accord fair treatment to all its stakeholders, which include not only the company's shareholders, but also its employees, suppliers and customers. Unfortunately, the guiding principle of CA 2016 is the shareholder theory, which is to maximise profits for shareholders. A calculated decision was made not to incorporate the company's social obligations or the regulation of the relationship between a company and its creditors and employees in the Act. Nevertheless, as we have seen in the above chapters, the pandemic COVID-19 has exposed the importance of considering the interests of stakeholders in the good governance of a company. All should be given fair and ethical treatment. Further, the pandemic has introduced new norms to curb the spread of the virus. These new norms should be adopted by all even if they might cause inconvenience or disruption to companies in carrying on with their businesses. It would only be ethical and proper to comply with the measures introduced to curb the spread of the virus. Thus, the debate whether non-compliance tantamount to a criminal liability should not have arisen, for everyone including companies should make a concerted effort to keep in check the spread of the virus for the good of all.

In the arena of environmental responsibility, it is envisaged that the use of ICT would reduce carbon footprint. Electronic lodgement of documents and communication will require only softcopy of documents thus eliminating printing. Attending meetings on online platforms will reduce travelling. Similarly, digitalising the company records, both financial and non-financial ones, and storing them in the cloud will reduce the usage of paper and physical storage space.

At the level of philanthropic responsibility, the COVID-19 pandemic has messed up the lives of many. Many could not make ends meet and had to wave the white flag to call for help. The crux of the matter is whether companies could donate to charitable causes. Unlike the position under the Companies Act 1965 which S. 19(1)(a) provided that the powers of the company included making donations for patriotic or for charitable purposes, the CA 2016 is silent on the power of a company to make donation. Consideration should be made to revert to the former position, otherwise directors who authorised the donations could be held liable for breaching their fiduciary duties.

Epilogue

The COVID-19 pandemic has brought forth much sorrow. It has also shown the way forward and quicken the process of implementing good practices. Due to the MCOs, people were forced to adopt ICT to communicate, otherwise they would be left out. The learning curve was steep and the benefits gained were exposed to the extent that many had expressed support to continue with virtual or hybrid meetings.

The pandemic has also brought to light the weaknesses of anchoring the company law framework on shareholder theory. It has shown that the interests of other stakeholders are just as important. A company is part of a community. Its actions have an impact on those connected to it, and vice versa. Thus, support from all quarters is necessary for its sustainability. In return, the company should uphold others in the chain during both good and bad times. This brings to mind the proverb "No man is an island".

References

1. Ayamany, Keertan. "After McDonald's 'Fry-tening' Shortage, KFC Malaysia Also Confirms Some Items Taken Off Menu." *The Malay Mail,* January 28, 2022.
2. Bank Negara Malaysia. *Annual Report 2020.* Accessed January 10, 2022. https://www.bnm.gov.my/o/ar2020/index.html.
3. Companies Commission of Malaysia. *CLRC Consultative Document No 5 Clarifying and Reformulating the Directors' Role and Duties.* https://www.ssm.com.my/Pages/Publication/CLRC/Consultation_Documents/cd5%20(1).pdf.
4. Loh, Siew Cheang. *Corporate Powers Accountability.* Petaling Jaya: LexisNexis, 2018.
5. Malayan Banking Bhd. Minutes of the 61st Adjourned Annual General Meeting. Accessed January 10, 2022. https://www.maybank.com/iwov-resources/corporate_new/document/my/en/pdf/agm-egm/2020/Minutes-of-AGM-2021.pdf.
6. Malaysian Institute of Accountants. "Circular to Members No. MF22/2021. Further Updates on the Operation of Firms During Total Lockdown".
7. "Summary of Findings: Special Survey Effects of COVID-19 on Economy and Companies/Business Firms (Round 1)." Department of Statistics Malaysia. Accessed January 10, 2022. https://www.dosm.gov.my/v1/uploads/files/covid-19/Infographic.pdf.

The manufacturer's authorised representative in the EU is Springer Nature Customer Service Centre GmbH, Europaplatz 3, 69115 Heidelberg, Germany. If you have any concerns regarding our products, please contact ProductSafety@springernature.com

Printed and bound by CPI Group (UK) Ltd, Croydon, CR0 4YY
01/10/2026
02226418-0001